The Buddha's Midwife

The Buddha's Midwife

Paul Carus and the Spread of Buddhism in America

JOHN S. HALLER, JR.

OPEN UNIVERSE
Chicago

To find out more about Open Universe books, visit our website at www.carusbooks.com.

Printed and bound in the United States of America. Printed on acid-free paper.

The Buddha's Midwife: Paul Carus and the Spread of Buddhism in America

ISBN: 978-1-63770-041-9

This book is also available as an e-book (978-1-63770-042-6).

An earlier edition of this book, under the title *Buddha's Midwife: Paul Carus and the Open Court Publishing Company*, was self-published by the author in 2020. This new Open Universe edition has been thoroughly checked and revised in detail, with some new material.

The photographs on the front cover and pages 13, 37, 59, 81, 107, 125, and 153 are reproduced by permission of the Carus family.

Library of Congress Control Number 2022944935

What is philosophical in Buddhism is no more than a preliminary step toward what is practical in it. Every religion, if it deserves the name, must be essentially practical and conducive in the promotion of the general welfare and to the realization of Reason.

—Shaku Soyen, *Sermons of a Buddhist Abbot,* 1906

Contents

Acknowledgments

Among the many debts I incurred in writing this book are Dean John Politz and the staff of the Morris Library at Southern Illinois University Carbondale, especially Nicholas Guardiano, Tony Bittle, Aaron Lisec, Anne Marie Hamilton-Brehm, Matt Gorzalski, and Walter Ray in its Special Collections Research Center. This excellent team assisted me in accessing the files of the Open Court Publishing Company, founded in 1887 by Edward Hegeler, with Dr. Paul Carus serving as editor and author until his death in 1919. The company's copious books, articles and journals were instrumental in spreading Eastern thought, especially Buddhism, throughout the western world. As the official repository for the Open Court Publishing Company, the Special Collections Research Center of Morris Library has made the full run of *The Open Court* magazine available online at OpenSIUC, https://opensiuc.lib.siu.edu/ocj.

Family-owned, the Open Court Publishing Company long stood unique within the nation's publishing industry. Its publishing mission is now being continued by Carus Books, with the imprints Open Universe and Carus Education. In this regard, I appreciate the courtesies provided by Blouke Carus, publisher of Carus Books, and the company's CEO and Editorial Director Dr. David Ramsay Steele, in facilitating the publication of the book through Carus Books.

I am also grateful to JSTOR, Google Books, Guttenberg, and the Hathi Trust for their facilitation of books, articles, and other important documentation.

Lastly, I express my deep appreciation to Robin, my wife of fifty-plus years, for her unstinting support of my work. Without her encouragement, criticism, suggestions, editing, and indexing, none of what I have accomplished in my career would have been possible. Once my student, she has since become my helpmate, anchor, and teacher for whom I am forever appreciative.

Introduction

Among Buddhists in the United States today, the preponderance are immigrants from South and Southeast Asia. These outnumber older Asian American Buddhist communities and help to explain why there are so many differences in their temples, centers, organizations, and literature. For these groups, the beliefs and practices of their Buddhism reflect not only class, ethnicity, and social organizations, but each group's experiences in both their native lands and in their new home.

It is not the intent of this book, to study Buddhism from an immigrant or ethnic point of view but to focus on those Euro-Americans who count themselves as converted followers, as well as any who find themselves acknowledging its traditions without necessarily attending its services or accepting its doctrines. This includes those Euro-Americans who identify with Buddhist traditions because of their intellectual curiosity, their readings, trips abroad, or other influences. Among these, Buddhism can be accepted as a cultural leaning distinct from religion, which is to say that Euro-Americans often choose to self-identify as Buddhists with nothing more substantive or definitional. Indeed, this study is simply interested in those who demonstrate American interest in Buddhism whether it elicits a response, positive or negative.

The earliest Euro-American interest in Buddhism took flight in the spiritual journeys, poetry, translations, and references by Ralph Waldo Emerson, Henry David Thoreau, and their fellow Transcendentalists eager to introduce eastern cultures and religions to the public. For others, it spread through esoteric literature shared among members of the Philosophical Society in St. Louis; the American Akadēmē in Jacksonville, Illinois; the attendees of programs offered by the Concord School of Philosophy; and expressed by writers and lecturers contributing to the ground-breaking movements of Theosophy and New Thought. According to Thomas A. Tweed, most late-Victorians favored "a hybrid Buddhism that blended occult traditions (i.e., Swedenborgianism and Theosophy) with strands of Asian Buddhism (i.e., Sri Lankan Theravada and Japanese Mahayana)."[1]

A return to less esoteric representations of eastern religions and philosophies occurred with the papers delivered by Buddhist delegates to the World's Parliament of Religions in 1893, and the subsequent contributions of Paul Carus and the Open Court Publishing Company through its books and the pages of *The Open Court* and *The Monist* magazines. This was followed by the igniting of scholarly interest in courses on comparative religions, interpretations of newly translated literature from the East, and lectures given by Buddhist priests and scholars across the country. Not to be overlooked in the East's appeal was Buddhism's organic relationship with the environment, its lack of mythology, and the elasticity of its language.

Buddhism's full presence was not felt until the 1950s when Zen popularizers Daisetsu Teitaro Suzuki, John Cage, Jack Kerouac, and Alan Watts gave substance to the Beat counter-culture movement. Historian Thomas A. Tweed refers to those belonging to this latter category as "night-stand Buddhists" in that they have little affiliation with Asian-American Buddhists, and why Peter N. Gregory suggested that "it is not at all clear that we are entitled to talk about Buddhism in the singular."[2] Unlike Asian-American immigrants whose beliefs serve as a binding tool reinforcing their ethnic identity and culture within an increasingly pluralistic society, counter-culture Buddhists more often than not represented a rebellion against the very family and community values into which they were born. In other words, rather than using their new-found beliefs to reinforce their identity with family and community, their Buddhism was more than likely an expression of personal fulfillment. For this group, explains Gregory, Buddhism is "not so much a set of beliefs whose truth is to be affirmed as a practice through which 'truth' is to be uncovered."[3]

It is the intent of this book to examine those Euro-Americans who identified with Buddhist philosophy and religion in the period between the World's Parliament of Religions in 1893 and the First World War. During this time, Asian religions and philosophies made a significant impact among educated Americans, causing profound challenges in the way they thought about themselves, of Christianity and its relationship to the sciences, of self-fulfillment, and lastly, of their combined relevance in the modern age. More so than any other religion, Buddhism became a crutch for those who, in the final decades of the nineteenth century, became disillusioned with Christianity's social-Darwinistic claim to superiority over all other faiths. This estrangement within Christian ranks caused some to despair, while others looked East, believing like Emerson and Henry David Thoreau before them, that there was much to be discovered in the vastness of Asia's subcontinent.

Those who shared this feeling of estrangement from Christianity attributed the breakdown to multiple causes: the theory of evolution, (with conflicting claims of skepticism, agnosticism, and atheism), the higher criticism, the uncertainty of Christian teleology, and the rejection of militant missionary attitudes and practices. Questions arose as to where Christianity's true compass pointed. Perhaps the most telling example of this disillusionment came from a Japanese scholar at the World's Parliament of Religions in 1893 when he remarked: "I was baptized by a Congregationalist missionary, but I never meant in so doing to be baptized a Congregationalist, but a Christian. What we want in Japan is not Methodism, nor Presbyterianism, nor Protestantism, nor Catholicism, but the pure Religion of Jesus Christ and of His Word! Where shall we find it?"[4]

Multiple efforts were made during the period from 1893 to the First World War to compare and contrast Buddhism with Christianity. This resulted in Buddhism sometimes being presented to the West as the originator of Christianity, or ranked as a sophisticated rival, factors that pointed to its philosophical significance, its focus on the here and now, and its movement away from beliefs, dogmas, rituals, superstition and a personal deity. As Buddhism grew in popularity, America's religious leaders gave grudging recognition to those areas of complementarity between Christian beliefs and Buddhism. "To our mind there has plainly been a misconception of Buddhism," admitted Rev. Gilbert Reid of the International Institute of China in Shanghai, who decided to point out those features of Buddhism for which "the Christian can justifiably express appreciation." This included 1. viewing both as reforming religions; 2. recognizing their sympathetic stance toward the suffering of people worldwide and their efforts to replace it with happiness and peace; 3. accepting their common signs of compassion and their ideas of deliverance or salvation to save mankind from suffering; 4. knowing that both Buddha and Christ received prayer, adoration, and trust in bringing salvation by faith; 5. admitting to their common emphasis on a righteous life, both internally and externally; 6. using a common set of rules and prohibitions to build character; 7. holding to the law of cause and effect when applied to morals; 8. recognizing the distinctions made by both between the self and the better self; 9. recognizing the distinction between reality and unreality, between the real and the unreal; and 10. accepting the existence of the eternal and omnipresent spirit or universal soul.[5]

In his function as the Buddha's midwife, Paul Carus, editor of *The Open Court* (1887–1919) and *The Monist* (1890–1919), and eventual owner of the Open Court Publishing Company, not only brought Buddhist thought to the United States through his writings and edited translations, he also facilitated the role of numerous philologists, historians, and philosophers to do the same. In the years following the Parliament of Religions, Carus presented Buddhism as having a foundation in rationalistic and scientific philosophy whose principles aligned with a broad range of liberal elements in Protestantism and in the Enlightenment. His enduring significance, explained Martin Verhoeven, was "in introducing and interpreting others' thoughts, particularly the religious thought of Asia, to an American audience."[6] In so doing, Carus deliberately downplayed those occult characteristics highlighted in Theosophy. The correct method for evaluating religion, he reasoned, was to "fearlessly apply scientific methods to religious doctrines" while, at the same time, "to search for and hold fast to the spirit of religion which is the truth contained in the several religious doctrines."[7] The intent of science was not in destroying religion but purifying and deepening the God-idea. Carus considered the age to be one of transition, marked by the disintegration of dogma with its persecutions and heresy trials, and the beginnings of reconstruction based on the forces of evolution in the domains of civilization, religion, and morality. Although the future "must be built upon the past," it also "must evolve the living present by way of progress and reform."[8] Carus was indifferent to whether this God-man was called Christ or Buddha. Both had sought to reveal the laws of universal love, righteousness, and goodwill. The God of science did not mean the negation of the older belief in God, but "its completion and perfection."[9]

Between 1887 and his death in 1919, Carus oversaw the publication of 732 issues of *The Open Court* and 113 issues of *The Monist.* During that period, the Open Court published more than 500 books on a range of topics—from mathematics and biblical criticism to poetry, translations of Oriental writings, Zoroastrian love, and psychology—of which Carus wrote, edited, or co-authored 74 books and over 1,500 articles. At least fifteen of his own books and thirty-nine of his articles were on Eastern philosophy and religion. Between 1887 and 1907, a period of time that best represented Carus's greatest interest in Asian religions and philosophy, the Open Court Publishing Company published eleven books on China and Japan; thirteen on Christianity and Liberal Religion; six on comparative religions; two on Islam; four on Hinduism, ten on Buddhism, three on Zoroastrianism, thirteen on psychology and the soul, six on Egyptian polytheism, one on Mithraism, eight on Judaism, one on Pantheism, and one on Shintoism.

The American writer Percival Lowell remarked once that "the Far-East holds up the mirror to our own civilization,— a mirror that like all mirrors gives us back left for right."[10] His observation requires an answer, perhaps several, since Buddhism's attraction covers so many different people and purposes, beginning when it was first portrayed as the death mask of lost civilizations, to when it became Carus's Religion of Science. Like so many intellectuals during the late nineteenth and early twentieth century, Carus was endeavoring to find a path from the older theologies into a new secular world and its uncertain future. This book will examine Carus's role as the principal contributor to the spread of Buddhist thinking in American culture at the turn of the nineteenth and the early twentieth century.

1
Mingling the Waters

> Surrender the grasping disposition of selfishness, and you will attain to that calm state of mind which conveys perfect peace, goodness, and wisdom.
>
> —Paul Carus, *The Gospel of Buddha,* 1894

The founding by Sir William James in 1784 of the Asiatic Society of Bengal, a scholarly organization of civil servants under the umbrella authority of the East India Trading Company, signaled the beginnings of an effort to convey to Westerners the historical greatness of the vast knowledge produced in the Indian subcontinent. Ironically, noted Alan D. Hodder, the very same colonial apparatus which spurred political and economic expansion into South and East Asia, was responsible for the discovery, investigation, and scholarly appreciation of its traditions and cultures. Contributors included Charles Wilkins, Thomas Colebrooke, Horace H. Wilson, and Brian Houghton Hodgson whose translations of Sanskrit manuscripts contributed to understanding the origins of Buddhism.

Many of these early translations tended to lump the different traditions together without discrimination, dismissing them as misguided efforts to address humankind's universal concerns over love, death, suffering, and fear.[1] According to Donald S. Lopez, Professor of Buddhist and Tibetan Studies at the University of Michigan, not until 1801 did the Oxford English Dictionary introduce the term "Buddhism" into the canon of Asian literature. Until then, it was generally thought that the beliefs and traditions observed among the native peoples of the East were simply different forms of idolatry. In 1816, the word was applied to the title of Edward Upham's book, *The History of the Doctrine of Buddhism.* With its naming came other components including a founder, a community of followers, and its own sacred scriptures. [2]

Early Accounts

Except for Columbus who set sail in search of Asian markets, and several commercial and cultural communications in the 1780s when American merchants began trading actively in Asia, few substantive exchanges existed before the nineteenth century. Puritan minister Cotton Mather corresponded with missionaries in Madras, English theologian Joseph Priestly wrote one of the earliest studies of Asian religions in America, and religious historian Hannah Adams expressed a curiosity about Asia's religious and philosophical traditions, albeit much of it derogatory in nature, centering around practices such as sati (widow burning), superstitions, mysticism, asceticism, maritime contacts, trade policies, and travel reports.[3]

It seems somewhat ironic that so many Americans would express their distaste for Oriental philosophy (anatman, or doctrine of the "non-self") because of its presumed preoccupation with pessimism when its own genteel culture was so consumed with the prospect of death as evident in its fascination with séances, death poetry, and unusually morbid funereal practices that prevailed from the Civil War to World War I. The difference, perhaps, can be explained in the deep-seated American belief in progress and acknowledgment that each person retained an immortal soul after death.

From accounts of early missionaries such as Adoniram Judson, to the founding of the American Oriental Society in

1842, one of the oldest learned societies in the United States, to the beginnings of research in Oriental religions and literature, Asia became an increasingly popular topic of discussion—some good, but mostly negative.[4] Helped by the scholarly contributions of the distinguished Sanskritists Edward E. Salisbury and William Dwight Whitney at Yale; the fusion of eastern and western philosophy in the works of Amos Bronson Alcott at the Concord School of Philosophy; the writings of George Bush, professor of Hebrew and Oriental Literature at New York University; and Henry David Thoreau's translations into English of French Orientalist Eugène Burnouf's work on Buddhism, the Occidental view of the Orient gradually tilted away from demonic, atheistic, nihilist, and pessimist depictions long held by Christian missionaries and civil bureaucrats.

Among educated Americans in the 1840s and 1850s, particularly those living in the northeastern seaboard states whose interests aligned with the literary and religious movements of Transcendentalism and Unitarianism, Buddhism became a topic of increased interest. Though no stranger to early prejudices of Indian ritualism and traditions, including child marriage and caste restrictions, Ralph Waldo Emerson became decidedly supportive after reading Victor Cousin's survey of world philosophies, and the accounts of Ram Mohan Roy, founder of the Brahmo Somaj ("Society of God"), a theistic movement within Hinduism similar to American Unitarianism.[5] After assuming editorship of *The Dial* in 1842, Emerson acquainted its subscribers with admiring articles, translations, and references to non-Western sources, including Charles Wilkins's translation of the *Bhagavad Gita* (1785) which was initially mistaken for a book on Buddhism instead of a Hindu dialogue between the Prince Arjuna and his friend Krishna in the first or second century A.D.[6] Despite Buddhism's being perceived as distant from the prevailing American values of individualism and optimism, there was a growing tendency to applaud if not embrace its moral and civilizing influence on the Orient's mass populations.[7]

The Transcendentalists pored through the *Bhagavad Gita* and the *Laws of Manu,* not as discerning scholars but as spiritual seekers reinforcing intuitional truths they already claimed. Thoreau, one of the brightest luminaries of Transcendentalism, translated portions of the *Saddharma-pudarika Sutra,* or "Lotus Sutra" from the French for the *Dial,* thus securing a prominent place in the movement's admiration of Asian thought, opposition to materialism, rebellion against formalism, and the desire to experience directly communion with the spirit in humanity.

> In the morning I bathe my intellect in the stupendous and cosmogonal philosophy of the Bhagavat Geeta, since whose composition years of the gods have elapsed, and in comparison with which our modern world and its literature seem puny and trivial; and I doubt if that philosophy is not to be referred to a previous state of existence, so remote is its sublimity from our conceptions. I lay down the book and go to my well for water, and lo! there I meet the servant of the Brahmin, priest of Brahma, and Vishnu and Indra, who still sits in his temple on the Ganges reading the Vedas, or dwells at the root of a tree with his crust and water-jug.[8]

Many of these and similar writings became compatible references for Emerson's essay on Plato in *Representative Men* (1850) which reflected his assimilation of Hindu texts. In Emerson's poetry ("Hametreya," 1847; and "Brahma," 1856) and Hindu reflections in *The Conduct of Life* (1860) and *Society and Solitude* (1870), he carried forward a positive view of Eastern thought. Before long, he and his Concord colleagues were examining Horace H. Wilson's translation of the *Vishnu Purana* (1840) and E. Roer's edited English translation of the *Upanishads* (1853).[9] Equally important, the Transcendentalists were the first major group of intellectuals to include Oriental thought in their worldview. As Thoreau revealed in his *Journal,* "I cannot read a sentence in the book of the Hindoos without being elevated as upon the table-land of the Ghauts. It has such a rhythm as the winds of the desert, such a tide as the Ganges, and seems as superior to criticism as the Himmaleh Mounts."[10]

The Transcendentalists were not alone in their admiration. Accompanying them on their spiritual journey of enlightenment were Deists and Unitarians who, dissenting from the Great Awakening, questioned the surety of Christian dogmas and creeds over the importance of inductive reasoning. As dissenters, they constructed a whole new foundation for their beliefs which argued against man's natural depravity and the concept of predestination, replacing the omnipresence of a harsh and demanding God with mounting optimism that humanity's future lay in its own hands. For many of these doubters, Asia's religions, most of which predated Christianity, became the subject of increasing admiration.[11]

For American and European romanticists, the cultural richness of China and the Indian subcontinent came as a welcome windfall. Samuel Johnson's three-volume *Oriental Religions and Their Relation to Universal Religion* (1872–85), which included volumes on India, China, and Persia, showed little, if any, religious bias. An independent clergyman and transcendentalist, he went out of his way to avoid labeling or otherwise judging Buddhism apart from its compatibility with other world religions and emphasis on personal moral responsibility.[12] The same applied to the works of Buddhist specialist Robert Spence Hardy, writer and poet James d'Alwis, German Indologist Albrecht Weber, and Sanskrit linguist Friedrich Max Müller whose fifty-volume set of English translations of the *Sacred Books of the East* (1879–1910) interpreted rather than passed judgment on eastern cultures and religions.[13]

By the late 1870s and 1880s, increased numbers of scholarly books were being published on Buddhism, including Hermann Oldenberg's *The Buddha, His Life, His Doctrine, His Community* (1881); Thomas Rhys Davids's *Buddhist Birth-Stories: Jataka Tales* (1878), *Buddhism: Being a Sketch of the Life and Teachings of Gautama* (1877), and *Buddhism: Its History and Literature* (1896); William Rockhill's *Life of the Buddha and the Early History of His Order* (1884); and Henry Clarke Warren's *Buddhism in Translations* (1896).

Also, during these years, Herman Vetterling, also known as Philangi Dasa, sought in his *Swedenborg the Buddhist* (1887) to demonstrate that the scientist and mystic Emanuel Swedenborg was a Buddhist at heart and that Buddhism aligned with both Theosophy and Swedenborgianism.[14]

America's cultural roots in individualism, activism, and optimism made it difficult to discuss concepts such as the anatman and Nirvana, or suppress characterizations of Buddhists as atheistic, nihilistic, and pessimistic. The same applied to understanding and appreciating the new discipline of comparative religions. Symptomatic of this view was the Reverend Edward Hungerford who wrote in 1874 that Buddhism was neither a religion nor a philosophy, finding in its canon "no God, no soul, no Savior from sin, no love, no heaven."[15] Given such gloomy answers to humankind's needs, critics and proponents alike were at a loss to explain Buddhism's continued growth worldwide. For Max Müller, it remained "a riddle which no one has been able to solve."[16] Eventually, its critics amended their findings, pointing sympathetically to Buddha as an exemplary moral teacher and reformer—a tendency that, while insufficiently expressed, suggested the beginnings of tolerance over animosity.[17]

In 1871, James Freeman Clarke published *Ten Great Religions. An Essay in Comparative Theology,* the first six chapters of which were serialized in the *Atlantic Monthly*. The book offered one of the earliest efforts to explain the similarities rather than the differences between and among the major religions. Buddhism reminded Clarke of the Roman Catholic Church. "For so numerous are the resemblances between the customs of this system and those of the Romish Church that the first Catholic missionaries who encountered the priests of Buddha were confounded and thought that Satan had been mocking their sacred rites."[18] Clarke noted that Jesuit missionaries attributed these striking similarities to the influence of Nestorian missionaries who traveled into China. However, skeptics of that scenario were quick to point out that Buddhism was five hundred years older than Christianity and that many of the characteristics Christians extolled actually belonged to the age of the Buddhist emperor Asoka who ruled India around 250 B.C.[19]

Clarke's chapter titled "Buddhism, or the Protestantism of the East," depicted an even closer resemblance of Buddhism to Protestantism in that they took exception to the oppressions of the priestly class with its sacerdotal emphasis; emphasized salvation dependent on personal character; treated the body as an enemy of the soul; and recognized the laws of nature. Essentially, both advocated "a revolt of nature against spirit, of humanity against caste, of individual freedom against the despotism of an order, of salvation by faith against salvation by sacraments." While the mass was the central feature of the Roman Church, for Buddhism, as for Protestantism, the sermon acted as the exhortative instrument by which souls were saved. Similarly, while the priestly class retained its authoritative role in the Roman Church, the laity succeeded in protecting their rights in Buddhism and Protestantism. For Clarke, "notwithstanding the external resemblance of Buddhist rites and ceremonies to those of the Roman Catholic Church, the internal resemblance is to Protestantism."[20]

The Platonists

Another more esoteric channel that carried the philosophies and religions of the East into the American mind was the popular Plato Club in Jacksonville, Illinois, which formed in 1866 and flourished for more than thirty years, attracting a broad array of lecturers including Emerson, Bronson Alcott, William T. Harris, Denton J. Snider, Horace H. Morgan, and Thomas Davidson. It is difficult to find a good explanation to account for the town's attraction to non-western literature other than the presence of Hiram K. Jones, a physician who preached abolitionism and sheltered runaway slaves. Known as "the modern Plato," he lectured on philosophy at Illinois College, the town's private liberal arts school affiliated with the United Church of Christ and the Presbyterian Church, and shared his passion for metaphysics with all who would listen, drawing from a broad band of literature and religions to illuminate his lectures.[21]

Equally significant in his influence on American thought was Vermont native General Ethan Allen Hitchcock, a West Point graduate and career officer in the United States Army and known to his friends as the "Hermetic Initiate." A dedicated writer whose interests covered the disciplines of science, philosophy, and mysticism, his *Remarks on Alchemy and the Alchemists, Indicating a Method of Discovering the True Nature of Hermetic Philosophy* (1857) and *Swedenborg, a Hermetic Philosopher* (1858), argued that alchemy belonged to a legitimate field of allegory setting forth the transformation of the human soul.[22] As Hitchcock explained, the Alchemists, or Hermetic Philosophers, had not actually pursued rare metals, but wisdom, a thesis that had him looking at the broader issue of intent. He concluded that the alchemists were universally misunderstood to be seeking to transform base metals into gold and silver. Instead, their works were a product of symbolic writing, much like *Gulliver's Travels* (1726) or the adventures of *Robinson Crusoe* (1719). Teaching by means of similitude, parable, fable, allegory, and symbolism, they brought innovative ideas and opinions before the public using guarded language to avoid the consequences of civil or religious retribution. Books dealing with the "elixir of life" and the "philosopher's stone" were written to avoid discovery at a time when intellectuals found it more expedient to communicate with symbols. The alchemists were Protestants at a time when their beliefs could not be practiced openly. Neither pretenders nor imposters, they searched after truth, believing that true knowledge of the One could not be openly taught and so they resorted to numbers, figures, and allegories.[23]

Another prominent idealist of the day was the attorney Thomas Moore Johnson of Osceola, Missouri, president of the Council of the Hermetic Brotherhood of Luxor and editor of *The Platonist* (1884–88). Published monthly, the magazine stood at the forefront of a national revival elucidating the practical application of Platonic ethics. According to Johnson, who was also an early member of the Theosophical Society (1875), Platonism was a method of discipline more so than a system. Though held in low esteem among those who favored scientific knowledge, it discriminated the permanent from the changing, and the absolute from the relative, valuing the whole body of facts and not just the few.[24]

The Platonist highlighted Oriental and Theosophical philosophy, philological investigations, translations, interpretations, and utterances of gifted individuals—all intended to demonstrate a harmony between Christianity and the esoteric doctrines of ancient faiths.[25] Exemplary articles included reviews of George Wyld's *Theosophy and the Higher Life* (1880); Giles B. Stebbins's *After Dogmatic Theology, What? Materialism, or a Spiritual Philosophy and Natural Religion* (1880); William Oxley's *The Philosophy of Spirit* (1881); Alfred Percy Sinnett's *The Occult World* (1881) which described the Adepts who wielded the scepter of occultism in India; and reprints from *The Theosophist* published in India by Helena Blavatsky and Henry Steel Olcott. According to Theosophy, the occult philosophers of old—Egyptian priests, Chaldean Magi, Essenes, Gnostics, Neo-Platonists—kept their knowledge secret. The sole exception was a group of monks in the highlands of Tibet who comingled the wisdom of the ancient world with modern science for the purpose of advancing humanity's comprehension of the forces of nature.[26]

Still another important source of Platonism was Alexander Wilder whose writings and translations emphasized perception over reductionist science. Given that Numa, Zoroaster, Mohammed, and Swedenborg claimed communion with the higher spirits, he thought it essential for people to understand how an individual arrived at a state of oneness with the Divine. Calling his belief system *Entheasm,* or participation in the divine nature together with prophetic inspiration and illumination, Wilder explained that the *entheastic* condition indicated a life lived beyond the physical senses.

It was a state of illumination, the participation of the individual in the nature, spirit, and power of the Divine Purpose. Such events that occurred in the external world were expressive of experiences of the human soul, making connections between the ethics of Aristotle and the Law of Moses; the Pentateuch and the doctrines of Pythagoras and the Academy; and the Essenes of Carmel and the Therapeutea of Egypt.[27]

Concord School

The Concord School of Philosophy, which dates from 1842 when Bronson Alcott met with several philosophers to discuss organizing a summer program built around Platonic Idealism, did not materialize until 1879. Incentivized by memories of the Transcendentalist movement, the school opened with financial support from William T. Harris of St. Louis and Louisa May Alcott. Based on the idea of Plato's Academy, it offered lectures on the Transcendentalists, Neo-Platonists, and Hegelians. Decidedly more high-brow than the Chautauqua movement founded in 1874 by Lewis Miller and John Heyl Vincent, the school represented a marriage of convenience between New England Transcendentalists and the circle of Midwest Platonists under the leadership of Harris, founder of the Philosophical Society in St. Louis and editor of the *Journal of Speculative Philosophy*.[28] By years three and four, Concord's summer program had expanded to include Harris lecturing on Gnosticism, Neo-Platonism, and the philosophy of the *Bhagavad Gita*; Hiram K. Jones on platonic cosmology, cosmogony, physics, Spiritualism ancient and modern, and metaphysics; William H. Channing on true Buddhism and Oriental and mystical philosophy; Protap Chunder Mozoomdar on "Emerson as Seen from India"; Franklin B. Sanborn on Persian and Christian Oracles; Alexander Wilder on Alexandrian Platonism; John Steinfort Kedney on the higher criticism; and Mrs. Ednah D. Cheney on an understanding of Nirvana.[29]

When the Concord School refused to relocate its program further west to accommodate its midwestern associates, Jones founded the American Akadēmē in Jacksonville in 1883. The organization resulted from conversations between Jones and Wilder who viewed it as a school of philosophy dedicated to personal improvement and the pursuit of truth. Distinct from Concord's summer program, it convened the third Tuesday of each month from September through June at the residence of Dr. Jones.[30] Within a year it claimed 180 members; by 1892 there were 422, including members from France and Australia.[31]

Theosophy

Still another channel of esotericism involved the so-called theosophists, a group of spiritualists from among America's urban elite who purported to represent the wisdom of the world's most revered religious prophets (Moses, Krishna, Lao-tzu, Confucius, Buddha, and Christ) whose beliefs had been brought together in the writings and remarks of Helena Petrovna Blavatsky, Henry Steel Olcott and William Quan Judge, co-founders of the Theosophical Society in 1875. Author of *Isis Unveiled: A Master-Key to the Mysteries of Ancient and Modern Science and Theology* (1877) and *The Secret Doctrine: The Synthesis of Science, Religion and Philosophy* (1888), Blavatsky claimed to be founder of a syncretic system of Eastern and Western religious and philosophical thought based on a belief that the universe evolved through seven distinct stages and whose humanity went through an ascending process of reincarnation before arriving at pure consciousness.[32]

Like Hinduism and mind-cure, Theosophy places great emphasis on the consciousness of the moment. In theory, the source of religious knowledge is not reason but an interior illumination or vision from oneness with the universal Spirit. Identified by Alfred Percy Sinnett as "Esoteric Buddhism," though by no means divorced from other creeds like Hinduism which he admitted had equal claim to many truths, he insisted that Buddhism "remained in closer union with the esoteric doctrine than any other popular religion." Not only did Buddha trace the principle of life from its original first cause in the cosmos but taught that the soul went through successive incarnations of improvement or devolution based on Darwinian law.[33]

Alexander Wilder edited *Isis Unveiled* for publication and wrote the introduction in which he took issue with the progress claimed by the competing interests of Christianity and the "bright lamp of modern science." The struggle between science and theology for infallibility had shown both with feet of clay.[34] Looking at the ruins left from their battles, Wilder suggested that Platonic philosophy offered the only true refuge. Plato, the greatest philosopher of the pre-Christian world, faithfully mirrored the minds of the ancient world beginning with the Vedic philosophers who lived thousands of years before him, and others who left their imprint during the intervening centuries. Not only did Plato teach justice as the greatest good but that the single most important object of attainment was *real* knowledge which existed in contrast to modernity's more transitory knowledge. Beyond all secondary causes, laws, ideas, and principles was the lawgiver, the supreme Good which stood on the permanent principle of unity beneath the forms and changes in the universe. *Nous,* or the rational soul of man, possessed a love of wisdom and a nature like the supreme mind making man capable of understanding the eternal realities. However, like the captives in the Plato's cave, man perceived only the shadows of objects, thinking them to be real. It was the province of philosophy that broke man from the bondage of the senses to experience the eternal world of truth, goodness, and beauty.[35]

Wilder explained that the object of *Isis Unveiled* was not to force on the reader the personal theories of the author or to give her ideas the imprimatur of scientific truth. Rather, the book offered a summary of the religions, philosophies, secret doctrines, and traditions that had reached Christendom by various routes over the centuries, explaining that many had braved persecution and prejudice in their efforts to convey this knowledge. While some chose to view these conveyers as charlatans and treated them with contempt, it was to their credit that the secret doctrines were

The young Paul Carus, not long after his arrival in La Salle.

preserved to enlighten mankind. Spiritualism was an expression of the occult tradition that dated back to the ancient wisdom of the Egyptians and the hermetic philosophies of the Renaissance, but the true fountainhead of ancient wisdom derived from India.[36]

As a western adaptation of Eastern religion and philosophy, Theosophy represented a high-brow variation of modern Spiritualism which had its origins in the so-called Hydesville and Rochester rappings that took place in western New York in 1848 and the efforts assembled by its proponents to provide a reasoned explanation of the phenomenon. Claiming validation by committees of educated professionals and scientists as well as reliance on pseudo-sciences such as mesmerism, phrenopathy, sarcognomy, and psychometry, the rappings were judged to be 'scientific' proof of religious promises made over the centuries of an afterlife. Now, science had at long last produced a psychological and therapeutic breakthrough that proponents believed would heal social wrongs, build moral character, and propel humanity toward a more perfect society. The rappings marked a transition from understanding death as a predominantly religious phenomenon not knowing with any assurance whether God had elected the individual for salvation, to a secular view of death as part of a natural process independent of any religion-bound eschatology. Spiritualism provided an otherworldly existence free from the punitive God of the Judeo-Christian tradition, a change due in no small measure to the staggering loss of lives in the Crimea and the American Civil War.[37]

Theosophy agreed with the reality of Spiritualism's manifestations but disagreed on the source of intelligence behind it. Whereas spiritualists maintained that communications from the 'other world' could come from any departed spirit, Theosophists claimed a single source, that of the Tibetan Brotherhood (Adepts) who explained the world in a manner beyond rational thinking. Thus, instead of mediums using darkened rooms and theatrical props to bring forth disembodied spirits answering questions from the mundane to the serious using rappings and slate-writing, the Theosophist's information arrived in the form of "materialized letters" addressing issues of moral import for the improvement of society.[38]

As explained by Alfred Percy Sinnett, the occult philosophers of old—the Egyptian priests, Chaldean Magi, Essenes, Gnostics, Neo-Platonists, and others—who kept their knowledge secret in order to protect themselves from enemies, shrouded their work as if they were displays of magic. It was this system of knowledge, cultivated in secret, that was inherited by the Adepts. Given that the West was preoccupied with material progress, it remained ignorant of much of this knowledge. The most the West was able to realize had been the manifestations which mediums produced through the phenomena of Spiritualism. However, this was but a minuscule aspect of the occult. The "spirit-raps" produced by the work of mediums were nowhere near what was possible, and although Sinnett had no intention "to make war on spiritualists," he wanted the public to understand that the phenomena of Spiritualism were primitive compared to Theosophy whose Adepts passed on their secrets to the world through "psychological telegraphy."[39]

This had not always been the case. According to Sinnett, Blavatsky had communicated with the spirit world using "raps" as late as 1880 but then came to regard the Brotherhood of Adepts as a more reliant source of spiritual knowledge. Since then, "wherever Madame Blavatsky is, there the Brothers . . . can and constantly do produce phenomena of the most overwhelming sort, with the production of which she herself has little or nothing to do." Sinnett claimed his own connections with the Brotherhood through messages he received from "Koot Hoomi," who first communicated to him in a letter that fell from the ceiling while he was talking with Blavatsky. "We were sitting at different sides of a large square table in the middle of the room, and the full daylight was shining. There was no one else in the room. Suddenly, down upon the table before me, but to my right hand, Madame Blavatsky being to my left, there fell a thick letter . . . out of nothing, so to speak; it was materialized, or reintegrated in the air before my eyes."[40] Referred to simply as "K.H.," Hoomi corresponded with both Sinnett and Allan

Octavian Hume, a Theosophist and member of the Indian Civil Service. Their communications were published in the book *The Mahatma Letters to AP. Sinnett* (1923).[41]

As a member of New York's metropolitan society, Henry Olcott reflected the bourgeois values of the city's patrician gentry with their admiration of Emerson, Whitman and Swedenborg; their curiosity concerning the mysteries of the Orient, including an open mind to the occult; and their favorable disposition towards social reform. Revered as the "White Buddhist," Olcott brokered a religious tradition that, while Buddhist in name, combined the religious beliefs and behaviors of America's Protestant communities, the contributions of academic Orientalists, and the social and political predilections of the city's gentry class. Olcott had a penchant for the work of Thomas Rhys Davids and Max Müller who had successfully transformed their Oriental interests into academic fields of study. Drawing from their research, he reconstructed a modern manifestation of Brahmanism and Buddhism out of what remained of their ancient truths. As Stephen Prothero explained, "Olcott set himself up as Asia's savior, the outsider hero who would sweep in at the end of the drama to save a disenchanted subcontinent from spiritual death." In doing so, he joined with other reform Orientalists in defining Eastern religions in ethical and moral terms rather than in ritualistic creeds.[42]

In 1878 Olcott and Blavatsky moved their headquarters to India, settling in Adyar, a suburb of Madras, to continue their work. Before long, differences arose between the two co-founders. Blavatsky, who insisted that all religions were true, distanced herself from Olcott's growing affinity for Buddhism. In place of her combination of Spiritualism and science, Olcott introduced a mixture of Buddhism and scientific reasoning. Viewing the Buddha as an ethical reformer who opposed the oppressiveness of the caste system, promoted self-reliance, and rejected rituals and ceremonialism, he transformed classical Buddhism into a modern religion.[43]

While Blavatsky's Theosophy operated at the intersection of science, occult research, and the law of progressive evolution, focusing on the individual and not a reform agenda, Olcott's Buddhism represented a combination of German romanticism, Victorian occultism, Christian liberalism, Enlightenment philosophy, and neo-Darwinian theories of evolution aimed at social transformation. With their approaches divided, the two labored independently of the other, with Blavatsky venting her thoughts in the organization's London magazine *Lucifer* (1887–97), while Olcott pursued a more structured and less secretive exposition of religion in *The Theosophist* (1879–present). Despite their differences, both emphasized science, evolution, and cosmic laws, and saw in Eastern traditions a degree of wisdom that had long been lacking in the materialistic West.[44]

Olcott remained fixated on the scientific investigation of both science and religion, believing it possible to identify a "neutral ground" where their differences could be sorted out.[45] According to David McMahan, "Olcott allied Buddhism with scientific rationalism in implicit criticism of orthodox Christianity but went well beyond the tenets of conventional science in extrapolating from . . . 'occult sciences' of the nineteenth century."[46] In his claim that Buddhism was a scientific rather than a revealed religion, he accepted mesmerism (hypnotism) as a legitimate empirical science and not simply a form of occult metaphysics. He also accepted psychometry, a form of extrasensory perception proposed by Joseph Rodes Buchanan that permitted a person to sense (read) the history of an object by holding or touching it; and odic force proposed by the Austrian chemist and philosopher Baron Karl Ludwig Von Reichenbach and Dr. H. Baraduc, a French parapsychologist and author of *Human Soul, Its Lights, and the Iconography of the Fluidic Invisible* (1896). Baraduc claimed this force was visible as an aura or halo surrounding all human beings, animals, trees, plants, and even stones. Olcott used this science to explain the textual descriptions of the Buddha with buddharansi rays or auric light emanating from the head. Belief in the powers attributed to the Buddha (or the Adepts in Theosophy) derived not from unquestioned faith or miracles but an alternative world of occult science centered on the unseen forces of magnetism, clairvoyance, mediumship, auras, and similar paranormal claims.[47]

In 1881, Olcott authored *The Buddhist Catechism* linking Buddhist beliefs with a combination of scientific rationalism and the occult sciences. Much like its Christian counterparts in both Catholic and Protestant denominations, the catechism employed a question-and-answer approach to explain Buddhist beliefs. Compiled by Olcott while living in Ceylon, it distinguished the basic principles of Buddhist doctrine from commonly held customs, some of which derived from Hinduism and primitive nature-worship. Purporting to decry all idolatry, astrology, omens, and other corruptions as non-Buddhistic, the catechism became the accepted authority in Ceylon and subsequently translated into French (1883), English (1885), and German (1886).

After Blavatsky's death in 1891, Theosophy split into several groups, with Annie Besant taking over leadership of the society based in Adyar; Katherine Tingley assuming leadership over those from the New York branch who resettled in Loma Linda, California; Austrian Rudolf Steiner who broke with Besant over her allegiance to Indian messianic spiritual leader Jiddu Krishnamurti; and Olcott who formally converted to Buddhism in 1880 and became the principal revivalist of Buddhism in Sri Lanka. By the early decades of the twentieth century, Theosophy claimed to be a worldwide movement drawing into its fold luminaries like George Bernard Shaw, Lyman Frank Baum, James Henry Cousins, William Butler Yeats, Lewis Carroll, Sir Arthur Conan Doyle, Jack London, James Joyce, D.H. Lawrence, T.S. Eliot, Thornton Wilder, Kurt Vonnegut, Susan B. Anthony, and Thomas Edison.[48] By the time of the World's Parliament of Religions in 1893, Theosophy had become an accepted companion in America's journey into selflessness and transcendence.

New Thought

While skeptics assailed Blavatsky's claim to paranormal powers as pretentious nonsense, a movement developed out of New England in the 1890s known as New Thought, advancing a set of beliefs connecting Western and Eastern elements of churched and unchurched spirituality. Described by Horatio Dresser, one of its founders, as a "kindred movement" to Theosophy, its stable of writers borrowed from Emerson and a host of lesser-known thinkers to explain how the human soul transitioned to a higher attainment—connecting self-fulfillment with transcendence.[49] New Thought could not have existed without the influence of Emerson whose message of individualism and self-reliance provided inspiration for the soul being immortal, spiritual, and free. Behind the veil of the physical world lay a spiritual universe of incomprehensible proportions where Christ or Buddha as the God-appointed mediator—not a secretive Brotherhood of Adepts—served as the channel of communication. With ideas that traced back to Scripture, Transcendentalism, Idealism, Spiritualism, Hinduism, Buddhism, and evolutionism, the New Thought movement began as a form of mind-cure healing before evolving into a philosophy of positive-thinking and eventually for some, into a misguided prosperity gospel. New Thought brought together a cluster of cultural symbols—both native and foreign—applying them in novel ways. It stood as a metaphor for people wanting to discover not only their innermost selves, but in doing so, finding God.[50]

The passage of American metaphysical thinking from Calvinism to New Thought began with the private medical practice of Phineas Parkhurst Quimby in Belfast, Maine, before breaking into the late nineteenth and twentieth century in the form of both church and unchurched spokespersons. Built on principles centered around healing, self-discovery, and empowerment, its gifted writers and teachers—Warren Felt Evans, Horatio Dresser, William Walker Atkinson, Bruce Barton, Sarah J. Farmer, Dale Carnegie, Emma Curtis Hopkins, Luther M. Marsden, Annie Rix Militz, Ralph Waldo Trine, and others—constructed a philosophy of free spirits seeking personal and collective growth. Over time, its philosophy preached the practical over the theoretical, of self-sufficiency over surrender, of instant over delayed gratification, and cash value as the measure of personal success.

Acclaimed as devotees of the scientific method, New Thoughters employed those portions of the Bible they judged agreeable to their needs but saw no reason why God would speak only through Moses or Jesus, and not through Whitman, Emerson, Buddha, or even a Jack Kerouac or Deepak Chopra. As for the lessons learned from Asia's religions, all were of equal importance to Scripture. Out of each, readers learned to respect individual choice, oppose textual literalists, reject the imposition of mind and spirit on others, and approached God through benevolence toward Being. To cultivate the awareness of the divine, New Thoughters used a combination of breathing exercises, word repetition, "entering the silence," meditation, yoga, and language drawn from Hindu and Buddhist texts.[51]

Seicho No Ie, a syncretic, monotheistic, non-denominational branch of the New Thought movement includes both Buddhist and Taoist Thought. With a reported 1.6 million adherents, mostly in Japan, it represents the largest New Thought organization in the world. Founded in 1930 by Masaharu Taniguchi, an English translator in Tokyo who studied world philosophies, it emphasizes the need for realizing God consciousness within everyone through the power of mind and replacing all negativism with positive thoughts. [52]

Meiji Rule

Official interest in the East, especially Japan, caught the attention of more sober-minded Americans following Commodore Matthew Perry's visit to the island nation with an armada of eleven ships in 1853. Soon afterwards, the Japanese government's policy of seclusion officially ended. Under Meiji leadership (1868–1912), Japan became a much-visited nation, including a small circle of Buddhist enthusiasts like Earnest Fenollosa, Curator of Far Eastern Art at the Boston

Museum, who lived in Japan from 1878 to 1890, and Japanese art collector William Sturgis Bigelow. The two, sometimes referred to as the "Boston Buddhists," urged the blending of Eastern spirituality with Western science. Bigelow was appointed lecturer in Buddhist Doctrine at Harvard where he created a fund to support Buddhist studies. Others like Henry Adams, zoologist and Orientalist Edward Sylvester Morse, translator Lafcadio Hearn, and astronomer and mathematician Percival Lowell, traveled throughout Asia to experience firsthand its many cultures and traditions. As religious skeptics and vocal critics of materialism, they drew individuals like painter and muralist John La Farge, and gifted statesman John Hay into their orbit of Japanese and Buddhist culture. So great had been this influence that Adams wrote: "Buddhist contemplation of the infinite seems the only natural mode of life."[53] One example was the sculptor Augustus Saint-Gaudens's rendition of Buddhist devotional art in the memorial commissioned by Adams for his wife Marian who took her life in 1886. Located in Rock Creek Cemetery in Washington, D.C., the monument grew out of a trip Adams made to Japan with La Farge in the summer after his wife's death to find inspiration for her memorial. A blend of Asian and European ideals, the memorial was meant to symbolize the Buddhist icon Kuan-yin who is regarded as the quintessence of compassion.[54]

* * *

All the above served as a prelude to the tectonic impact of the World's Parliament of Religions which convened September 11–28 as an auxiliary congress to the Columbian Exhibition held in Chicago from May 1st through October 31st, 1893. For its participants and observers, the Parliament proved to be a brilliant success, due in large measure to the popularity of its non-Christian speakers, especially its Buddhist and Hindu delegates, who touted their religions as better suited than Christianity to meet the challenges of the modern age. The Parliament's success was also due to its capable architects, the lawyer and judge Charles Carroll Bonney, and Presbyterian clergyman Rev. John Henry Barrows. However, it fell to the labors of Paul Carus, editor, publicist, and writer for the Open Court Publishing Company in LaSalle, Illinois, to give Buddhism a place of honor. To him belongs the title of midwife to Buddhism's success as both a philosophy and a religion, presenting it to the western world as a rational and scientific philosophy whose principles aligned with the most liberal elements of Protestantism and the Enlightenment.

2
Apprentice Years

> If a traveler does not meet with one who is his better, or his equal, let him firmly keep to his solitary journey; there is no companionship with fools.
>
> —PAUL CARUS, *The Gospel of Buddha,* 1894

Paul Carus, the son of Dr. Gustav and Laura (Krueger) Carus, was born July 18th, 1852, in the town of Ilsenburg, located at the north foot of the Harz Mountains in Saxony-Anhalt. His father, a prominent Lutheran minister and pulpit orator who rose through the ranks to become Superintendent of the State Church of Eastern Prussia, set a high standard for his son by sending him to the gymnasia in Posen and then Stettin to study mathematics and classics under the tutelage of Indologist and polymath scholar Hermann Günther Grassmann, author of *Die Lineale Ausdehnungslehre, ein neuer Zweig der Mathematik* (The Theory of Linear Extension: A New Branch of Mathematics). Grassmann, whose mastery of mathematics would later influence the British mathematician and philosopher Alfred North Whitehead, introduced Carus to the philosophy of forms, meaning the determining principle of a thing as distinguished from matter. From the gymnasium, Carus pursued his studies at the universities of Greifswald, Strasbourg, and then Tübingen, whose school of theology had become a prominent source of the higher criticism.

Though intending to follow his father's footsteps into the ministry, Carus instead faced a crisis of faith due to Christianity's flawed credibility in the light of higher criticism, the first of several devastating trials that shattered its paradigmatic role in the West. Another came with Darwin's theory of natural selection which undermined the long-held teleological basis upon which natural theology stood. The world of reductionist reasoning, once the bugbear of religion's faithful in the debate between materialism and vitalism, became the normative basis for identifying demonstrable truths. Unable to subscribe to his father's beliefs, Carus would spend his professional career seeking a world-view compatible with what he found in philosophy, philology, and the natural sciences. Having rejected the German orthodox religion of his father which emphasized revelation and the concept of God as an anthropomorphic Being, he instead conceived of God as the intrinsic source of universal order and of man's moral aspirations. Furthermore, he considered the issue of the historical Jesus solved by the reverent but scientific and critical research of the gospels conducted by Heinrich Julius Holtzmann, professor of theology at the University of Strasbourg. In accepting an optimistic view of science, he felt assurance that its methods, when applied to the different disciplines, would result in humankind's steady progression.

The Academy

After earning his PhD in classical philology from Tübingen in 1876, Carus served briefly in the Twelfth Saxon Artillery Regiment in Mertz before accepting an appointment to the gymnasium in Dresden and then to the military academy of the Royal Saxon Cadet Corps where he held the position of *Oberlehrer* teaching Latin, German, and history. In 1882, Carus published *Lieder eines Buddhisten* (Songs of a Buddhist) suggesting that, like other German intellectuals, he had been drawn to Buddhist philosophy and ethics through the treatises and translations of Eugène Burnouf's *Introduction à L'histoire du bouddhisme indien* (1844); Arthur Schopenhauer's *The World as Will and Representation* (1818); Paul Deussen's study of the Vedanta; August Wilhelm Schlegel's work in Sanskrit; and Johann Wolfgang von Goethe's *Faust* (1808; 1831).[1]

While at the academy, Carus published several articles on religious and philosophical topics, one of which angered the school's director for questioning the literalness of Scripture. Faced with prospect of writing no further expressions of his liberal views, he chose to leave the academy. In a testimonial given on his departure from the corps, his colleagues wrote: "He resigns because his religious views are not in harmony with the Christian spirit, in accordance with which the training and education of the Corps of Cadets should be conducted . . . But he has in no wise—neither in his teaching nor on other occasions—obtruded these opinions."[2]

Recognizing the limitations placed on his future by remaining in his homeland, Carus decided to emigrate to the United States. Before leaving, he traveled the continent and resided for a brief time in Great Britain where he acquired the basics of English. Not unlike many young adults in Continental Europe, he intended to test his abilities and aspirations in America, believing it offered the opportune place and time to make his mark in the world. Arriving in 1884, he found work tutoring in Boston before moving to New York where he obtained employment as co-editor of *Zickel's Novellen-schatz and Familien-Blätter.* With time on his hands, he also wrote articles and poetry for several magazines, one of which was *The Index*, a publication of Boston's Free Religious Association co-edited by Benjamin Franklin Underwood.

Monism and Meliorism

In 1885, Carus published *Monism and Meliorism, A Philosophical Essay on Causality and Ethics,* an eighty-three page monograph in which he proposed a philosophical system comprised of two key words: *monism* which stood for a conception of the world, tracing everything to a single source or principle, and *meliorism* which advocated a view of life that, rejecting both optimism and pessimism, found purpose in the "aspiration of a constant progress to some higher state of existence." Monism related closely to the positions taken by Ernst Mach and Ernst Haeckel in that they rejected Cartesian dualism as unscientific, proclaiming instead a oneness of truth and the unity of the universe. Drawn to the philosophy of *forms* and God as the *principle* of form, Carus set out to find truth in both religion (when approached scientifically) and science, viewing them as two sides of the same coin. Confident in what he termed the "Religion of Science," he felt that a proper study of science and religion would result in a single result—monism.[3]

Carus began his study with an analysis of Immanuel Kant's *Critique of Pure Reason* (1781) which had marked the beginning of a new era in the study of philosophy. In his attempt to solve the problem of dualism and the unknowability of the "thing-in-itself," Kant looked to monism to connect subject and object. As Carus explained, "What Luther did for religion, and Copernicus for science, Kant has done for philosophic thought." He had taken the development of human thought in a new direction, clearing away the "rotten edifice" of metaphysics, filled as it was by the antagonistic principles of Bishop George Berkeley's spiritualism, John Locke's sensualism, David Hume's skepticism, August Comte's positivism, Gottfried Wilhelm Leibnitz's idealism, and Paul-Henri Thiry d'Holbach's materialism. Some of the above were tied to creed and faith, others to atheism and the "nonsense" of the Neo-Platonists, while Kant "stood above parties and showed his greatness by embracing them all."[4]

Kant explained that time and space were no realities and, consequently, the world was a mere phenomenon while the soul along with God were noumena, i.e., concepts. Thus, when "we perceive in the world certain purposes proving the premeditative wisdom of a creator . . . such a teleology or doctrine of purposes is an imagination and simply a paralogism of pure reason; for it is only according to the law of causality that the affairs of the world are regulated." Despite his atheism, Kant felt that the idea of God contained a kernel of truth, namely, that there was but one law ruling the world (causality). Concluding, however, that Kant had failed to find the "higher unity," Carus laid claim to solving what Kant had failed to accomplish. By no means shy of the task before him, he remarked: "If Kant compared his work to that of Copernicus, I may fairly liken mine to that of Kepler who filled out the Copernican system and reduced the law of motion of planets to simple mathematical formulae."[5]

Carus rejected the idea of a *first cause* in the sense of a Creator, God, or law governing the universe as the ground on which everything rested. This represented the God of the theist or what Spencer called the "Unknowable." As for the term "final cause," which he also rejected, it was invented on the supposition that there existed two kinds of causality: one regulated by chance, and the other by some conscious will. For himself, Carus could accept neither. Finding it an "unfortunate expression," he proposed the term *finis* in place of any implied theology. "We find a *finis* wherever we observe causation," he wrote. "Everywhere in the world therefore we meet with some development; it is found in history as well as in natural science." *Finis* implied an aim or purpose in the universe. The faculty of mind which enabled persons to perceive the aim or purpose was reason which produced understanding, and judgment. It represented a cause that operated without interference, reflecting a progressive evolution "toward a higher plan and a better arrangement."[6]

Carus discounted the ethics expounded by both the theologian-based morals of religionists and the utilitarian's principle of happiness. Nevertheless, ethics (he preferred the term *virtue*) formed an essential part of his meliorism which he considered not a regulative law but a natural law at the very core and inmost quality of the world. The purpose, aim, and end of an organism's existence was not in itself but in something higher. "This principle pervades all organic nature. Organisms cannot exist but under this condition; and *this principle is ethical.*"[7]

> So man and the society of man rest on the same principle. The first higher unity is the family; families grow into tribes, and tribes form nations. The love of parents has broadened into patriotism, and no doubt the next higher ideal will be that of humanity. The next higher stage to which development ever tends is the *ideal,* and there will be no rest in the minds of the single individuals until this ideal is realized. After that, new ideals arise and lead on the interminable, infinite path of progress, not as Darwin says, merely ruled by the famous law of the struggle for life but enhanced by the *strife for the ideal.*[8]

Carus considered meliorism a concept in keeping with the values of his newly chosen homeland and evident in the writings and speeches of its philosophers and progressive thinkers. From John Winthrop's "A Model of Christian Charity," a sermon delivered in 1630 at Holyrood Church in Southampton, to Emerson's "The American Scholar," delivered before the Phi Beta Kappa Society at Cambridge in 1837, meliorism offered a cautiously optimistic view of life that turned away from any foreordained fate. Carus was inclined to believe that this law ruled in the organic world as well—a law of primordial matter, of single atoms and clusters of nebulae whose chaos and turmoil eventually gave way to order.[9]

Edward Carl Hegeler

In the meantime, Edward Carl Hegeler and his schoolmate and business partner Frederick William Matthiessen, both graduates of the School of Mines in Freiberg, Saxony, immigrated to the United States in 1857 with the idea of partnering in a business enterprise. After working in a zinc operation in Friedensville, in Lehigh County, Pennsylvania, where they manufactured zinc on a small scale, they looked for opportunities to invest their own capital in a similar enterprise. After exploring possibilities in Pittsburgh and Johnsville in Bucks

County, Pennsylvania, as well as in southeastern Missouri, they selected La Salle, Illinois, as the ideal location due to its proximity to the zinc and coal deposits at Mineral Point, Wisconsin. Their company, the Matthiessen and Hegeler Zinc Company (M&H Zinc), grew rapidly because of the need for zinc cartridges in the Civil War and quickly became a highly successful business enterprise. By the late 1880s, the company employed approximately three hundred workers producing eight million pounds of zinc annually.[10]

On a return visit to Germany in 1860, Hegeler married Camilla Weisbach, the daughter of one of his teachers at Freiberg. Together they had ten children, the oldest of whom was Mary Henriette who at age sixteen began working in the assay office of M&H Zinc. She went on to major in mathematics and chemistry at the University of Michigan and, following her graduation in 1882, attended lectures on metallurgy at Freiberg before returning to La Salle to work in the plant. In 1886 she became a director at M&H Zinc, thereby allowing her father to devote his time to philosophical interests. Already known and respected for his generous support of liberal organizations, Hegeler intended to utilize the framework of monism to promote his personal philosophical, moral, and religious ideas which meant placing religion and ethics on a scientific basis.[11]

Benjamin Franklin Underwood, an outspoken agnostic and representative of the freethought movement and editor of *The Index*, a Unitarian magazine published by the Free Religious Association, wrote Hegeler in June 1886, asking for support for the magazine which required at least a thousand dollars in addition to receipts from subscriptions to cover its annual expenses.[12] The respected author of *Darwinism: What It Is and the Proofs in Favor of It* (1875), *The Crimes and Cruelties of Christianity* (1877), and *Woman: Her Past and Present, Her Rights and Wrongs* (1877), Underwood received instead a proposal to consider moving *The Index* to Chicago where Hegeler offered to underwrite its expenses provided it could be tailored to monism. Alternatively, he offered Underwood the job as editor of an entirely new journal that would replace *The Index* and provide the world with a philosophy that harmonized with his monistic views.[13] Hegeler was single-minded in his beliefs. "His strategic plan," explained Nicholas L. Guardiano, "was to recruit a mix of specialists in science, religion, philosophy, and other disciplines to set them on the common task of developing the doctrine of monism." Despite being freethinkers and champions of materialism, Underwood and his wife Sara seemed the most likely match.[14]

After Hegeler and Underwood met in New York to discuss their mutual interests, including the decision by the trustees of the Free Religious Association to close *The Index* rather than move it to Chicago, they began several months of correspondence involving possible names for the new journal which included "Dawn," "The Radical," "Reasoner," "The Meliorist," "The Contemporary," "The Monist," and "The Monist's Open Court." They eventually settled on *The Open Court* as the most easily understood for those religious ideas "that affect the building up of religion on the basis of science." The title came partly by accident due to a misunderstanding (the first but certainly not the last) between the two men as Hegeler had preferred the title "The Monist" (which he would later title his second journal). Not surprisingly, differences arose almost immediately due to Underwood's atheism as well as his insistence that he have complete control over the management of the magazine, and Hegeler's insistence on being more than just the publisher.[15] Committed to the goal of finding a connection between science and religion, Hegeler founded the Open Court Publishing Company in February 1887. That same month, *The Open Court* made its inaugural issue as a fortnightly magazine on February 17, 1887, from the company's offices in the Nixon Building at 175 La Salle Street in downtown Chicago (later moved to 324 Dearborn and then 1322 Wabash Avenue). In it, Hegeler expressed his intent "to establish religion on the basis of science and in connection therewith it will present the Monistic philosophy . . . which embraces all that is true and good in the religion that was taught in childhood . . . . "[16] Surprised, however, by the language in the masthead ("Devoted to the Work of Establishing Ethics and Religion upon a Scientific Basis") and in the magazine's content which Hegeler believed had been expressly agreed upon, he asked for a meeting with Underwood and directed his attorney, Charles K. Whipple, to attend at which time specific directions were again given regarding the publisher's expectations.

With the publication of the first issue, most readers of *The Index* transferred their support to the new magazine, giving it a foundation on which to build new subscribers. Nevertheless, the conflicting views of Hegeler and his editor/manager continued to reflect an increasingly tense relationship between the two men. Behaving the part of a schoolmaster in expressing his objections to Hegeler's frequent suggestions, Underwood reminded the publisher repeatedly that he expected "unhampered control" over the editorial and management aspects of the paper.[17]

Ironically, it was Underwood who introduced Carus to Hegeler, giving the publisher a book of poems titled *Ein Leben in Liedern, Gedichte eines Heimathlosen* (A Life in Song: Poems of a Homeless Person) that Carus had written. Even before then, Hegeler had come across a copy of Carus's *Monism and Meliorism*. Impressed by the breadth and depth of the content in the two publications, Hegeler reached out to the young man, offering him employment as a tutor to his older children and as associate editor of *The Open Court*, sharing the title and responsibilities with Underwood's wife. Hegeler suggested that Carus's assistance would be helpful in managing correspondence with German scholars and the translation of their articles into English. He even considered asking for Carus's assistance in establishing a college for philosophy and scientific religion in America, an idea he had been considering for some time. For his part, Carus suggested adding a new section to the magazine titled "Transatlantic Review" to incorporate articles on European thought. Carus welcomed the offer to join the Hegeler family and when asked to assist Carus with his English, Mary Hegeler became quite taken by the family's handsome new tutor.[18]

When Hegeler announced his appointment of Carus as associate editor and spokesperson for the publisher's views in subsequent issues, Underwood took exception to the decision as it had been made without his involvement. The action, which clearly violated the contract, brought a new and unexpected challenge to the editor's relationship with Hegeler and with Carus. Since Carus lived with the Hegeler family in La Salle and was courting the eldest daughter Mary while the Underwoods worked out of the company's office in Chicago nearly one hundred miles north-northeast of La Salle their differences, both real and perceived, became increasingly difficult to resolve.[19]

Soon after Carus's appointment, the magazine published his article "Monism, Dualism, and Agnosticism." Written in collaboration with Hegeler, it expressed their strong opinions toward monism and their rejection of both dualism and agnosticism. "For Hegeler," explained Guardiano, "the problem with agnosticism is that it denies the possibility of knowledge of a spiritual reality, and thus it is the ultimate antithesis to his faith in religion and consequently his religious monism."[20] According to historian Harold Henderson, Hegeler intended for Carus's articles to be one of the more important additions to the magazine while, for Underwood, "they were an irritation and an embarrassment." Underwood insisted on preserving the journal's philosophical neutrality, a position that ran counter to the publisher's missionary bias towards monism which he believed would eventually become a religion. As both men were strong-willed, it seemed only a matter of time before the discord between the two became intolerable.[21] Objecting to the journal being used in this manner as it violated the very definition of the word *open* in in the magazine's title, Underwood wrote Hegeler on October 28th 1887, tendering his and his wife's resignation to take effect at the end of the year.[22] In the November 24th 1887 issue, the Underwoods offered their farewell comments to readers.

> It is sufficient, perhaps, to say that the immediate cause of the editors' resignation is Mr. Hegeler's expressed desire and purpose

> to make a place on THE OPEN COURT for Dr. Paul Carus, who never had, it should here be said, any editorial connection with the paper, who never wrote a line for it except as a contributor and as Mr. Hegeler's secretary, and who was unknown to Mr. Hegeler when his contract with the editors was made. To the request that Dr. Carus be accepted as an associate editor, the present editors, for good and sufficient reasons, have unhesitatingly refused to accede, and although always willing to make concessions when required in the interests of the paper, a point is now reached where they feel compelled by self-respect to sever all relations with this journal rather than yield to Mr. Hegeler's latest requirement. At the same time the editors acquit the proprietor of the paper of any intentional injustice in this matter, and appreciate his high purpose in founding and sustaining THE OPEN COURT. May its future fulfil his highest expectations.[23]

Editor and Publisher

In the December 22, 1887, issue of *The Open Court*, the new editor and manager, Paul Carus, announced his (and Hegeler's) intention of using the journal to combine religion and science in the philosophy of monism—a philosophy intended to remove the superstitions and falsehoods from religion by establishing a more spiritualized and scientifically verifiable faith. Its new masthead ("A Fortnightly Journal Devoted to the Work of Conciliating Religion and Science") communicated to its readers a clear distinction from the journal edited and managed by Benjamin Underwood.[24] Both publisher and editor considered themselves theological/scientific system-builders who believed in evolution and in the possibility of a religion purified by science that would eventually embrace all religions. Neither considered their reformist ideas as advocating atheism or agnosticism; rather, they viewed their collective efforts to be the establishment of religion and ethics on a scientific basis. This remained the core of their thinking. Acting as Hegeler's ghost-writer, Carus explained to the magazine's readership that his aim was to publish for discussion the "philosophical problems of God and soul, of life and death, and life after death, the problems of the origin of man and the significance of religion, and the nature of morality, occasionally including political and social life without, however, entering into party questions." Implied in this statement was his intent for the magazine to become a vehicle for religious reform and to perform that responsibility devotedly and dispassionately. Not until Carus's initiation into the world of Asian religions by way of his involvement in the World Parliament of Religions in 1893 did he and Hegeler bring a change in direction to the magazine by choosing Buddhism to breach the shattered divide within Christianity between science and religion.[25]

Carus and Mary Hegeler were married on March 28th, 1888. For the next thirty-two years, Carus worked out of the family home in La Salle editing and managing *The Open Court* and its sister journal, *The Monist*, which he started in 1890. In addition, he wrote and edited an array of books produced by the Open Court Publishing Company.

The Open Court Publishing Company, as explained by its new editor, was now the operational center for the reformation of religion under the influence of science as foreordained by the law of evolution. Science was slowly transforming all aspects of life with truths verified by rational proof, experience, and experiment. While doing away with ignorance and bigotry, it was not as some critics claimed, ushering in an age of irreligion. Instead, it was proving to the world the human origin of Scripture, the outdated anthropomorphism of the old God-conception, and discrediting the traditional theory of a soul-entity. In true Comtean fashion, he saw the path to truth passing through periods of myth and allegory, as well as through parables, mysticism, and other approximations of scientific understanding. This path was in conformity with the law of evolution which, as a general principle, meant not the destruction of the old but the building of a higher and truer interpretation of religion. "We are too much convinced of the truth of evolution as a general principle of all life, not to apply it also to the spiritual domains of civilization, morality and religion."[26]

Carus did not follow his father into the ministry as he originally intended, but with encouragement from Hegeler, his employer and father-in-law, he became a missionary for a religion of science, believing monism would not only replace but fulfill the purposes of orthodox Christianity.[27] "Carus's radical convictions," explained Henderson, "were governed by a conservative instinct. Thus, the religion of science . . . was radical in substance, conservative in style: radical in its rejection of traditional dogmas, conservative in reinterpreting them 'scientifically' and in retaining such terms as *God* and *immortality*."[28] As Carus explained:

> When I took charge of *The Open Court* in 1888, it was regarded as an ultra-radical and even shockingly blasphemous periodical. I thought then that the time would slowly come when the very orthodox of our traditional religion would finally fall back on the interpretation which I then advocated. The time has come more quickly than I expected. A new orthodoxy has arisen, and the philosophical interpretation of religion will gradually but surely become recognized as the true conception of a scientific theology; in other words, *theonomy*, with its scientific conception of God, will replace the old bigoted views of an antiquated theology.[29]

Markers

Over the next several years, Carus's articles and books not only tightened the relationship he had with his father-in-law, they became markers for his editorial approach until the World's Parliament of Religions. These included "The Unknowable" (1887), "Science and Religion" (1887), "Monism and Religion" (1888), "The Religious Character of Monism: In Reply to the Criticism of Dr. Gustav Carus" (1888), followed by the monographs *The Idea of God* (1888), *Fundamental Problems* (1891), *The Soul of Man* (1891), *Homilies of Science* (1892), *Primer of Philosophy* (1893), and *The Religion of Science* (1893).

One of Carus's more memorable articles involved a response to his own father who questioned his son's advocacy of monism, claiming it not only denied a personal God but compelled the notion that the world was a product of accident. This denial, in turn, forced believers to renounce the existence of the soul, freedom of will, immortality, and every dignity pertaining to humanity. As Dr. Gustav Carus explained,

> The quibbling sophistries that delight in renouncing God, the Freedom of the Will, and the Immortality of the Soul, are long since recognized as the marks of a degenerate and imperfect culture that can only stifle the vigor and energy of life, and which must stunt in a people the sense of the true worth of human life, should these irreligious and unethical principles ever assume a serious front and no longer remain the mere mental freaks of literary adepts. For irreligious and unethical they certainly are, even though by a misuse of language they be called religious and ethical. There is no religion without a personal God; and without free will, without accountability for acts and omissions, there is likewise no morality.[30]

Carus vigorously but politely denied his father's assumptions concerning the tenets of *The Open Court,* particularly his claim that it was an organ of freethought. Nor did he accept his father's claim that he viewed the world as the fortuitous result of blind forces. Freedom of the will and the self-determination of rational beings, explained Carus in his rebuttal, were not annihilated by the fact that "events in the world proceed necessarily from their conditions." Monism not only accepted the doctrine of the freedom of will but rejected any assumption that implied a fortuitous outcome of chance. "What man feels as an *ought,* or categoric imperative for his *conduct,* does not proceed from a mysterious power but is the natural outgrowth of his rational nature. It is a necessary result of life's evolution on earth; and the *ought* must . . . lead humanity onward on the path of progress." The God of monism had a living presence but was no longer recognized "as an ego like ourselves with successive states of consciousness."[31]

In another essay titled "The Idea of God" which Carus read before the Society for Ethical Culture of Chicago in

Zinc manufacturer Edward C. Hegeler (1835–1910) founded The Open Court *and* The Monist *and became Paul Carus's father-in-law.*

1888 and later expanded into a monograph, he spoke glowingly of the term *God* which he identified as "one of the most wonderful expressions in our language." As to the question whether the idea of God was a truth or a hallucination of the mind, he insisted that the term was an abstract idea which nevertheless possessed a reality in the human mind. "Our view of God is not theism, not pantheism and not atheism. It does not teach that God is a person above the world, nor does it identify God with nature, or deny God's existence altogether. If our view must be labeled and registered among the different 'isms,' I must form a new word and call it *Entheism*, which clearly denotes the conception of a monistic God, who is immanent, not transcendent, who is in many respects different from and superior to nature, yet pervades all nature." Even so, Carus did not concern himself with discarding the use of the personal *he* when referring to God. There was no need to dispose of the word provided one was aware of the simile just as Christ when he spoke of God as his *father.*[32]

Carus preferred to address the God-idea as one of historical growth, the product of evolution representing aspirations moving forward in a definite direction. Whether the aspirations were conservative, reactionary, progressive, or radical, they all existed in the realm of the unconscious soul-life that originated in the traditions of the past. The God-idea was neither irrelevant nor an aberration, even for agnosticism which Carus characterized as a "bankruptcy of thought." He judged as reactionary the views of anyone who said that questions concerning the soul, its immortality, the existence of God, creation, or the ultimate purpose of being were "beyond the reach of reason."[33]

Carus proceeded to build a "God-conception" that he promised would "prove tenable not only before the most critical tribunal of science, but even the atheist will be unable to refute or reject it." Starting with the premise that "uniformities" existed in nature that made the world both classifiable and comprehensible through the use of reason, and that these uniformities "in their totality constitute a grand harmony which is commonly called the cosmic order," the question became whether these uniformities were ordained or accidental. This was at the core of the God-problem and Carus answered the question by saying that neither explanation was correct; instead, the uniformities were "intrinsically necessary" much like 1 + 1 = 2. It was an action of purely mental logic which, when applied to the material world, could be used to classify its phenomena. These uniformities, when combined, constituted "one great system" and became the "formative factors of the world." Carus considered the God-conception in Christianity as a form of paganism which in no way applied to the God-being. Instead, God was the "Allhood of existence," the formative factor of the world-order which included "the laws of nature and of ethical norms which are indispensable factors in the evolution of mankind."[34]

While admitting to having passed through numerous stages of belief, Carus still claimed to cherish "the sacred Godward longings of a childlike mind" even as he investigated the imperfections of past creeds. Life was evolution and it took time for humankind to progress from its mythological beliefs through the metaphysical to the purely scientific. "God is different only in so far as our conception of Him is purified." Having lost the supernatural religion of his youth and finding little satisfaction in either skepticism or atheism, he retraced his way back to the inspiring and spiritual significance of the term "God" but without its personal or anthropomorphic attributes. There was neither an individual God nor was there an individual man who survived his mortal remains.[35] Having shunned any and all speculation on the nature of God, whether in terms applicable to orthodoxy, theism, pantheism, agnosticism, or atheism, Carus seemed most comfortable likening God to that law, form, or principle which stood for the moral or natural law.[36] God was the "author of the moral ought."[37]

Homilies of Science

In his *Homilies of Science* (1892), a collection of editorials written for *The Open Court* which preached an ethical system based upon truth alone, Carus dedicated the publication to his deceased father, a decision that conveyed a sentiment he had been reluctant to reveal when the two had sparred over the issue of monism. He insisted that his homilies were hostile only to those religions that survived on pious frauds and dogmatic conceptions and not toward natural religion or religion of science which stood on the facts of nature. Such a natural religion could be called cosmic insofar as its ethics rested on a belief in the elevation, progress, and amelioration of the whole of mankind. It could also be called a "religion of life," a "religion of science," or "religion of immortality" since it concerned the salvation of the human soul as a living presence for future generations. He remained hopeful that all religions would drop their sectarian dogmas and mature into a cosmic religion.[38]

Carus explained that his ideas were iconoclastic and yet "tenaciously conservative and religious." Having lost his faith in dogma and viewed by some as "an enemy of Christianity," he nonetheless remained thoroughly religious and feeling instinctively "that some golden grain must be amongst the chaff."

> I have lost the dross only, the slags and ashes, but my religious ideals have been purified. My life was such that I could not help becoming a missionary, but I became a missionary of that religion which knows of no dogmas, which can never come in conflict with science, which is based on simple and demonstrable truth. This religion is not in conflict with Christianity. Nor is it in conflict with Judaism or Mohammedanism, or Buddhism, or any other religion. For it is the goal and aim of all religions.[39]

Carus saw himself a preacher who belonged to no church, dogma or creed; instead, he claimed to represent a religion of humanity and reason, pledging to be faithful to only those facts that could be verified by experiment and capable of being repeated again and again. “If Christianity means the dogmatism of the Church, it is an historical religion which will disappear in the course of time; if it means the doctrine of Christ, the fulfillment of the law through love, it will be the religion of mankind.” He insisted that the often made description that the God of old religion was dead and whose leaves of dogmatic opinion were falling to the ground was not a dreary depiction of a future empty of purpose, ideals, or hope in life’s enjoyments, but a sign that a new religion was stirring in the tree of humanity whose branches would soon grow in the hearts of mankind. The new religion would be an ethical one—realistic for its love of truth and its ennoblement of human life. Carus placed his hopes on a religion of science which taught ethics not founded on the authority of a power foreign to humanity but “upon a more correct understanding of man and man’s natural tendency to progress and raise himself to a higher plane of work, and to a nobler activity.” The hoped-for triumph of a better future did not mean revolution or disrespect for the old but rather an evolution with “due reverence for the merits of the past.”[40]

The so-called religious problem of the modern world did not imply doubting the commandments; rather, it meant ceasing to believe in Christianity’s crude anthropomorphism and dogmas such as God making the world out of nothing, the fairyland of heaven beyond the skies, and miracles. When sectarian ceremonies, antiquated rites, and customs were dispensed with, and humanity returned to the moral law (“Thou shalt love they neighbor as thyself”), only then would there no longer be a religious problem. Carus objected to both the orthodox believer and the agnostic who argued that because he could not know, he must not believe. Both were misguided by not allowing for evolution to a higher understanding in conformity with science.[41]

In looking at Christianity in his day, Carus was struck by the realization that many of its preachers no longer believed in the particulars of their creed and treated them as absurdities. Yet, surprisingly, few felt obliged to inform their congregants of having joined the vanguard of science. Ideas once sanctified by tradition were hard to remove, even if recognized as untrue. "Why can it not be acknowledged," he asked, "that tenets which our fathers considered as truths of divine revelation, were after all their personal and private opinions only?" At one time Christianity was the religion of progress. Over the centuries, however, dogmatism and preaching the letter of the gospels had made it barren, choking its spirit. But the dogmatic and miraculous faiths of the past were gone. Rent by the effects of the higher criticism and challenged by the implications of natural selection, church doctrines appeared as so many ancient artifacts dragged along in the baggage as humanity marched into the future. "If Christianity means the dogmatism of the Church, it is an historical religion which will disappear in the course of time; if it means the doctrine of Christ, the fulfillment of the law through love, it will be the religion of mankind."[42] As the moral instructor of mankind, Carus urged the churches "not to be dragged along behind the triumphant march of humanity but should deploy in front with the vanguard of science!"[43]

Primer of Philosophy

In 1893, Carus published *Primer of Philosophy* intended to reconcile rival philosophies without acquiescing to Huxley's agnosticism or to Spencer's Unknowable. Believing that philosophy existed to open humanity's eyes to the deeper significance of science—and not get lost in its specialties—Carus thought it possible to seek out "new fields of noble work and practical usefulness." There were three key principles of philosophy: Positivism, Monism, and Meliorism. Positivism was not that of the Comtean school but what he called "the new positivism" which took its stand upon facts that could be proved and observed and admitting to a constant revision by experiment. Monism stood for the principle that there was but one truth which was eternal. Its aim was "a methodical arrangement of experience so as to present a unitary or consistent conception of the world." Monistic positivism abandoned the speculations of former ages by changing philosophy into "a systematization of positive knowledge." True monism was recognition of the inseparable oneness of all, while meliorism was the ethics derived from the philosophy of systematized facts. Carus did not share in the illusion that, because of evolution, all would become good and perfect over time. Meliorism was not about the value of life in "pleasurable feelings" but in "worthy actions."[44]

Carus identified positivism and monism as the two philosophical systems that dominated modern thought, with the former being complementary to the latter. True positivism was monistic and positive. "Instead of solving the basic problems of philosophy, Comte and his school declared them to be insolvable." By contrast, monism conceived the world as "one inseparable and indivisible entirety" which was constantly corroborated by the progress of science.[45]

The Religion of Science

In 1893, Carus published *The Religion of Science* in which he advocated for the preservation of all that was good and true in the old religions while discarding its irrational elements and errors. Believing that America's churches were "not as conservative and stationary as their dogmas pretend to be," he hoped with his book to create a belief system which kept "the warmth of religious enthusiasm" but used the spirit of criticism and scientific research to rid religion of its "sectarian narrowness and dogmatic crudities." The book represented a "protest against the idolatry of our churches and against their pagan spirit which alone brings them into conflict with science." Rather than incite a schism, he urged the creation of an "invisible church" whose members "believe in the religion of truth, who acknowledge that truth has not been revealed once and once only . . . and that the scientific method of searching for truth is the same in religious matters as in other fields."[46] Those who professed these principles could call themselves Christians, Jews, Buddhists, Moslems, or simply Freethinkers.

Carus was indifferent to the historical Jesus, focusing instead on the Christ-ideal with its legends and poetical visions that formed Christianity. The investigations of science were in no way a threat to the Christ-ideal which represented mankind's aspirations towards perfection. "Christ is an invisible and superpersonal influence in human society," he explained, "guiding and leading mankind to higher aims and a nobler morality. . . . and we are Christians in the measure that his soul has taken its abode in us." Implied in his remark was a distinction between the Christ-ideal and the Christian worship of Christ which amounted to paganism. Most Christians, he observed, had made their religion a "fetish worship" significantly different than the actual injunctions of Christ. "They believe in the letter of mythological traditions, and fail to recognize the spirit of the truth." In their blind confessions of faith, supplications, and odd practices, they ignored the simple fact that "Christ is the way, the truth, and the life"—the very spirit of evolution. Unfortunately, most Christians demanded blind belief instead of investigation. Their distrust of the inductive sciences ("sense-information") made their acceptance of God's revelation one-sided, accepting the wisdom of Isaiah but rejecting that of Darwin.[47]

With religion which he defined as "a conviction that regulates man's conduct, affords, comfort in affliction, and consecrates all the purposes of life," and science as "the methodical search for truth" which represented a correct and concise statement of facts, Carus viewed the Religion of Science as "that religion wherein man aspires to find the truth by the most reliable and truly scientific methods." It was a religion that accepted no revelations, dogmas, creeds, or rituals, but did recognize certain principles and ethical codes.[47] Trusting that most of America's churches were moving away from their sectarian narrowness and "dogmatic crudities," he saw movement toward "one cosmical religion" which he predicted would be the only true catholic faith which he called Monism, New Positivism, New Realism, or simply the Philosophy of Science. The God of the Religion of Science was not a new God, but the old God of the Jews and Gentiles without the literalness of belief.[48]

Carus was forced to face the question of immortality since most individuals felt the need to look for something beyond physical death. This notion had led to numerous interpretations of the soul and its purported existence after death. Carus described the soul as impulses, dispositions, and ideas manifested in consciousness and formed by a living being's individual experience. The soul neither began with birth nor ended with death. Instead, it existed "wherever the ideas of which we consist were thought and shall exist wherever they are thought again; for not only our body is our self, but mainly our ideas. Our true self is of a spiritual nature." Seen in this light, each individual soul-life was part of a "greater whole" which, in the scheme of evolution, rose to ever higher planes of spiritual existence. The soul's immortality was a scientific truth whose continuance was not to be found in the Christian dogma of the resurrection of the body but in the incarnation of God in "the soul of our soul," a difficult concept not because of its reasonableness but "in feeling that our soul is not our individual self, but God in us."[49]

From Carus's perspective, there was no ego-soul. The soul was not our own but belonged to mankind which is to say that it "is from God, it develops in God, and all its aspirations and yearnings are to God." Not only was man's soul the continuance of former generations of souls, but their continuance into the future. "The souls of our beloved are always with us and will remain among us until the end of the world." The posthumous existence of man's soul was consistent with the facts of science. "Not only do the souls of our dead continue to communicate with those who still live in the flesh, but they are present in their minds, and they will form parts of the souls of generations to come." Every thought was never gone but remained in the soul-life of the whole which consisted of "the immortalized precipitate of the sentiments, ideas, and acts done in past years, dating back to the beginning of soul-life upon earth." Every thought remained part of the whole. The past lived on in the soul-life which was real.[50]

* * *

Carus faced harsh criticism for his beliefs which one naysayer described as a "conglomeration of self-contradictory ideas."[51] Nevertheless, he insisted there was a power in the world which man was obliged to recognize as the "norm of truth and the standard of right conduct." Claiming that his life's work was to uphold the "religious conception" of God ("cosmic order" or "universal Logos") as the eternal abiding reality of the moral law, he declared God a "super-individual reality" provable by science which, unlike old orthodoxy, was not a human invention.[52] Science could not be fashioned as man pleased. Instead, it was "stern and unalterable," producing revelations that must be discovered. Contempt for science was a sin against the spirit of genuine religion. Genuine science was not of human origin, but divine. Scientists do not make science; they instead discover it. "Science is a revelation in the true and original sense of the word." With the ascendancy of science, which included the law of evolution, it was possible for humanity to make science divine and the truths of science the revelations of God. "Through science God speaks to us; by science he shows us the glory of his works; and in science he teaches us his will."[53] This was Carus's Religion of Science. As Donald Meyer explained, Carus published scores of books and articles on the subject, and confident that science provided the answer, "he elaborated his Religion of Science with great vigor, bewildering complexity, much repetition and amazing naiveté."[54]

3
Parliament of Religions

> There are two kinds of Christianity. One is love and charity; it wants the truth brought out and desires to see it practically applied in daily life. It is animated by the spirit of Jesus and tends to broaden the minds of men. The other is pervaded with exclusiveness and bigotry; it does not aspire through Christ to the truth; but takes Christ, as tradition has shaped his life and doctrines, to be the truth itself.
>
> —Paul Carus, *The Dawn of a New Religious Era and Other Essays*, 1899

From May 1st to October 31st, 1893, nearly twenty-eight million people visited the World's Fair in Chicago. Popularly known as the Columbian Exposition to celebrate the four-hundredth anniversary of the discovery of the New World, the fair took place on 686 acres on the shoreline of Lake Michigan. Built at a cost of $28 million, it involved 65,000 exhibits from fifty nations and twenty-six colonies.[1] The site, designed in the Greek classical style, was nicknamed the "White City" because of the introduction of electric lights which shone across the white-painted buildings at night. Presented as a utopian depiction of Western civilization, the Exposition contrasted the material triumphs of the western world, like Edison's moving picture kinetograph, against portrayals of North African villages, Venetian gondolas, bazaars, and spectacles of primitive cultures complete with native peoples. The Exposition represented a mythic rendition of the West's self-image by allowing large sections of its history to slip by under the guise of survival of the fittest.

World's Congress Auxiliary

Ancillary to the Exposition was the World's Congress Auxiliary proposed by Charles C. Bonney in an article first printed in the *Statesman Magazine* in September 1889. A lawyer, judge, orator, and Swedenborgian, it was Bonney's idea that along with the material accomplishments displayed at the Exposition, its planning committee should also consider highlighting the intellectual and progressive spirit of the age. This meant broadening the displays of the West's material accomplishments by including break-through achievements in twenty general Departments: Woman's Progress, the Public Press, Medicine and Surgery, Temperance, Religion, Moral and Social Reform, Commerce and Finance, Music, Literature, Education, Engineering, Art, Government, Science and Philosophy, Social and Economic Science, Labor, Religion, Sunday Rest, Public Health, and Agriculture.[2] Having succeeded in obtaining public support for the idea, the Exposition's Planning Committee assigned Bonney to preside over the World's Congress Auxiliary. Ultimately, nearly 700,000 of the Fair's visitors would attend speeches, meetings, and symposia provided in these additional events.

Organized in a two-fold manner, the Auxiliary offered a series of general congresses intended for the public to promote "the intelligence, culture and elevation of the people of all countries." There would also be smaller symposia for the discussion of topics by specialists in the different departments. In all, approximately two hundred separate congresses were organized to highlight an assortment of themes in its twenty different departments. One example was the presentation titled "The Significance of the Frontier in American History" given by Wisconsin historian Frederick Jackson Turner before the World's Historical Congress.

Turner advanced the hypothesis that as the frontier moved westward across the continent, the nation's democratic institutions formed at the confluence (the frontier line) of savagery and civilization. His "Frontier Thesis" was based on the notion of the Caucasian's ascendency and authority over the savage, half-civilized, and bankrupt civilizations of the New and Old World. Mimicking this solipsism two decades later, Henry Adams remarked that "[American] Society offered the profile of a long, straggling caravan stretching loosely toward the prairies, its few scores of leaders far in advance and its millions of immigrants, negroes [sic], and Indians far in the rear, somewhere in archaic time."[3] In another example, the Congress of the Psychical Sciences met to discuss the most recent findings in psychical research. Much of the conversation focused on connecting the wireless telegraph with messages sent from departed spirits to mediums holding forth in séances. Its speakers wanted the public to understand that the wireless telegraph and telepathy were two sides of the same coin.[4]

Of all the General Congresses that met during the six months of the Exposition's operation, the World's Congress [Parliament] of Religions had the most impact nationally and internationally. As president of the Auxiliary, Bonney expressed his dream of bringing together leaders from the world's major religions to share their beliefs in a spirit of brotherhood. Talk of such a gathering had been mentioned over the years but nothing had materialized. The concept was not original, as earlier gatherings had involved the Religious Council of Buddhists called by the Mauryan emperor Asoka at Palatiputra (now Patna) in 242 B.C.; the Council of Nicaea in 325 A.D. which permitted only a select group of proto-orthodox Christians to attend; and the convocation called by the Mughal Emperor Akbar the Great at Delhi in the sixteenth century to unite his empire around religion. Tennyson later immortalized this meeting in his poem "Akbar's Dream."[5]

Bonney insisted that the Parliament was not a scheme to form a new religion; nor was it a trap to place the representatives of any faith in a false or embarrassing position. Instead, he intended it as "a royal feast to which the representatives of every faith were asked to bring the richest fruits and the fairest flowers of their religion." By this, he intended for the Parliament to end religious persecution, protect the sacred right to worship, and ensure that "no participant was asked to surrender any conviction of what he believed to be truth and duty."[6] To accomplish these objectives, Bonney appointed his friend, the liberal Rev. John Henry Barrows of Chicago's First Presbyterian Church, to chair the sixteen-member World's Parliament of Religions Planning Committee. A graduate of Yale Divinity School, Union Theological Seminary, and Andover Theological Seminary, Barrows would later become president of Oberlin College. With Bonney's encouragement and oversight, Barrows set out to plan, capture, and embrace the ecumenical potential of the moment.

Among the rules Bonney gave to delegates, "each representative was asked to present the very best things he could offer for those on whose behalf he spoke, and was admonished that nothing was desired from him in the way of attack on any other person, system, or creed." It was the "rigorous exclusion" of this behavior that made the Parliament a success. To control what was spoken, Bonney insisted on his right to review the papers ahead of time. Although discord had been slight, he admitted to prohibiting a Parsee delegate from condemning Christianity for the tortures of the Inquisition; preventing a Universalist from challenging the Calvinist dogma of infant damnation; and refusing to permit a Quaker to criticize the excessive use of rites and ceremonies by Episcopalians. In addition, debate, rebuttal, and votes of censure or approval by the delegates were forbidden. Because Bonney provided the official history of the Parliament, he took liberties not only to edit the papers presented but omitting some entirely from the written record. Consequently, F.T. Neely's edition of the Parliament offered a more complete record of the presentations.[7]

As a member of the Auxiliary's Advisory Council, an attendee, and contributing speaker to three separate Congresses, Paul Carus expressed genuine surprise that the Parliament of Religions took place at all, much less involve so many of the world's great religions. His uncertainty had been due to concerns that the Catholic Church might use its growing antimodernist feelings to oppose the gathering. To the surprise of many, the three most notable faces in the American Catholic Church—Archbishop Patrick Feehan of Chicago, who was a member of the General Committee; James Cardinal Gibbons, the Archbishop of Baltimore; and Father John Keane, rector of Catholic University in Washington, D.C.—agreed to participate and send delegates. The fiercely conservative side of American Catholicism would emerge after the Parliament in the personages of physician Thomas Dwight and Monsignor Robert John Seton to attack the Parliament as a symbol of modernism's key threats: the higher criticism and evolution.[8]

In the meantime, more immediate opposition to the Parliament came from the Presbyterian Church of the United States, the European Catholic hierarchy, evangelical leader Dwight Moody, and the Sultan of Turkey. The Rev. Ernst Johann Eitel, a member of the Evangelical-Lutheran Church and Inspector of Schools for the Hong Kong Government, warned his fellow Christians that by agreeing to attend the Parliament they were "unconsciously planning treason against Christ."[9] Eitel's opposition was anticipated, but to the surprise of almost everyone, it was the Archbishop of Canterbury, a liberal-minded prelate, who decided that England's Anglican Church would not participate.

> I am afraid that I cannot write the letter which, in yours of March 20th, you wish me to write, expressing a sense of the importance of the proposed Conference, without its appearing to be an approval of the scheme. The difficulties which I myself feel are not questions of distance and convenience, but rest on the fact that the Christian religion is the one religion. I do not understand how that religion can be regarded as a member of a Parliament of Religions without assuming the equality of the other intended members and the parity of their position and claims.[10]

The Opening

After two years of preparation and more than ten thousand letters and forty thousand documents mailed, the delegates gathered on September 11th, 1893, to hear President Bonney open the Parliament. To symbolize the moment, a bell rang ten times in the grand Hall of Columbus (now known as the Art Institute of Chicago) to acknowledge the ten historic religions: Buddhism, Confucianism, Hinduism/Brahmanism, Islam, Jainism, Judaism, Zoroastrianism, Shinto, Taoism, and Christianity. Gathered around them were forty-one additional denominations and sects (including Greek and Russian Orthodoxy, Roman Catholicism, Theosophy, Church of the New Jerusalem, and Christian Science).[11] Almost overnight, the Parliament became the spiritual expression of the Exposition, far exceeding any of the other congresses due to the eagerness with which the world's religious leaders showed their willingness to participate. The Parliament's intended purpose, as explained by Carus, was "to unite all religion against all irreligion; to make the Golden Rule the basis of this union; [and] to present to the world . . . the substantial unity of many religions in the good deeds of the religious life."[12]

The spectacle of brightly colored robes, vestments, turbans, and hats delighted the press and visitors who attended the events. In fact, the diversity among the participating delegations became a source of pride. There was Swami Vivekananda, the smartly turbaned "orange monk" from Bengal; the handsome Ceylonese Buddhist Anagarika Dharmapala in his long white robe; the bearded master of eloquence Protap Chunder Mozoomdar from the Brahmo Somaj Society in India; and the richly colored robes of the Japanese Buddhists. From Carus's perspective, the very existence of the Parliament was a manifestation of religious yearnings for unity and understanding. "How small are we mortal men who took an active part in the Parliament in comparison with the movement which it inaugurated!" Rather than a sign of drift toward an irreligious future, it signified to him that humanity was becoming less sectarian and more indifferent to theological subtleties. The event proved greater than anything he had ever dreamt possible.[13] For a period of seventeen days, the program addressed the topics of revelation, immortality, the incarnation of God, the universal elements in religion, the ethical unity of different religious systems, and the relationship of religion to morals, marriage, education, science, philosophy, evolution, music, labor, government, peace, and war. Often, the organizers had to accommodate the overflow of visitors using the adjoining Hall of Washington in which case the program had to be presented twice, while smaller halls were set aside to discuss more specialized conversations among the delegates.

The Events

Of the 216 major addresses given at the Parliament, forty-one were by Asian delegates whose presentations of the Tao, Lord Krishna, the Divine Mother, Ahura Mazda, the Buddhist dharma, the Shinto kami, and the Mahatmas of Tibet were accomplished with both passion and sophistication.[14] It seemed to many attendees that the age of blind belief and obedience—whether in the form of orthodoxy or sheer fanaticism—was at last drawing to a close. Remembering a remark from Buddha to his disciples: "I forbid you to believe anything simply because I said it," struck at the heart of what Carus viewed as the desire by humanity to expect a reason for every belief. Dogma no longer sufficed.[15]

Besides being the first global gathering of its kind in the modern world, the Parliament, through its discussion of missionary work, westernization, science, evolution, industrialization, colonialism, imperialism, comparative religions, and racism, left a legacy by shifting the marginally understood history and culture of Asia into the forefront of global thinking. For those Asian delegates educated in missionary schools and acquainted with the West's hegemonic ideologies, hidden behind their rhetoric of brotherhood and goodwill were nationalistic challenges to the West's presumptive claim to dominance. Admitting that the East had much to learn about the Christ of Christianity, Brahmo B.B. Nagarkar of Bombay decried that so much money was expended in spreading Christian dogma, bigotry, pride, and exclusiveness. He found it impossible for Christians to practice the humility they so liked to preach.[16]

Japan's Delegates

In its bid to claim its rightful place among the nations of the world, Japan was among the first Asian nations to set an example at the Parliament by claiming the reconciliation of its religion and culture with the modern world. Rather than sow discord, most of its delegates controlled their dialogue by portraying Japanese Buddhism as a harmonious religion that not only supported international peace and brotherhood but endorsed the spirit of science and evolutionary theory as a shield against narrow superstitions. Its delegates (four priests and two laymen who served as translators) asserted a status that had not been previously evident to the outside world. While western skeptics privately described Japan's delegates as "clever heathens" whose religion was without a soul or a God, what they accomplished by way of their positive presentations to the Parliament made it difficult for Christians to dissent. Here was a group of educated priests of the Meiji empire who identified with Western learning but whose intention, at the same time, supported nationalism, and by implication, a growing military and industrial future for their country. Confident in their self-esteem, they presented Northern or Mahayana Buddhism as scientific and even superior to the confusion evident in Christianity with its pro- and anti-scientific elements.[17]

Except for occasional journeys to China over the centuries, it was not until the nineteenth century that Japanese Buddhists traveled abroad for the expressed purpose of seeking knowledge of foreign lands. In 1872, decades prior to the gathering of delegates in Chicago, two separate groups of priests from the Nishi and Higashi Honganji sects journeyed to England, France, Germany, Switzerland, Italy, and the United States, before returning home through Greece, Turkey and India. Following the example of the Iwakura Mission (1871–73) sent by the Japanese government to examine government and non-government institutions in Europe and the United States, representatives of the two sects were dispatched to examine state/church relations. Specifically, they desired to understand how Christianity was interpreted in the West compared to the manner it was being taught in Japan. The Japanese also wished to learn the interaction of Christianity's different denominations with politics, its participation in public education, its conflict with the emerging sciences, and its involvement in social concerns such as temperance and suffrage. Much of this information would later be used to inform the delegates as they crafted their remarks for the Parliament.[18]

Ironically, there was no organized plan among the Japanese delegates. None received government funding or authorization; nor, for that matter, were they officially recognized by their respective temples. "The divisive nature of contemporaneous sectarian politics," observed James Ketelaar, "effectively prevented the Meiji Buddhist community from mounting a trans-sectarian selection of Buddhist notables for participation in the Parliament." Of the four Japanese priests (Shaku Soyen, Yatsubuchi Banryu, Toki Horin, Ashitsu Jitsunen), laymen and translators Kinza Hirai and Zenshori Noguchi, only two—Soyen (Rinzai Zen) and Yatsubuhi Banrya (Pure Land)—carried any rank.[19]

Speaking as translator for the Japanese priests at the Parliament, Zenshori Noguchi praised Commodore Perry for having opened the eyes of his countrymen to the industrialized nations of the West. It had been thirty-six years since he knocked on the "long-closed door of my country [and] awakened us from our long and undisturbed slumber." Calling Perry "the Knocker," Noguchi remarked that Japan owed him much. But Noguchi's speech caught Carus's attention for another reason, namely, his remark that "truth is only one," meaning that each sect had as its ultimate object "to attain truth." For the religions of the world to reach their full development, there could be no distinction "between faith and reason, religion and science."[20] These words were music to Carus's ears, observing how many of the delegates had chosen to adopt the concept. Symbolic of their promotion of Japanese Buddhism as distinct from the more pessimistic and monastic descriptions of Theravada Buddhism, the delegation distributed several thousand translations of Buddhist works including *Outlines of the Mahayana, as Taught by Buddha, A Brief Account of Shin-shu,* and *A Shin-shu Catechism.* All three works were written in Chinese, but Noguychi hoped they would eventually be translated into English. He also provided several hundred portraits of Shaka, the historical Buddha from the *Mahamaya Sutra.*[21]

The Mahayana Buddhism espoused by the Japanese delegates resonated with Carus's Religion of Science. Both intended not to destroy religion but to restore its intended purpose by integrating evolutionary science and the law of cause and effect into their respective beliefs. Those delegates who presented Mahayana Buddhism distinguished it from Southern Buddhism as well as the Northern Buddhism of China and Tibet. By the end of the Parliament, the West's preferred perception of Buddhism (to the extent that distinctions were made) was firmly anchored in Mahayana Buddhism, a modernized version that rejected ritual and the errors of oral and written tradition, replacing them with an emphasis on individual fulfillment. Life was a matter of will and intelligence. Rejecting excessive asceticism, it encouraged the mind to guide the individual on the path of rightness. It represented the victory of mind over body and the realization that human purposes and values allowed the individual to escape blind destinies.[22]

Noguchi was followed by Kinza Hirai who, in one of the few strident speeches at the Parliament, claimed that his nation suffered from a multitude of "unfair judgments." He explained why Christianity was not as warmly accepted as other religions in Japan because of its involvement in "a tragic and bloody rebellion" in 1637 that shocked the nation and took a year to finally suppress. Otherwise, he explained, Christianity would have been "eagerly embraced." Moreover, the 1858 Harris Treaty with the U.S. and the Anglo-Japanese Treaty of Amity and Commerce had placed Japan in a disturbingly "disadvantageous situation," depriving it of its lawful rights and privileges by allowing, among other things, the right of extra-territoriality for its resident aliens. To make matters worse, the United States government prevented its immigrants from entering the public schools, forced them into unemployment due to pressure from unions, and deprived them of the right of suffrage. "If such be the Christian ethics," Hirai warned his audience, "we are perfectly satisfied to be heathen." Unless the people of the United States cast away their prejudices, they have no claim to morality, much less the "highest humanity and noblest generosity."[23]

Toki Horin's first speech on the "History of Buddhism and its Sects in Japan," took note of Buddha's birth in India some 2,020 years earlier and dying in the city of Kushi at age seventy-nine. Pointing to the differences between Mahayana and Hinayana doctrines, he made it clear that despite their distinguishing characteristics, there was no diminution in their truths. Those countries where the Hinayana prevailed were in southern and central parts of Asia covering Siam, Anam, Burma, Ceylon, Chittagong, and Arakan, while the Mahayana doctrines prevailed in Japan, China, Korea, Manchuria, and Tibet. He cautioned, however that Buddhism in Manchuria and Tibet was more accurately called Lamaism because it differed in its origin from the Mahayana doctrines. Southern Buddhism emphasized strict obedience to rules while Northern Buddhism focused on mental harmony and moral precepts. It was the purpose of Mahayana Buddhism to enlighten all beings, guiding them to the plane of Buddha with sympathy and humanity. In Buddhism, the soul was in all beings and without beginning or end, transmigrated through past, present, and future according to one's conduct.[24] In all, Horin explained, Japanese Buddhism was divided into nine ancient and six modern sects, the former reflective of the time when the imperial power was at its height, while the latter reflected the new age of military power. He concluded that "it is time to remodel the Japanese Buddhism—that is, the happy herald is at our gates informing us that the Buddhism of perfected intellect and emption, synthesizing the ancient and modern sects, is now coming."[25]

In his second lecture, "What Buddhism has Done for Japan," Horin insisted that Buddhism had no quarrel concerning the truth. If any religion taught the truth, he considered it a Buddhist religion in disguise. "Buddhism never cares what the outside garment might do," he informed his audience. "It only aims to promote the purity and morality of mankind." With the Japanese guided by the truth of the Buddha, he saw the spirit of his nation rising in recognition. Fearing its loss of nationality and spirit, Japan should glory in the originality of its fine arts, literature, architecture, language, and other areas of achievement. The rumor, however, that Japan's conflicting philosophies were on a collision course was wrong in every manner.[26]

Next among Japan's speakers, Yatsubuchi Banryu informed his audience that the Buddha was a man and not the Creator; nor did he have the power to destroy the laws of the universe. Instead, he exercised the power of knowledge and worked through wisdom and mercy to the extent that he or she could be called a "Savior." Before his enlightenment, Buddha was simply an incomplete man. "The only difference between Buddha and all other beings is in his supreme enlightenment." There was no single Buddha; they are numerous and are simply humans who attained Buddhahood through the perfection of virtue and wisdom.[27]

Rinzai Zen monk Shaku Soyen, arguably the most eminent of the Buddhist representatives at the Parliament, was Abbott of Engakuji, one of the oldest Zen monasteries in Kamakura. Having received a Western-style education in science, philosophy, and religion at Keio University following his Rinzai Zen training under Imakita Kosen, he distanced himself from the nation's traditional Buddhism for one that was more attached to the imperial and industrial needs of the Meiji government. Soyen spent two years, from 1887 to

A scene at one of the sessions of the World's Parliament of Religions held in Chicago during the World's Fair of 1893. Paul Carus served as Secretary of the Parliament.

1889, in Ceylon where he was ordained a Theravada monk and where Henry Steel Olcott was girding Ceylonese Buddhism to be more hardened in its ability to face the modern world. Like Olcott who sought to counter Christian missionary influence by reconciling Northern and Southern Buddhism, Soyen regarded Christian proselytizing as a similar threat in Japan and hoped for a more united Buddhism to counter its effects.[28]

Because Soyen could neither read nor write English, his speech, "The Law of Cause and Effect, as Taught by Buddha," was translated into English by his disciple Daisetsu Teitaro Suzuki and read to the audience by the Rev. John Henry Barrows.[29] In it, Soyen stressed Buddhism's sublime compatibility with the theory of evolution and in the endless progression of causal law. The Buddha was not the creator of this law of nature but the first to explain life's endless progression. Each cause was preceded by another cause and each effect followed by another effect. There was no beginning or end to the universe. "Like as the waters of rivers evaporate and form clouds, and the latter change their form into rain, thus returning once more into the original form of waters, causal law is in a logical circle changing from cause to effect, effect to the cause." The same applied to the sphere of human conduct where man enjoys or suffers from the effects of his past life. The happiness or misery that one faces in the future is the result of an individual's present actions. "No other cause than our own actions . . . make us happy or unhappy." All religions referred to the causal law in the sphere of human conduct but only Buddhism applied it to past, present, and future. It was not just education or experience that made an individual wise, but the totality of one's past life.[30]

Compared to the Christian God whose ontological presence made him out of step with Western science's understanding of the causal nature of phenomena, Soyen rejected the concept of an inscrutable God acting arbitrarily and with seemingly disregard of the individual. In place of this mysterious first cause, he made humanity's destiny rest solely on the shoulders of each and everyone. "There is no other cause," he explained, "than our own actions which make us happy or unhappy."[31]

In his second speech before the Parliament on "Arbitration Instead of War," Soyen noted that "The truth is only one. There must be no distinction, and all must be equal before the light of truth." He went on to discuss universal brotherhood, explaining that "all rivers flowing into the sea become alike." Universal love and fraternity were present not only in Buddha, but in Christ, as well as in Confucius—all followers of truth. Wars, on the other hand, take place because of the ambitions of a few men who choose to disturb the social peace and the course of truth. Referring to the present state of the European powers, he questioned the purpose of the Triple Alliance and wondered if it existed for the promotion of peace. "We are born to enlighten our wisdom and cultivate our virtues according to the guidance of truth," he explained. Provided humankind did not make distinctions among the races, civilizations, and creeds, we all become "sisters and brothers" for the promotion of peace and love. By implication, Soyen indicated there was a moral duty to treat all nations equally. "You must not say 'go away' because we are not Christians. You must not say 'go away' because we are yellow people."[32]

Siamese and Ceylonese Delegates

Besides the Japanese delegates, other notable representatives of Buddhism came from Siam and Ceylon. The most titled was Chandradat Chudhadharn, brother to the king of Siam, who recounted the four noble truths of Buddha and the eight paths that lead to the cessation of lust.[33] The prince was followed by the Rev. H. Sumangala, High Priest of the Southern Buddhist Church of Ceylon, who regarded Southern Buddhism as the oldest of the missionary religions. Though its monks were now focused on quiet study in their monasteries, at one time they were actively spreading the word. Admitting that education in Ceylon had once been considered backward by Western standards, he informed his listeners that this had been remedied by the work of Colonel Olcott to whom they were beholden for *The Buddhist Catechism* which authorities were now using to teach the principles of religion. With this new tool, Sumangala predicted that Buddhists would once again carry abroad the teachings of the Gautama.[34]

The highlight speaker among the non-Japanese Buddhist delegates was the personage of Anagarika Dharmapala. Born into a wealthy Sinhalese family and educated at a succession of Catholic and Protestant missionary schools in his native Ceylon, he learned firsthand the sacred books of Christianity. During that time, he also came to feel a special kinship with the poets Keats and Shelley while acquiring a decided distaste for western religions. Like Hirai from Japan, Prince Chandradat from Siam, and the Venerable H. Sumangala from Widyodaya College in Ceylon, he had been attracted to Blavatsky and Olcott whom he met when only fourteen and was initiated into the Theosophical Society. He even traveled with Olcott and Charles Leadbeater to Japan where Olcott delivered over seventy lectures during their three-month visit. Unusually prescient for his age, Dharmapala worried that Japanese Buddhism carried with it an unusual degree of nationalism and militarism. He interpreted the reform thinking within the New Buddhism as protecting the nation through religious activism, loyalty to the emperor, social criticism, modernization, and support of science.[35]

Dharmapala brought to the Parliament the wishes and blessings of 475,000,000 Buddhists worldwide and re-echoed Emperor Asoka's call twenty-four centuries earlier for a council that met in the city of Patma where a thousand scholars remained in session for seven months after which they embarked as missionaries across the known world. In his several addresses before the delegates, Dharmapala explained how much more capable Buddhism was than Christianity in repairing the divide between science and religion. His choice and those made by others among the Buddhist delegates to use the language of evolution helped undermine the condescending behavior of their American hosts.[36]

Dharmapala revitalized Buddhism in the eyes of Western scholars by characterizing it as ethical, rational, scientific, reform-minded, deeply personal, optimistic, altruistic, and suited to the challenges of the modern age. "The Message of the Buddha that I have to bring to you is free from theology, priest craft, rituals ceremonies, dogmas, heavens, hells, and other theological shibboleths. The Buddhism taught to the civilized Aryans of India twenty-five centuries ago was a scientific religion containing the highest individualistic and altruistic ethics, a philosophy built on psychological mysticism and a cosmology in harmony with geology, astronomy, radioactivity and reality."[37]

In his lecture "The World's Debt to Buddha," Dharmapala further ingratiated himself to the Parliament's audience by expressing his indebtedness to Thomas Rhys Davids, who founded the Pali Text Society in London in 1881 and brought the wisdom of Pali literature to the West. He also referenced Max Müller who once remarked that if asked to find the most comprehensive literature addressing the problems of human life, he would point to the galaxy of brilliant Buddhist teachers in India and the labors of Buddhist scholars from the West. Dharmapala spoke approvingly of Eugène Burnouf, Edwin Arnold, Hermann Oldenberg, Henry Thomas Buckle, Robert C. Childers, Daniel John Gogerly, and Robert Spence Hardy for their work on Pali literature. Similarly, he praised Blavatsky, Thomas Huxley, and William W. Hunter for their appreciation of the wisdom of Buddha and of the Buddhist Scriptures.[38] By giving praise to American and European intellectuals, Dharmapala quickly became a favorite among the visitors to the Parliament. As Lewis Pile Mercer noted, "all eyes turn to one of the most winning figures on the platform, tall, clad in white, soft and closely clinging robes, idealistic face, gentle eyes, waving black hair and scanty beard—the gentle and lovable Dharmapala of Ceylon."[39]

Dharmapala became the spokesperson and leader of Ceylonese Buddhist revival, using his masterful command of the English language to proclaim the Buddhist dharma, not Christianity, as the ideal representation of modernity and the scientific spirit.[40] As a teacher and lecturer, he connected Buddhism to evolution. Referring to Grant Allen and his popular account of *Charles Darwin* (1885), he reinforced the western belief that this great law controlled the entire universe.[41] Presenting Darwin's theory which he mischaracterized as "life passing onward and upward through a series of constantly improving forms toward the Better and the Best," he won over his listeners by inviting all to share in the idea of brotherhood, the oneness of life, and the usefulness of doing good to self and humanity. And to those enamored by Spiritualism, he spoke positively of thought transference, clairvoyance, and the projection of the sub-conscious self. By the same token, he spoke of faith, pure life, and receptivity of the mind to liberality, wisdom, and all that was good and beautiful. On the other hand, Dharmapala mistook Spencerian evolution for Darwin's natural selection (a mistake made by many) and failed to discriminate between the proven sciences and the proto- and pseudo-sciences. He accepted all as equally meritorious in their validity.[42]

In the debate over foreign missionary methods, Dharmapala criticized the Christian intent to evangelize the non-Christian world, pointing out that it was only in the last three centuries that Christianity had attempted to propagate in the East. For Christianity to succeed in the East, its missionaries must demonstrate a spirit of self-sacrifice as well as that of charity, tolerance, and meekness exemplified in the life of Jesus. Instead, its missionaries conveyed an intolerant and selfish behavior that was mean, crass, and unwanted. Unlike the Buddhist missionaries of the past and present, Western missionaries arrived with the Bible in one hand and a bottle of rum in the other. "I warn you that if you want to establish Christianity in the East," he advised, "it can only be done on the principles of Christ's love and meekness. Let the missionary study all the religions; let them be a type of meekness and lowliness and they will find a welcome in all lands."[43]

Repeatedly, Dharmapala returned to the practical objectives of Buddha's teachings: the consequences of individual actions; the pursuit of virtue; the code of practical morality as the means of salvation, self-sacrifice and kindness to others; and reverence for the life of all creatures. Whenever the opportunity arose, he compared Buddhist teachings with the words of Jesus, showing their similarity in seeking the state of holiness. Quoting Henry Buckle, author of the *History of Civilization* (1857) that "knowledge of Buddhism is necessary to the right understanding of Christianity," he explained that no true scholar of religion could ignore the moral teachings and precepts of Buddhism and the connection between the two religions. Given the intrinsic relationship between these religions in their scientific, religious, and literary ideas, there was no reason to ignore the fact that long before the birth of Christ, Buddhist ideas and precepts had penetrated the Greek world. For many of the visitors attending the Parliament, this was the first time they had heard the possibility of Buddhism's contributions to Christianity.[44]

Dharmapala's reformist thinking is often associated with so-called "Protestant Buddhism," a western invention intended to foster the marriage of Buddhism with post-Enlightenment science. In its simplest terms, it represented the most modern manifestation of inductive thinking and the most genuine representation of science. Unlike Europe which remained victim of ignorant superstition until the Enlightenment, it was argued that India possessed a scientific worldview and a scientific religion that preceded the Enlightenment by centuries. Because of this assertion, Judith Snodgrass points out that Buddhism held a "unique place" among the religions at the Parliament. In effect, Buddhism represented the "other" Christianity, meaning that there was much in it that was comparable, even though it differed "precisely on those points at issue in the debates of the time."[45]

La Salle's Delegate

Carus presented himself to the delegates at the Parliament as a non-Christian and non-creedal idealist grounded in empirical and evolutionary science. In doing so, he delivered three papers before three different congresses: "The Philosophy of the Tool" before the Congress of Manual and Art Education; "Our Need of Philosophy" before the Congress of Science and Philosophy; and "Religion in Its Relation to the Natural Sciences" read before the Parliament of Religions.

In his lecture "The Philosophy of the Tool" he praised the work of Benjamin Franklin who, as the epitome of the American thinker, preferred the use of applied reason rather than theorizing as it represented the employment of tools as the great educator for humanity. While the origin of man's reasoning remained a mystery, every rational being was in possession of this tool and the language that accompanied it, meaning "no reason without language [and] no language without reason." The invention of tools played a significant role in the growth of the human mind.[46]

Carus's second address which he read before the Congress of Science and Philosophy noted that philosophy along with religion, the arts, and the sciences were the "most important possessions of mankind." For its role, philosophy provided a clear and distinct understanding of the spirit or wisdom of a given age, i.e., those foundation blocks which constituted the framework of a people's ideas, knowledge, aspirations, and character. A true philosopher should be able to feel the pulse of a people and instruct them on how to discriminate between error and truth, enforce the authority of science, raise the standards of education, and "combine dignity with obligation, duty with rights, and self-discipline with self-assertion."[47]

In his final paper which he read before the Parliament of Religions, Carus reported that many of the theological questions of past ages had disappeared from popular discourse. Consequently, the Copernican system and the theory of evolution were now providing a the most recent understanding of the universe. The religious horizon, which the Enlightenment had augmented with science, now extended worldwide. However, what Henry Buckle, William Edward H. Lecky, and Jean-Marie Guyau predicted would be a transition to an irreligious age, had instead improved religion by cleansing it of past errors. The God of modern religion was not the God of the old dogmas but of "the moral ought." Consequently, both science and religion had much to contribute to the world. Even if science could prove that God was not a person, it could not deny the existence of a power which enforced conduct. In a word, God was the "authority of conduct." In former times, religion found its truths by insight, inspiration, and intuition—methods common among prophets and sages like Zarathustra, Confucius, Buddha, Socrates, and Moses. Now, it was important for humankind to appreciate the contributions and grandeur of science; the more one studied it, the more one discovered that it preserved the spirit of religion and enhanced its truths.[48]

Like Victor Cousin, the French philosopher of eclecticism, Carus celebrated the pluralism of religions. In each he found elements of justice and good will toward a set of common universal themes that no one religion owned exclusively. The bible represented only a small part of God's revelation. It was but a groping for the right path. God also revealed himself in the works of Shakespeare, Goethe, Lamarck, Darwin, Guttenberg, and Edison. Each contributed toward the establishment of a single religion destined to be truly orthodox because it was scientifically true. Unlike the more conservative elements of society who regarded science as destructive of religion, those who were truly reform-minded understood that science actually purified religion.[49]

Carus argued for a "new orthodoxy" whose propositions did not surrender to the illusion of blind faith nor fall into the hands of the fashionable philosophy of agnosticism which tended to discredit all faiths, whether scientific or religious. "We must never lose faith in the ideal of Orthodoxy," he wrote.

> Science has made many new discoveries in this century and has established truths which widen our spiritual horizon and deepen our philosophical understanding. Under the conditions it is but natural that our religious beliefs, too, will have to be revised and restated. They must be purified in the furnace of scientific critique, and I trust that thereby they will not lose in religious significance. On the contrary, they can only gain in every respect; and after the fusing and refining religion will be purer and shine brighter than ever.[50]

It was no use defending old orthodoxy or agnosticism. Neither was relevant any longer. Only that orthodoxy which reconciled with science had any future. "We must broaden both our science and our religion until our religion becomes scientific, and our science religious." True science cannot be anti-religious and true religion cannot be anti-scientific. "If you want a Religion that is truly catholic, let it be in accord with Science." In their respective roles, science searched for Truth and formulated the facts of experience into natural laws, while Religion sought to apply Truth to life. Without religion, science fell prey to agnosticism and pessimism; and without science, religion became mere superstition. Science was the equivalent of Jacob's ladder which "at its bottom touches the world of sense, while its top reaches into the heaven of spirit."[51]

Carus applauded the results of the higher criticism, and although it seemed to some to threaten the roots of Christianity, he insisted that the very power that destroyed the errors of the past was the same power that purified religion and opened up a new epoch in the evolution of religious life. To that end, the Parliament proved that churches were "becoming more truly religious, as they are becoming less sectarian." The type of Christianity that once shaped life and fortified it with biblical passages, councils, tracts, and papal bulls was fading into the background. There were few who continued to breathe this narrow form of Christianity, and the same was true among the other religions which were now presenting themselves as mild and rational. A very visible outcome of harmony in matters of faith and consciousness had taken hold. He hoped this feeling would spread among all believers and that narrow-minded religionists of all stripes would show a more "simple-minded piety."[52]

The two factors necessary for establishing a scientific truth included sense experience and a method for handling material identified by sense activity. This meant classifying, measuring, tracing cause and effect, and arranging outcomes in an understandable and harmonious system. Arriving at a scientific truth meant distinguishing between the formal sciences (such as arithmetic, geometry, pure mechanics, and logic) and those sciences that investigated concrete things (such as chemistry, physiology). The formal sciences constituted the organ of thought that supplied the concrete phenomena and a method to arrive at conviction. Once experience verified the results of the sciences, one could be assured there would be no conflict for the world was a unitary system, not one of chaos. Once a truth is proven to be true, it remained true forever. The consistency of the world was universal and eternal. Not only did Carus believe it was possible to arrive at truth, but the advances occurring through day-to-day enquiry were preparing the modern mind for this eventual conception. Every success in man's scientific enquiry became grounds for repudiating agnosticism. As Carus explained, "We may confidently hope that the future which the present generation is preparing will be the age of science."[53]

Outcomes

The seventeen-day Parliament won widespread endorsements from most Protestant denominations and was celebrated in newspapers and magazines across the country. So great had been the enthusiasm that Max Müller, who along with Thomas Rhys Davids was a conspicuous absentee at the meeting, described the Parliament as standing "unprecedented in the whole history of the world."[54] Most of the religious representatives from Asia also praised the meeting, and before returning to their native countries, many embarked on speaking tours which included the distribution of literature and the founding of organizations, centers, and temples. In their remarks, they continued to reinforce the message that their doctrines were not only in step with modernity but fully tailored to the world's vision of evolution as the mechanism for human progress. Rather than take a defensive role against Western belief systems, those Buddhists on tour in the United States continued to define their religion as morally superior and with a longer tradition of supporting science than religion in the West.[55]

It is fair to say that the Parliament turned out to be "a great surprise to the world," a spectacle of dramatic proportions in that it brought the most powerful religions into the same tent while smaller religions entered if not on a level of equality, at least one of forbearance; and if not of tolerance, then one of temporary truce; and if not one of comparison, at least not one of ridicule. There was a genuine feeling that the major religions had become less sectarian, more ecumenical, and less territorial regarding their respective dogmas. Carus described the Parliament as "the most noteworthy event of this decade . . . . A holy intoxication overcame its speakers as well as the audience; and no one can conceive how impressive the whole proceeding was, unless he himself saw the eager faces of the people and imbibed the enthusiasm that enraptured the multitudes."[56]

Despite an overall positive response, the Parliament meant different things to different people. Not counting those who refused to attend for some protean fear of corruption of principles, Müller, Carus, and Barrows described it as one of the most extraordinary events of the post-Enlightenment and internationally significant for generations to come in that it laid the foundation for a more unifying global paradigm. For mainstream religious historians such as Sydney Ahlstrom, Edwin Gaustad, Martin Marty, and Sidney Mead, the Parliament laid the groundwork for a pluralistic approach to religion rather than one of unity, while Protestant missionaries and those on the fringes of the major denominations judged the Parliament as an interesting but momentary event that would soon be forgotten.

Then again, there were those who viewed it as an incentive for comparative religious studies; or, like historian Paul Carter, who interpreted the event as the finale to a century of schisms, the rise of the social gospel, and the impact of evolutionary philosophies on mainstream Protestantism. Finally, there were the approaches taken by Rick Fields in *How the Swans Came to the Lake* (1980) and Carl T. Jackson in *The Oriental Religions and American Thought* (1981) who observed that the Parliament offered the first opportunity for

Asians to speak publicly about their faiths and whose accounts interestingly circled back to the discussions of the Concord transcendentalists.[57]

* * *

Christianity's face-to-face encounter with Eastern religions at the Parliament and in its aftermath, would eventually lead to the unraveling of the West's self-inflicted narcissism. There among the delegates from the great historical religions, Christians heard emotionally-charged criticisms of the destructive nature of their colonialism, with its dross view of humans and the prejudices that accompanied its missionaries.

Carus viewed the Parliament as having "stirred the spirits" of the religious mind. Although it was a "child of the old religions," with Christianity as its "leading star," the faults of Christianity were "more severely rebuked" than any other religion. Rather than view this negatively, he interpreted it as a symptom of Christianity's purification. It was a sign that the religions of the future would have to rid themselves of their narrowness, their dogmatisms, and their sectarian spirit. Instead, they needed to reconcile their creeds with the principles of science. Why? Because "science is divine, and the truth of science is a revelation of God. Through science God speaks to us; by science he shows us the glory of his works; and in science he teaches us his will."[58]

For those Americans and Europeans who had come to view traditional Christianity as scientifically untrue, pernicious in its effects on social progress, filled with incongruities and unreasonable beliefs and practices, and extending divine legitimization to human cruelties, Buddhism became a winning response.

4
The Wise Men

> Please tell Maganlalbhai [Gandhi's nephew] that I would advise him to read Emerson's essays. They can be had for nine pence in Durban. There is a cheap reprint out. Those essays are worth studying. He should read them, mark the important passages and then finally copy them out in a notebook. The essays to my mind contain the teaching of Indian wisdom in a Western garb.
>
> —Mahatma Gandhi, letter to his son, March 25, 1907

Over the seventeen days of the Parliament with its formal meetings and presentations in the Hall of Columbus and smaller gatherings in the Hall of Washington, Carus made numerous personal and professional connections, including Protap Chunder Mozoomdar, leader of the Hindu reform movement and author of *The Oriental Christ* (1883); the Indian Hindu monk Swami Vivekananda, a nationalist credited with raising Hinduism to a major world status in India; Anagarika Dharmapala, the Ceylonese Buddhist of the Theravada tradition (a school of Hinayana Buddhism) and co-creator of the Theosophical Society in Ceylon; and Shaku Soyen, the Lord Abbot of a Japanese monastery and representative of the Zen Buddhist tradition. Some, like Vivekananda, a disciple of the Indian mystic Ramakrishna, went on tour immediately in the United States, drawing sympathetic seekers to Hinduism and to his Vedanta Society. Others, like Soyen, Dharmapala, and Mozoomdar, would visit the Hegeler-Carus mansion at La Salle before returning home. "Suffice it to say," remarked Richard Segar, "if the Parliament was a modern feast for Protestants, Catholics, Jews, Humanists, and a good for many women, the Asians were the men who came to dinner, tarried over cognac and cigars, and then never went away."[1]

Protap Chunder Mozoomdar

One of the visitors to La Salle was Protap Chunder Mozoomdar, leader of the Brahmo Somaj, a Hindu reform movement in Bengal, who was already well known from an earlier visit to the United States when he endeared himself to audiences with his expressions of love for Christ. During three-months of travel in 1883, he visited over sixty Unitarian and Congregationalist churches in New England, New York, Chicago, San Francisco, and the District of Columbia. He lectured at Alcott's Concord School of Philosophy where he praised Emerson for understanding India and Hinduism more so than any other Westerner. His "sense of homogeneity with the woods and wilderness. The tranquil landscape and the distant line of the horizon gave him that perception of occult relationship between man and all things which is the key to the sublime culture known as yoga in the history of Hindoo philosophy."[2]

Following his tour, he authored *The Oriental Christ* (1883) which recalled his prayerful endeavors as a young man wandering in "dark isolations and seasons of spiritual exile." Sensing a deep unworthiness influenced by Christian doctrines spread by missionaries in his native land, he looked for "a personal affinity to the spirit of Christ."[3] The most painful period of his spiritual isolation occurred in 1867 when his travails reached crisis stage. It was then that he found Jesus in his heart as "an unpurchased treasure to which I was freely invited."[4]

Even with his religion now outside the fold of Christianity, Mozoomdar never doubted that the ministry of Christ remained as important as it had been in his youth. In fact, it was Christ's continued presence in his life that caused him to point out in *The Oriental Christ* that the West's picture of Jesus was distorted in that his teachings had been colored by European theology which failed to attract the spiritual sympathies belonging to the Hindu religion. "When we speak of an Eastern Christ, we speak of the incarnation of unbounded love and grace," Mozoomdar explained, "and when we speak of the Western Christ, we speak of the incarnation of theology, formalism, ethical and physical force." The former Christ was a stranger to learned books and his sentiments were of simple utterances about brotherhood of all races and his love invited all to the spirit and expanse of his nature. The latter, on the other hand, was well versed in the principles of a theology that were exclusive and arbitrary, condemned humanity to eternal darkness, considered innocent children "the progeny of deadly sin," hurled invectives at other faiths, and judged all scriptures outside of its dispensation as false.[5]

Mozoomdar went on to explain that the evangelical theology taught by European missionaries was only suggestive of Christ's teachings but failed to touch the deeper meanings of his character. Christianity was an Eastern, not a European religion and therefore was best understood by those closest to Oriental life and feeling. Christianity originated in Asia and was therefore more congenial to its habits of thought and feeling. Evangelical Christianity had sent a "Western Christ" to Asia, a false prophet who invaded and subverted Hindu society. "It is an Asiatic only who can teach religion to Asiatics," Mozoomdar insisted. The Western Christ was like the "setting sun" while the Eastern Christ was "fresh and resplendent." Jesus manifested the divine attributes of holiness, love, and wisdom, but "it was never meant to be held that the infinite perfections of the absolute Godhead had ever descended into Jesus or any other man." Jesus was an "exemplar of a model man" showing what the human soul could be in the world.[6]

On his second trip to the United States in 1893, Mozoomdar attended the Parliament of Religions during which time he presented a paper discussing the work of the Brahmo Samaj founded by Ram Mohun Roy who traveled to Tibet to study the lore of the lamas, labored to abolish the custom of sati and advocated for public morality and the remarriage of widows. He also lectured on "The World's Religious Debt to Asia," quoting from physicist John Tyndall that "true religion once came from the East, and from the East it shall come again."[7] Following the close of the Parliament and his visit to La Salle, he went on to Indianapolis, Buffalo, Boston, New York, and the District of Columbia. He would make a third trip in 1900, visiting Unitarian churches in New England and along the eastern seaboard stimulating a strong Brahmo-Unitarian connection.

Swami Vivekananda

Another delegate to the Parliament and guest of Carus and Hegeler was Swami Vivekananda, leader of the Ramakrishna mystic order of monks and a member of the Brahmo Samaj which embraced Unitarian concepts as part of their overall reform agenda. His popular presentations at the Parliament brought him back to the United States on numerous lecture tours. Like Mozoomdar, he made frequent references to Emerson and the inspiration he received from the *Bhagavad Gita*. "If you want to know the sources of Emerson's inspiration, it is this book [that is] responsible for the Concord Movement."[8]

Vivekananda was born into a Bengali family whose father was a prosperous lawyer. After earning his BA in Calcutta in 1884, he immersed himself in Western philosophy and science, focusing principally on the writings of Kant, Hegel, Comte, Spencer, and Darwin. Following the death of his father in 1884, he left the legal profession for religion, turning to Ramakrishna for spiritual guidance. Invited to be a representative of the Brahmo Samaj branch of Hinduism at the Parliament of Religions, his message to the mostly American audience began with the words, "Sisters and Brothers of America!" which drew a standing ovation. Once into his address, he spoke of both the universal nature of truth and the acceptance of evolution theory as it applied to religion. Vivekananda's short but succinct speeches resonated with his audiences and attracted attention in and outside the halls of the Parliament. Taking advantage of his popularity, he criticized Christian missionaries for offering sectarian creeds instead of bread and building churches instead of distributing food to famine-starved populations. "How much more effective would Christian missionaries be if they taught religion instead of dogmas, and love of truth instead of blind faith."[9] After quoting from passages of Hindu scripture, Vivekananda continued:

> Sad will be the day for India when Christian missionaries cease to come; for we have much to learn about Christ and Christian civilization. They do some good work. But if converts are the measures of their success, we have to say that their work is a failure. Little do you dream that your money is expended in spreading abroad nothing but Christian dogmatism, Christian bigotry, Christian pride, and Christian exclusiveness. I entreat you to expend one-tenth only of your vast sacrifices in sending out to our country unsectarian, broad missionaries who will devote their energy to educating our men and women. Educated men will understand Christ better than those whom you convert to the narrow creed of some cant Christianity.[10]

In several papers he presented before the Parliament, Vivekananda sought to impress upon the Western world the universality of the Hindu Faith and the richness of its contents. He even spoke encouragingly of Buddhism, remarking that "Hinduism cannot live without Buddhism nor Buddhism without Hinduism." After the close of the Parliament, he visited cities in the Eastern and Mid-Western states, lecturing almost always extempore. Sometimes outspoken in his criticism, he was not reluctant to identify the faults and defects in Western religion. "One thing I would tell you, and I do not mean any unkind criticism," he explained in one of his lectures in Detroit in February 1894, "You train and educate and clothe and pay men to do what?—to come over to my country and curse and abuse all my forefathers, my religion and my everything. . . . If you want to live, go back to Christ. You are not Christians. No, as a nation, you are not."[11]

During a visit to Boston, Vivekananda met William James who had quoted extensively from him in his *Varieties of Religious Experience* (1902). An admirer of James's pragmatism, Vivekananda was nevertheless a monist who opposed James's pluralistic approach to religion and truth.[12] The Ramakrishna monk founded the Vedanta Society of New York in 1894, lectured at Greenacre, and attracted a number of admirers including Josiah Royce, Robert G. Ingersoll, Ella Wheeler Wilcox, and Sarah Bernhardt. He returned in 1899 before attending the Congress of Religions in Paris in 1900. A nationalist, he is credited with raising Hinduism to a major world status in India.

Dharmapala

In response to the negative impact of American and European colonialism, especially the missionary activities of their churches on native populations, a cadre of Western and Eastern intellectuals began a discourse on whether Buddhism was better suited to the needs of the emerging scientific world. While Christianity continued to struggle with the existential challenges resulting from the higher criticism and Darwin's theory of natural selection, Buddhism offered a smorgasbord of beliefs that minimized the tensions arising from modernity. Time and again during the Parliament's proceedings, Buddhist delegates took advantage of the moment to advance their cause. As noted by David L. McMahan, "perhaps no major tradition has attempted to adopt scientific discourse more vigorously than Buddhism."[13]

But Buddhism is no monolithic religion. It encompasses different variants, some of which are distinctly modern, others modern and western in their approach and practices, and still others which remain highly traditional and mythological. Perhaps the best example of the middle group was represented in the pioneering work of Dharmapala of Ceylon whose beliefs were strongly influenced by the activity of Colonel Olcott and Madame Blavatsky who had moved to Ceylon in 1880 to support the cause of Theosophy. Ceylon had become a British territory in 1796 and, although its colonial governors promised to respect native religions, British policy eventually became one of conversion. Because of his association with Theosophy and promotion of a vision of Buddhism that was compatible with western science, Dharmapala embraced freedom of conscience and direct insight (an internalized spirituality) rather than public rituals; emphasized personal responsibility and meditation; saw everyday life as sacred; and drew heavily from the work of laypeople rather than monks and priests. Having entered the brotherhood of the Anagarika, an order of the homeless (one who gave away most of his worldly possessions), he soon rose among its ranks to become leader of the Buddhist protest and reform movement.[14]

Audiences warmed to Dharmapala's brand of Buddhism due in part to his generous use of English-language concepts to support the theory of evolution and the significance of cause and effect. Quoting from Western popularizers of the empirical sciences, he explained that Buddhism (meaning "Protestant Buddhism)[15] had accepted scientific ideas twenty-four centuries earlier than the West, which was now only beginning to embrace them, albeit with numerous caveats due to its late start. The popular conception that the historical relationship between science and religion was one of all-out conflict is best depicted in John William Draper's best-selling *History of the Conflict Between Religion and Science* (1874). This work alone was sufficient justification for Dharmapala's argument that, unlike Christianity, Buddhism was not only compatible with the sciences, but superior to the West for engaging in it so early. Dharmapala's views resonated with Carus who found little sympathy for the evangelical biases of old-style Christianity.[15] As Carus explained to the Rev. W. Subhuti in Ceylon, "there are men who are cleverer and more scholarly than H. Dharmapala" but he had gained the hearts of many on account of his religion. "While

Vivekananda, the Brahman delegate to the Religious Parliament, is very bright and very ingenious, and while Gandhi, the Jain representative, is a man of great culture, Dharmapala excels both, but especially the former, in sincerity and unselfishness."[16]

After speaking at the Parliament, Dharmapala embarked on a three-month tour of the United States acting as a missionary on behalf of Buddhism and a spokesman for Ceylon nationalism against the colonialism of the West. His tour not only solidified his importance as a representative of Buddhism but strengthened his standing among his own countrymen. The Ceylonese followed his talks, and on his return home, he became a celebrated leader in helping to advance its culture and nationalism.[17]

Carus remained in contact with Dharmapala in the ensuing years and followed his efforts to create a center for Buddhism in Bodh-Gaya, a town in northeastern India and home to the Mahabodhi Temple, one of the nation's four ancient Buddhist holy sites. His goal was to make the town what Rome became for the Roman Catholics, Benares to the Hindus, and Mecca to the Mohammedans. However, a pilgrimage to the temple in Bodh-Gaya was complicated. It involved a twenty-four-hour train ride from Calcutta to Bodh-Gaya, and then another six miles to the town of Gaya. According to Dharmapala, the Buddhists who visited the temple were put to great inconvenience by the government and by the Hindu High Priest who controlled the site. To counteract this obstructionism, Dharmapala filed a lawsuit against the Brahmin priests demanding protection for its pilgrims.[18]

Fearful of rising tensions between Buddhists and the Hindu majority, Carus wrote Dharmapala expressing personal concern over his attempts to purchase the Bodh-Gaya village. Carus pointed out that his efforts were not in the best interest of Buddhism. "Religion does not consist in keeping sacred certain days, or places, or relics, or in making pilgrimages to holy shrines," he advised. These attributes were the leftovers of paganism and, like the Crusades, "were a useless sacrifice of

The world-famous Buddhist scholar and author, Daisetsu (or Daisetz) Teitaro Suzuki (1870–1966). As a youthful protégé of Shaku Soyen, Suzuki lived for more than a decade in the Carus household in La Salle, helping Paul Carus with translations and other work. His first book, Outlines of Mahayana Buddhism, *was published by Open Court in 1908.*

much money and blood for a phantom—the possession of Jerusalem as the most sacred spot of Christianity." Such possessions were "curiosities" that were best forgotten.[19]

After learning that Dharmapala's efforts to buy the village had failed due to intrigues allegedly orchestrated by the British government, Carus encouraged him to return to the United States as a representative of Southern Buddhism and embark on a missionary tour through the country, promising that he would have far more converts in the United States than among the Hindus in India. Moreover, he could use the money he had already collected to establish homes and centers for Buddhist students at nearby universities. In 1896, three years after Dharmapala served as an official delegate at the Parliament, he returned to the United States to preach. To help pay his expenses, Carus sent him a draft for seventy-five pounds, payable in English gold. He also invited him to La Salle to meet D.T. Suzuki whom he expected would be arriving soon. Given that dharmapala advocated the Hinayana branch of Buddhism, and Suzuki the Mahayana branch in Japan, he thought such a meeting would prove fruitful.[20]

After arriving in New York in September 1896, Dharmapala traveled to La Salle where the two men spent days discussing philosophy. "I believe he has been too long in India among Indians and has imbibed too many of their philosophical notions," remarked Carus to C.T. Strauss, a Buddhist sympathizer from New York, "but I have great hope that he will become clearer when he sees things in the right light."[21] With Carus's encouragement and connections, Dharmapala preached at various churches in La Salle and Chicago where he met Charles Bonney, Lewis Pyle Mercer, Bishop Samuel Fallows, and William R. Harper, the president of the University of Chicago, whom he urged to create a chair of Pali and where he gave talks to students learning about comparative religions.[22]

During his visit, Dharmapala opened an American branch of the Maha Bodhi Society which he and the poet Sir Edwin Arnold had originally founded in 1891 to advance the cause of Buddhism in India and restoration of the temples at Bodh-Gaya, Sarnath, and Kushinara. Carus, whom Dharmapala appointed president of the American branch, accepted the responsibility for advancing Buddhism in the United States: "I am quite clear about the plans of making Buddhism known in this country and I pursue it accordingly." In that capacity, he cautioned Dharmapala for fear he might be moving too fast. "That you are impatient is quite natural, but you cannot make a movement go quicker by being busy in lines where the success is only temporary and incidental." Using monies collected by the Society and from his American supporters, Dharmapala set up scholarships and opened boarding houses near several universities.[23]

With Carus's encouragement, dharmapala used the Hegeler-Carus mansion as the base of operations for his tours which took him as far north as Guelph in southwestern Ontario. After being on the road for weeks at a time, he returned to La Salle where he rested before starting out on a new tour. Carus used these opportunities to advise him and even arranged for William Pipe to accompany Dharmapala and manage his tours. Both Carus and Pipe were concerned that Dharmapala lectured without notes, lacked a sense of timing, and often failed to understand the level of his audience's sophistication. In anticipation of his visit to San Francisco, for example, Carus warned that most of his attendees would be Theosophists, a group who "form circles of their own and are upon the whole intellectually second-class people." On the other hand, his audiences in Boston and at the Greenacre conferences in Maine were far different. "You will there have a critical and highly cultivated audience, and you should not speak there without thorough preparation."[24] Accordingly, he and Pipe persisted in urging Dharmapala to write out his lectures, never speak unprepared, and "become more business-like" in his presentation of subjects. Carus also advised him not to travel to California unless he had definite arrangements in advance of the trip. Until then, he should stay as a guest in La Salle where he could work quietly on his lectures in preparation for the tour. In many ways, Carus used Pipe to provide Dharmapala with this much needed advice.[25]

Despite being an excellent speaker, Dharmapala sometimes lacked a sense of proportionality when offered the opportunity to criticize Christianity. After noticing highly negative remarks in the newspapers to one of his lectures, Carus tried diplomatically to tutor him on how to present himself before American audiences.

> The charges which are made in these remarks against Christianity are not true, and even if they were true, they ought to be expressed in a different way. Buddha certainly would not have used this language, and would if he had found faults with an existing religion have looked upon it rather with compassion and sympathy than with scorn. . . . It is always advisable to adhere to the rules of the Religious Parliament which request everyone to state positively his own views to their best advantage without deprecating the views of others. . . . It is, of course, not impossible that the passages quoted in the *New York Herald* are not your own words. It is even probable that the newspaper has exaggerated any statement which you made so as to create a sensation, but you should, on that account be more careful with your expressions. Pardon me for calling your attention to these points but I believe it to be my duty to give you my views freely and candidly. I know that Mr. Bonney will be very much grieved when he sees this statement. Of one thing you may rest assured that if you wish to succeed you must avoid expressions such as were reported in the *New York Herald.*[26]

Informed that Dharmapala was considering entering politics as a prohibitionist, Carus again took strong exception. While sympathizing with his aspiration to teach the dangers of liquor and of his desire to join the Prohibitionist Party, he warned that being so public about such matters would jeopardize his mission. As for his suggestion that *The Open Court* become a prohibitionist paper, Carus responded: "We are . . . against any method of forcing morality by law, and we have adopted this principle not without good intentions. . . . While we are all working for the purification of morals, we cannot do so by the methods advocated by prohibitionists, which briefly means to make people good by removing by force any kind of temptation. All experiences in the past have been against this method and I should say it is a thoroughly un-Buddhist method. In its final consequences it leads to the principles of the Inquisition which makes people religious by the rack and faggot."[27]

Not having a chance to see Dharmapala before he returned to Ceylon following his tour in 1897, Carus wrote a letter congratulating him on the "good impression" he had left with the people and used the opportunity to give him one last piece of advice: "I conclude this long letter with my best wishes for your future welfare and hope that you will let me hear from you again. Be critical in all you do and undertake. Do not set your trust in acquirements of so-called supernatural powers. It will merely be a loss of energy and a disappointment."[28]

Dharmapala was not alone in receiving advice from Carus. In a letter to the Rev. P.A. Jinavaravansa in Ceylon in 1897, he urged him not to despair of the conditions in Buddhist countries but to come to the United States and speak for its cause. Because the U.S. was the "most important country at the present time," it behooved him to make his opinions known here as opposed to somewhere else, assuring him there was "no country in the world which is as open-minded as you will find the people of the United States." He furthermore advised him to come as a student rather than as a missionary, promising that he would find open doors everywhere. Nor was it necessary for him to be a scholar to speak about Buddhism. He reminded him that Dharmapala was neither a scholar nor an accomplished public speaker. "I have sometimes tried to induce him not to speak extemporary but to prepare a few speeches and to memorize them until he had acquired that familiarity which a public speaker ought to have. But I find it difficult to change him and I have left him as he is. . . . He does not control himself as a speaker but follows the spur of the moment." Carus went on to explain to Jinavaravansa that his idea of creating a union of all Buddhists under the protectorate of the King of Siam was not an impossibility but warned that doing so might cause politics to be mixed up with religion. For one thing, England would surely not favor the idea of having the King of Siam as the defender of Buddhism for those countries belonging to the British empire. "A religious union of the Buddhists should be strictly unpolitical and should be, if possible, established first in such countries as are not English, viz., in Japan or China."[29]

Shaku Soyen

The strongest influence on Carus during and after the Parliament was Shaku Soyen, the Zen master from Japan who spoke on causality from a Buddhist perspective, a subject dear to Carus because of his monograph *Monism and Meliorism*. Following the close of the Parliament, Soyen and Toki Horin visited La Salle where they stayed several days. On their arrival, they presented Carus and his father-in-law with several poems composed by Soyen and read at an evening session of the Parliament. They also prepared a poem on their train ride from Chicago to La Salle.

> (There are) several races of man, red, black, yellow, and white
> (But) truth (is) one (only), reigning (in the) South, North, East and West
> (If any one) doubt truth (being) one, (let him) look (at the) moon shining
> brightly (in the) skies.
> (There is) no place (in the) world (where her) pure light (does) not penetrate.[30]

Both Carus and Soyen were greatly impressed with the results of the Parliament and agreed on working together to advance the Religion of Science. Both saw opportunities. Believing that religion must have its roots in science, Soyen urged Carus to facilitate the popularization of Buddhist thinking in the United States, explaining that he was "a beachhead here for us. If . . . he [Carus] could be brought to understand the true meaning of Buddhism, it would be better than converting a hundred thousand ordinary people."[31] Similarly,

Carus saw Soyen as his passport to Asia, giving him access to religious and philosophical books that could be translated into English. In other words, Carus would use Soyen to bring Buddhism to America, convinced that he possessed a better than even chance of inspiring American audiences provided he could demonstrate the effects of science on Buddhism's beliefs and practices. The process, however, would require a 'makeover,' exchanging certain Buddhist qualities, images, and interpretations for a new set of conceptions.[32]

Following his return to Japan, Soyen wrote frequently to Carus regarding their mutual desire to establish a Religion of Science. "I am a Buddhist but far from being a conservative religionist, my interest is rather to stir a reformation movement in the religious world. . . . And I believe that if the present Christianity be reformed it will become the old Buddhism, and if the latter be reformed, it will become the future religion of science which is still in the womb of Truth, but which is steadily growing up there to be born with full power. The late Parliament I think is the forerunner of the future universal religion of science."[33]

In 1896, when Rev. John Henry Barrows presented a negative view of Buddhism in a presentation at the University of Chicago as part of the Haskell Lecture Series on Comparative Religions, Carus wrote to Soyen informing him of the presentation and remarking that Barrows "follows exactly the line of those Christian critics who know nothing of the spirit of Buddhism." Rather than respond personally to Barrows for fear it would cause a rift, he turned to Soyen to "set him right on the various points on which he is mistaken." Carus even drafted a statement for Soyen to consider sending under his own name. "I have put it in words which are as reverent as I could make it. If you feel like omitting them, do so, but I think it would do no harm."[34]

Soyen took Carus's advice and wrote Barrows chastising him for his remarks. "I was greatly disappointed," he explained, "seeing that you only repeat those errors which are common in the various Western books on Buddhism." He also criticized Barrows for remarking that Buddhism "groans under the dominion of inexorable and implacable laws." Not so, answered Soyen, Buddha's teachings agreed with the laws of modern science. Better that Christianity disavowed its miracles and notions of supernatural intervention before casting stones at Buddha's teachings.[35]

> I am anxious to know all that is good in Christianity and the significance of your dogmas, so that I may grow in a comprehension of truth, but I have not as yet been able to see that mankind can be benefited by believing that Jesus Christ performed miracles. I do not deny the miracles, nor do I believe them; I only claim that they are irrelevant. The beauty and the truth of many of Christ's sayings fascinate me, but truth does not become clearer by being pronounced by a man who works miracles. You say that, "We can explain Buddha without the miracles which later legends ascribe to him, but we cannot explain Christ—either his person or his influence—without granting the truth of his own claim that he did the supernatural works of his father." We may grant that Jesus Christ is the greatest master and teacher that appeared in the West after Buddha, but the picture of Jesus Christ as we find it in the Gospel is marred by the accounts of such miracles as the great draft of fishes, which involves a great and useless destruction of life (for we read that the fishermen followed Jesus, leaving the fish behind), and by the transformation of water into wine at the marriage-feast at Cana. Nor has Jesus Christ attained to the calmness and dignity of Buddha, for the passion of anger overtook him in the temple, when he drove out with rope in hand those that bargained in the holy place. How different would Buddha have behaved under similar conditions in the same place! Instead of whipping the evildoers he would have converted them, for kind words strike deeper than the whip.[36]

Evident in Soyen's response to Barrows was his clear distinction between Christianity which he viewed as decidedly unscientific in its perpetuation of miracles, and Buddha's teachings which agreed with the findings of modern science. In typical Soyen fashion, however, he asked that Barrows not take offense at his remarks but explained that he felt compelled to write in protest since Barrows should have had a better understanding of Buddhism than most because of his role in the Parliament. Soyen ended his letter asking that Barrows make public his protest so that the misconceptions and prejudices could be corrected. Carus published Soyen's response in *The Open Court* where it elicited a veritable feast of responses—both positive and negative.[37]

In 1905, Soyen returned to the United States as the guest of Mr. and Mrs. Alexander Russell of San Francisco and, using their home as his base, he toured the country with Suzuki who took a leave of absence from his editorial work at the Open Court Publishing Company in La Salle to serve as translator. In one of his lectures which included a collection of aphorisms drawn from the different canonical books brought into China by the first Buddhist missionaries from Central India, Soyen compared them with those he found in the Christian Gospels. In another lecture, "The God-Conception of Buddhism," he elucidated on the West's insistence that Buddhism was atheistic, or at best pantheistic, implying that it rejected the personal God of Christianity. Soyen explained that Buddhism avoided using the term God, preferring instead the word *Dharmakaya* which corresponded to wisdom. Repeatedly, Soyen quoted from Goethe or the Gospels of John, Mathew, and Luke to explain and visualize the different elements of Buddhism found in their writings. Other lectures addressed topics of immortality, faith, ethics, spiritual enlightenment, and the doctrine of the non-ego or anatman.[38]

Soyen's tour included a visit to Washington D.C., where he lectured before the National Geographic Society, insisting that there was more than one school or division of Buddhism. Properly speaking Buddhism, like Christianity, had gone through several stages of development before reaching its present state. As he explained, Hinayana Buddhism should be considered a preparatory phase of Mahayana Buddhism. At the present time, most of what the West knew of Buddhism was seen through the lens of Hinayana Buddhism. Because Hinayana was more pessimistic, ascetic, and monastical, it failed to satisfy man's spiritual yearnings. It was this form of Buddhism that still held sway in Ceylon, Burma, and Siam. The people of Japan, on the other hand, had turned to Mahayanistic Buddhism, which was more religious, humanistic, enlightened, satisfying, and free from superstition.[39]

When he left for Europe at the end of his speaking tour in April 1906, Soyen gave his lectures, many of which had been prepared from shorthand notes, to Suzuki to edit and revise for publication by the Open Court Company. Because some lectures were formal and others informal, Suzuki took the liberty of condensing several talks into a single lecture. Oftentimes, he simplified Soyen's thoughts to make them less technical and more easily understood by the American public.[40] The lectures, published under the title *Sermons of a Buddhist Abbot* (1906), included Soyen's letter to Barrows protesting the latter's misconception of the spirit of Buddhism, and another which addressed the Buddhist view of war following his visit to the battlefield of Nan-Shan Hill during the Russo-Japanese War. "War is an evil and a great one," he observed, "but war against evils must be unflinchingly prosecuted till we attain the final aim." It was the price paid for one's ideals. "Let us, then, though not without losing tenderness of heart, bravely confront our ordeal." War may be horrible in its particulars but provided it was fought for a "just and honorable cause," and for the "realization of noble ideals," it is justified for "the upholding of humanity and civilization."[41]

* * *

Before returning to their native country, many of the Buddhist and Hindu delegates to the Parliament of Religions embarked on speaking tours. Though not shy in pointing out the inconsistencies and questionable ethics of evangelical missionary work, and calling attention to western racism, imperialism, and materialism, the delegates were far more interested in proving to the West the modernity and sophistication of their respective cultures. Their religions were not only in step with modernity but fully tailored to the West's vision of evolution as the mechanism for human progress. Rather than take a defensive role against Western belief systems, Mozoomdar, Dharmapala, Vivekananda, and Soyen explained their religions as not only morally superior but with a longer tradition of supporting science than the West. Each played into the American psyche by wanting to revitalize the traditions of their respective nations at a time when nationalism and science were shaping the contours of the modern world.[42]

5
Open Sesame

> The nearer we approach to the great founders of the different schools of Buddhist thought, the more easily does the Christian have feelings of honest appreciation. 'Back to Buddha' needs to be said as well as 'Back to Christ.'
>
> —Gilbert Reid, "A Christian's Appreciation of Buddhism," 1916

As noted earlier, American interest in Indian philosophy, and Buddhism in particular, began with Transcendentalism and morphed through several schools of thought before becoming the avocation of Paul Carus who, until the Parliament of Religions, had used the pages of *The Open Court* to espouse the Religion of Science. What he anticipated would come incrementally, however, happened more quickly due to the public's response to the presentations and discussions among the delegates.

In the Parliament's aftermath, Carus became a self-appointed ambassador introducing Eastern religions and philosophies, particularly Buddhism, to the West. "For reasons that Carus himself only dimly sensed," observed Martin J. Verhoeven, his encounter with Asian Buddhists in Chicago "gave birth to a modern Buddhism in the United States, and one that would leave its imprint on the religious landscape well into the next century."[1]

After listening to presentations by delegates from India, Japan, and southeast Asia, Carus returned to La Salle convinced that Buddhism represented the most accurate expression of western rationalism, science, evolution, and cause and effect. The more he analyzed its inner workings, the more convinced he became that Buddhism anticipated Darwin's transformation of species and the fundamentals of modern psychology; that karma was "natural law translated into the ethical realm;" and most strikingly, that Buddha's exhortation to be "lamps unto yourselves" (verifying through experience) was far more important than blind belief. Consequently, over the next two decades, he invested heavily in the publication of thirty-eight books and a myriad of articles on Eastern philosophy and religion.[2] Carus felt that, as a religion, Buddhism could easily represent the centerpiece of his Religion of Science, confident that it stood for positivism and scientific methodology.[3] "It demands no belief in the impossible; it dispenses with miracles, [and] it assumes no authority except the illumination of a right comprehension of the facts of existence."[4] Buddhism was a "religion of enlightenment" whose Buddha Gautama was "the first positivist, the first humanitarian, the first radical freethinker, the first iconoclast, and the first prophet of the Religion of Science."[5] Moreover, judging from the letters he received following the Parliament, he found the public's interest was greatest when it concerned Buddhism.[6]

A New Centerpiece

The earliest pre-1893 article on Buddhism to appear in *The Open Court* was in 1887 with J.G.R. Forlong's "Through What Historical Channels did Buddhism Influence Early Christianity?" After the Parliament, however, articles on Eastern religions and philosophy rose rapidly until about 1906, when they leveled off before declining.[7] One of Carus's first books was *Karma: A Story of Buddhist Ethics* (1894) which went through six editions before 1917 and translated into multiple languages. Leo Tolstoy, who provided the Russian translation, explained in his preface that Buddhism shed light on two fundamental Buddhist and Christian principles, namely that "life exists only in the renunciation of one's personality," and that "the good of men is only in their union with God, and through God with one another."[8]

As a result of the contacts he made at the Parliament, Carus opened his journals and the Open Court Publishing Company to analyses of all forms of religious thought. His book contributors included Macahar Anesaki's *Gospel Parallels from Pali Texts;* Syed Ameer Ali's *Islam;* William George Asten, *The Religion of Ancient Japan;* L.D. Barrett's *Hinduism;* Albert J. Edmunds' *Buddhist and Christian Gospels;* Richard Garbe's *The Philosophy of Ancient India;* Hermann Oldenberg's *Ancient India: Its Language and Religions;* Shaku Soyen's *The Sermons of a Buddhist Abbot;* D.T. Suzuki's *Acyaghosha's Discourses on the Awakening of Faith in the Mahayana* and *Outlines of Mahayana Buddhism;* and Keichyu Yamada's *Scenes from the Life of Buddha.* Contributors of articles included the Asian scholar and Presbyterian minister George Foot Moore; E. Washburn Hopkins at Yale; James Barton, foreign secretary of the American Board of Commissioners for Foreign Missions; German Indologist Paul Jacob Deussen, author of *The Sutra of the Vedanta* (1906), *The Philosophy of the Upanishads* (1906), and *The System of the Vedanta* (1912); and Swami Vivekananda whose interpretation of Hinduism connected it with western esoteric traditions, especially Transcendentalism, New Thought, and Theosophy. Carus also acquired the publishing rights for George John Romanes's *Darwin and After Darwin* (1897) as well as his posthumous *Thoughts on Religion* (1912) because he recognized in the doctrine of evolution one of the more important truths, namely that science and religion were not two separate and distinct spheres. On the contrary, they both formed "integral parts" of humanity's spiritual existence. They were "the web and woof of our souls."[9]

From Harvard, Carus solicited articles from the philosopher and idealist Josiah Royce, author of *The World and the Individual* (1899), and the philosopher and psychologist

William James, whose *The Varieties of Religious Experience* (1902), the outcome of his Gifford Lectures delivered at the University of Edinburgh during 1901 and 1902, relied heavily on Eastern religious experiences. Additional contributions came from the Ceylonese Tamil philosopher Ananda Kentish Coomaraswamy of the Boston Museum of Fine arts; Indian philosopher and statesman Sarvepalli Radhakrishnan; and Indian philosopher Surendranath N. Dasgupta. According to Harold Henderson, *The Open Court* and *The Monist* "gave Eastern religions and societies more extensive and sympathetic coverage than any U.S. publications had before."[10]

The Gospel of Buddha

Between 1894 and 1907, Carus wrote or edited thirteen books on Asia as well as a spate of articles and reviews addressing the differences and similarities between Buddhism and Christianity, the merits of missionary work, Oriental art, and the post-Parliament influence of Oriental philosophy and religion in the western world. His list of books is worth noting for they indicate a definite change of interest that in many ways defines his character.

1. *Karma: A Story of Buddhist Ethics* (1894)
2. *The Gospel of Buddha* (1894; 1915; 2004)
3. *The Dharma, Or, The Religion of Enlightenment: An Exposition of Buddhism* (1896)
4. *Buddhism and Its Christian Critics* (1897)
5. *Lao-Tze's Tao Teh-King* (1898)
6. *The Canon of Reason and Virtue* (1898)
7. *Nirvana: A Story of Buddhist Psychology* (1902)
8. *Portfolio of Buddhist Art, Historical and Modern* (1906)
9. *Amitabha;: A Story of Buddhist Theology* (1906)
10. *T'ai-Shang Kan-Ying P'ien* (1906)
11. *Yin Chih Wen* (1906)
12. *Chinese Life and Customs* (1907)
13. *Chinese Thought; An Exposition of the Main Characteristic Features of the Chinese World-Conception* (1907)

According to D.T. Suzuki, the idea for *The Gospel of Buddha* (1894) originated from "lively discussions" between Shaku Soyen and Carus during the monk's visit to La Salle following the close of the Parliament.[11] When published, the book drew from a broad array of writings made accessible from Western scholarship and translations from Pali, Sanskrit, Chinese, and other languages. Being neither a Buddhist nor a scholar of comparative religions or of Asian languages, Carus relied heavily on the translations of Max Müller, Thomas Rhys Davids, and Samuel Beal for his understanding of the original Buddhist texts. "Suffice it to say," observed historian Martin J. Verhoeven, dean of academics at Dharma Realm Buddhist University in Berkeley, "Carus chose his European sources wisely."[12] This included Müller's fifty-one volumes of *Sacred Books of the East* (1879-1910); Beal's *Travels of Fah-hian ad Sung-Yun* (1869), *A Catena of Buddhist Scriptures from the Chinese* (1871), *The Romantic Legend of Sakya Buddha* (1875), *Buddhist Canon* (1878), *A Life of Buddha by Asvaghosha Bodhisattva* (1879), and *An Abstract of Four Lectures on Buddhist Literature in China* (1882); and Rhys Davids's *Buddhism* (1877), *Buddhist Suttas from the Pali* (1881), *Vinaya Texts* (1881–85) and *Questions of King Milinda* (1890–94) which he translated in collaboration with Hermann Oldenberg.

Of all the translations used by Carus, those by Müller were the most frequently cited. Müller taught that there was a science of language, but he was a great believer in a Science of Religion that could bring to light the treasury of human knowledge found in the ancient religious texts. The real critical study of Buddhism dated from 1824 when the British ethnologist Brian Houghton Hodgson announced that the original documents of the Buddhist canon had been preserved in Sanskrit in the monasteries of Nepal. From his labors, and those of Eugène Burnouf, Sándor Csoma de Körös in Tibet, and Isaak Jakob Schmidt in Mongolia, the world of Buddhist literature was made accessible to European scholars. Given the wealth of information now available, argued Müller, it was time to dispel those erroneous notions about Buddhism current among educated people. The most important aspects of Buddhism had always been its social and moral code, not just its metaphysical theories. "That moral code, taken by itself, is one of the most perfect which the world has ever known."[13]

A graduate of Leipzig University in 1843 in the field of Sanskrit, and one of the founders of comparative religions, Müller spent his professional life at Oxford until his death in 1900. Like Carus, he believed in religion grounded in science and looked to removing the layers of accretion in dogma and ritual that had corrupted the original purity of the great religions of the world. Both Carus and Müller exhibited a greater appreciation of Buddhism than their contemporaries, admiring its positive spirit and dismissing claims by European and American missionaries that Buddhism was unqualified to be identified as a religion. How could one deny its status as a religion, asked Müller, whose path to Nirvana consisted of "right faith (orthodoxy), right judgment (logic), right language (veracity), right purpose (honesty), right practice (religious life), right obedience (lawful life), right memory, and right meditation?"[14]

With his choice of texts, Carus presented to the Western world a view not of historical Buddhism but rather an advanced form of Buddhism intended to strengthen its compatibility with post-Enlightenment science. Even though Buddhism, like Christianity, was divided into numerous sects, Carus had no intention of giving equal time to each. Instead, he presented Mahayana Buddhism as the "ideal position upon which all true Buddhists may stand as upon common ground." It represented a compilation of the life of Buddha much as the fourth Gospel of the New Testament accounted for the life of Jesus. To achieve this objective, he arranged and sometimes rewrote texts to promote Buddhism's harmony with science and the modern world. Not only did *The Gospel of Buddha* replicate the Christian Gospels but it represented the ideal Religion of Science, demonstrating that Buddhism was the cosmic religion of the future—the same argument asserted over and over again by Buddhist delegates at the Parliament.[15] With the publication of the book, Carus became an advocate for so-called Modern Buddhism which integrated evolutionary science with the law of cause and effect, catapulting historical Buddhism from centuries of disparate teachings into a single transnational tradition compatible with the ideals of the European Enlightenment. More so than any other religion, it demonstrated Carus's ideal of a universal Religion of Science.

Carus's selection of texts fit comfortably with the Japanese, giving the book a degree of gravitas that added to its significance, particularly since it explained in practical terms how man should live rather than dwell on metaphysical propositions for virtuous behavior. For this reason, Carus found himself at odds with the very scholars whose translations he used for the book, including the meaning behind the terms Nirvana and atman. Except for Thomas Rhys Davids, most translators treated these terms as nihilistic and irreconcilable with Western concepts of a personal creator, an immortal self, and a heaven. By contrast, Carus argued that the atman belief corresponded to man's egotism, an illusion growing from man's vanity and the belief that the purpose of life lies in self. The Buddha, however, denied the self. Nirvana, the ideal state, consisted of no atman or ego entity. This was a cornerstone in Buddha's ethics.[16] Carus and Davids blamed the misinterpretations on the disparaging bias of Christian translators who, as explained by Verhoeven, "were influenced by their own parochial *Zeitgeist*" and therefore unable to view Buddhism through the eyes of a Buddhist.[17]

Until *The Gospel of Buddha,* Sir Edwin Arnold's poem, *The Light of Asia* (1879) had been the most successful and widely read publication on Eastern religion, selling more than a million copies in Britain and the United States alone. By contrast, Carus's first edition sold over three million copies and translated into more than a dozen languages. Yet, according to Verhoeven, neither work was a true representation of the Buddhist canon; rather, they were recasts of the Buddha in a manner intended to appeal to western readers and westernized Asians.[18]

Other Editions

As Carus prepared his texts for inclusion in *The Gospel of Buddha,* he sent advance sheets of his work to Soyen. The first point that attracted the monk's attention was Carus's view of Nirvana, noting that most interpretations were drawn from Hinayana Buddhism. "But happily it is not so in your case," wrote Soyen, "because you seem to understand it as relating to this life and as real, positive, altruistic, and rather optimistic, which is the true sense of Nirvana taught in the Mahayana." Impressed by Carus's work, the relationship between the two men blossomed, causing Soyen to remark: "I think you may well be said to be a second Columbus who is endeavoring to discover the new world of Truth."[19]

Shortly after *The Gospel of Buddha* came out in English, a Japanese translation titled *Budda no fukuin* followed. In his preface to the Japanese edition, Soyen explained his support for the work saying that it not only demonstrated the degree to which Buddhism was understood and appreciated by Western scholars, but that it represented a road for Japan's younger generation to study Buddhism and "sow widely the seeds" of its teachings. In other words, the book not only served the needs of Western audiences but also those educated Japanese in search of a national spirit. Here was a truly indigenous philosophy and not a substitute Western religion. Still, Soyen remained cautious in his praise of the book, suggesting that it might not be a truly reflective account of Buddhist philosophy.

> Many Buddhist scriptures have been translated, both from Sanskrit and Chinese, by Western scholars, and a dozen of books relating to Buddhism have also made their appearance, but only a few of them are read in our country. They are Max Müller's *Nirvana,* Olcott's *A Buddhist Catechism,* Arnold's *The Light of Asia,* and Swedenborg's *Buddhism.* Swedenborgianism entered the realm of Buddhism from his deep mysticism. Arnold from his beautiful poetical thoughts, Olcott from his mighty intellectual power, and Max Müller from his extensive knowledge of the elegant Sanskrit literature. Every one of them shines in his special department, accord-

> ing to the peculiar excellence of his genius. But as for the first and ultimate truth of Buddhism, I am not sure whether they have thoroughly understood it.[20]

By July 1895, when the English version entered its third printing, the Japanese translation had reached its second, and the high Buddhist authorities in Ceylon were recommending it as an English reader in their schools. In subsequent years, translations were made in Chinese, German, French, Spanish, Dutch, Russian, Czech, Italian, and Siamese.[21]

Until 1915, the numerous printings of the *Gospel of Buddha* remained the same, with no textual revisions or additions. In that year, a new revised edition appeared under a slightly different title *The Gospel of Buddha, Compiled from Ancient Records* and included illustrations by Munich artist Olga Kopetzky and a new preface by Carus. In it, he gave recognition to scholars like Robert Childers, Thomas Rhys Davids, Edouard Foucaux, Spence Hardy, Max Müller, Hermann Oldenberg, and D.M. Strong who had made the sacred books of Buddhism accessible to the world. He admitted copying from them quite literally, and at other times, "rather freely in order to make them intelligible to the present generation." Then again, he admitted to rearranging, abbreviating, and, in some instances, providing "purely original additions" which he did "with due consideration and always in the spirit of a legitimate development." He justified these modifications as nothing more than ideas for which "prototypes can be found somewhere among the traditions of Buddhism and have been introduced as elucidations of its main principles."[22]

According to Thomas Tweed, except for Henry Steel Olcott's *Catechism* which contributed to both the Indian Renaissance and the Sinhalese Buddhist Revival, Carus was probably "more influential in stimulating and sustaining American interest in Buddhism than any other person living in the United States."[23] As Verhoeven observed, Carus's encounter with Asian Buddhists in Chicago "gave birth to a modern Buddhism in the United States, and one that would leave its imprint on the religious landscape of America well into the next century." The book's success also played a role in the "second flowering" of Buddhism in the 1960s through the work of Suzuki at Columbia University and the Beat Generation's embrace of Eastern philosophy, especially Zen.

Over a hundred years later and into the fifth generation of the Hegeler-Carus family enterprise, Buddhism remained a centerpiece of Open Court's publishing interests with the 2004 new edition of *The Gospel of Buddha.* This newest edition, the book's third, includes illustrations by the Japanese artist Keichu Yamada found during the restoration of the Hegeler-Carus Mansion in La Salle. According to Blouke Carus, the son of Edward H. Carus (the oldest son of Paul Carus), the pictures of the talented Munich artist Olga Kopetzky used in the 1915 edition had probably been chosen over Yamada's paintings because of her more "western" (Greco-Roman) look which arguably resonated more with American readers.[24]

Carus's Critics

In an effusive letter, Charles Bonney congratulated Carus for his publication of *The Gospel of Buddha,* judging it not only as an important sign of the time but as a prophecy "of the coming unity of mankind in Jesus Christ." Having refused to give up on his preference for Christianity, Bonney insisted that scientists would find in Christ, not Buddha, the "harmony of nature and spirit, and the crown of evolution." It was the mission of Christianity to "found an empire of truth, the kingdom of heaven upon earth." The same applied to the Rev. John Henry Barrows who, despite his liberal reputation, predicted that Christianity, not Buddhism, would be the lone survivor in the competition between and among the world's religions.[25]

Unlike Bonney and Barrows who viewed Buddhism in the context of evolution, most scholars preferred to challenge Carus's choice of texts. George Stephen Goodspeed, a member of the editorial staff of the *Biblical World* and professor of Ancient History and Comparative Religion at Chicago, attacked Carus's method of text selection given the fact that he did not work in the original but only in translations. "To know what to choose at second-hand . . . is no ordinary qualification, and such knowledge is evident in the pages of this book," Goodspeed concluded. There were simply too many errors of judgment that resulted in misleading the very persons for whom the book was intended. Had he separated the book into two parts—one presenting the Hinayana sources and then material from the Mahayana writings—the book would have been worthwhile. The fact that he mixed them together caused the book to lose its trustworthiness. For these reasons, Goodspeed refused to recommend *The Gospel of Buddha* as a safe guide to the teachings of the Buddha.[26]

Joseph Estlin Carpenter of Manchester College, Oxford, placed the work in a class of well-meaning but wholly misleading books. Carus had read diligently "but without any perception of the historical development of the religion which he endeavors to exhibit." The bulk of his material came from different ages, different collections, and different countries, placing side by side books separated by centuries and still wider philosophic thought. In doing so, Carus had presented them as a rational, harmonious, and systematic arrangement. "The compiler has been struck with the ethical nobleness of many Buddhist sayings. His spirit is excellent, but his method is execrable."[27]

The American missionary, George W. Gilmore, claimed that Carus not only depended on second-hand knowledge but failed to demonstrate any understanding of what he read. Because of this limitation, the book lacked for clearness in its presentation. Better that individuals interested in understanding Buddhism look to Thomas Rhys Davids's *Hibbert Lectures* (1881) on the origin and growth of religion, or his *American Lectures* (1896) on the history of religions than concede ground to Carus's misrepresentation of the Buddhist religion. The only aspect of the book Gilmore praised was its neat binding.[28] Professor E. Washburn Hopkins of Yale took a similar view, arguing that the book's real purpose had been to claim Buddhism as a better religion than Christianity and that Buddhistic psychology was a scientific system that anticipated modern philosophy. Hopkins took issue with each of these assertions on the basis of Carus's unreliable interpretations. Although an "honest effort," it was a misleading attempt to make Buddhistic psychology scientific when it was founded on assumptions as unprovable as that of the soul-theory.[29]

As summarized by Judith Snodgrass a hundred years later, Carus "scandalized his academic contemporaries by dipping indiscriminately into texts ranging over 2,000 years and belonging to different cultural traditions." Presented to readers as a condensed and edited version of the Buddhist canon, *The Gospel of Buddha* was not much different from the Christian Gospels on which it had been modeled. As a patchwork of passages copied sometimes verbatim, and on other occasions, extrapolated to carry an idiosyncratic interpretation, it appealed to the general reader but failed to receive the academic validation Carus had desired.[30]

What Carus's scholarly critics failed to appreciate in his over-simplification of ideas and trivialization of doctrines was that the book, however inaccurate in its representation of traditional Buddhism, served the long-range strategic religious and political interests of Meiji Japan and other westernizing Buddhist countries by capturing in its historical literature the apologetics essential for a Buddhist revival that included the acceptance of science, evolution, and modernization. Japanese Buddhists drew from Carus's composite of Buddhist literature an understanding and justification of their religion. According to Snodgrass, Soyen "not only appropriated Carus's text for deployment in the contest over the religious future of Meiji Japan, he also took the opportunity in his preface to the Japanese publication to continue his participation in the formation of Western knowledge of Buddhism." Then again, the book illustrated in a backhanded way that Christianity was less relevant than Japanese Buddhism as a religion for the modern world. Even today, the book holds an honored place in Japan and other Buddhist countries because it characterizes the spirit of Buddhism as an endorsement of the positive relationship between religion and science that remained an open sore within Christianity.[31]

The Origin Controversy

Among Carus's many articles published subsequent to *The Gospel of Buddha* was "Buddhism and Christianity" which focused on the idea of a possible Buddhist origin of Christianity, noting that many of those most competent to speak on the subject were reticent to do so, or refused to countenance the idea. Carus admitted to clear differences between the two belief systems but found it remarkable that scholars would suppose no historical connection at all, reasoning instead that both Buddhists and Christians, facing the same problems of life, solved them "in a similar spirit although using different modes of expression." Countering this argument was the fact that Buddha lived in the fifth century before Christ and that the Buddhist canon had been settled by 250 B.C. While it remained possible in the later phases of Buddhism's development that some Christian ideas and modes of worship might have been imported into Northern India (the legend of St. Thomas's visit to India), it was just as likely that the story of St. Thomas was a Christianized Buddhist legend due to the commercial relations and exchange of thought between India and Judea before the appearance of Christ.

During Asoka's time, official legations had been dispatched from India to Western Asia for the purpose of spreading the Buddha's teachings. "There cannot be the slightest doubt," Carus argued, "that Buddhist missionaries were sent to Western Asia in the third century before the Christian era and must have made attempts to preach Buddhism. . . . It would be strange if Buddhist missionaries had gone to all neighboring countries except to Palestine, and that all kinds of Buddhist stories and wise saws were translated into other tongues, but not the essential doctrines of their sacred literature."[32] As explained by Thomas Rhys Davids, "We only know that at the end of the fourth, and still more in the third, century before Christ there was constant travelling to and fro between the Greek dominions in the East and the adjoining parts of India, which were then Buddhist, and that the birth stories were already popular among the Buddhists in Afghanistan, where the Greeks remained for a long time."[33]

Many of the attributions given to the influence of Buddhism on Christianity stemmed from Rudolf Seydel's *The Gospel of Jesus in Its Relation to Buddha-legend and Buddha-lore* (1882) and *Buddha-legends and the Life of Jesus According to the Gospels* (1897). This was followed by Otto Pfleiderer's *The Christ of Primitive Christian Faith in the Light of the History of Religions* (1903), G.A. van den Bergh van Eysinga's *Indian Influence on Gospel Narratives* (1909) and Albert J. Edmunds's *Buddhist and Christian Gospels* (1908–09). While the latter three dismissed the excessive dependence of Christianity on Buddhism attributed by Seydel, they admitted to rendering probable the influence of Buddhist materials on Christianity's oral traditions as distinct from the canonical Gospels.[34]

Despite Rhys Davids's rejection of any attempt to trace connections between Christianity and Buddhism in the New Testament, Edmunds countered, arguing that "the time is rapidly passing when scholars will feel compelled to adopt any hypothesis rather than admit the greatness of ancient India and the supremacy of Buddhism which, at the time of Christ, was the most powerful religion on the planet and the dominant spiritual force upon the continent of Asia." This meant that the formative years of Christianity were influenced not only by the Old Testament, the Greek mysteries, and the Philonian scriptural philosophy, but also by Hinayana Buddhism. After the first century, Christianity was sufficiently strong to influence Mahayana Buddhism which was itself a new religion and led to a "complex interchange between Christianity and Buddhism, both of them giving and taking."[35]

In identifying the similarities between Buddha and Christ, Carus compared their words and meanings, some of which

Paul Carus with Shaku Soyen, Toki Horin, and one other unidentified monk on their visit to La Salle, shortly after the World's Parliament of Religions.

were significant, others simply curious. In addition, he singled out the close alignment in the lives of Buddha and Christ, and in their belief systems. As for their respective lives:

- Both came from royal, but not priestly, lineage
- Both had their lives jeopardized as infants by massacres ordered of all children born the same time
- Both led lives of poverty and wandered without a home, family, or property
- Both preached to rich and poor alike a gospel of deliverance
- Both were hailed by prophets as saviors of the world
- Both excelled as teachers and powerful preachers
- Both tempted by the Evil One
- Both confessed a mission to establish a kingdom of righteousness
- Both refused to pander to superstitions
- Both walked on water
- Both helped entertain guests as a marriage feast
- Both tried asceticism for a time
- Both substituted a spirit of devotion and moral conduct for traditional rituals and prayers
- Both expressed their sentiments in paradoxes
- Both showed similarity in their parables
- Both showed graciousness toward women sinners
- Both were transfigured before death
- Both abandoned the traditional dualism and its pessimistic applications
- Both recognized that the purpose of life lay not in a material reality but in the realm of the mind
- Both taught that lust, vanity, and hatred resided not in the objects of the senses, but in the heart
- Both abandoned self-mortification
- Both preached that the way to the kingdom of heaven is from within

With regards to their respective religious beliefs and practices, Carus made the following observations of those aspects of Buddhism and Christianity which they shared in common. Both Buddhism and Christianity:

- Included the idea of a world Savior
- Advocated a sense of universality
- Sent out missionaries
- Used councils to settle disputes on matters of doctrine
- Developed a sacred literature containing their master's sayings
- Were revered by monks who wore similar garments; lived under similar restrictions; and used tonsures and rosaries
- Remembered the master in exaggerated legends and fables
- Had analogous sects and heresies
- Had processions, baptized adherents, used the confessional, and sprinkled holy water
- Shared doctrines that speak of three personalities of God and of Buddha
- Were similar despite Buddhist atheism and Christian theism
- Shared affinity in their art productions, such as the halo around the heads of certain individuals
- Were religions and not philosophies
- Shared a monistic world-conception[36]

Carus found it remarkable that so many Christian scholars chose to ignore the coincidences between these two great religions, insisting that Christianity alone possessed the truth. "This narrow view of Christianity is refuted by the mere existence of Buddhism," he wrote.

The essential moral truths of Christianity, like those of Buddhism, were deeply rooted in the cosmic order of the world. Unlike Buddhism, Christianity's doctrines contained contradictions that conflicted with science thereby estranging much of the educated class from the religion. By contrast, Buddhism "knows of no supernatural revelation, and proclaims doctrines that require no other argument than the 'come and see'." Accordingly, Buddhism had long been superior in distinguishing between symbol and meaning, dogma and religion, metaphysical theories and facts, and man-made ratiocinations and eternal truth. Carus hoped that the book would serve both religions in representing the spirit of their respective faiths. Outside their dogmatology and mythological accounts stood a nobler faith which aspired to be the religion of eternal truth. As the work of a publisher devoted to the prospect of reconciling the perceived polarities in the epistemological methods used by religion and science, *The Gospel of Buddha* provided an archetypical example of how Buddhism came closest of all the historical religions to approximate Carus's ideal for a future Religion of Science.[37]

Notwithstanding their similarity, Carus chose to regard the idea behind their similarities as only a hypothesis, focusing instead on those elements of Christianity that were probably borrowed from other sources: the idea of the Logos from Neo-Platonism; the God-idea from Jewish tradition; baptism from an Essene rite; and communion from a Dionysian cult. He pointed out that the Christian church of Jerusalem changed as it spread through the Roman Empire and changed again when it spread among the Teutonic races in the North.[38] Then, too, the Trinitarian theory, accepted by Christians as almost "a self-evident truth," was common to Egypt (Osiris, Isis, Hor), Babylonia (Ea, Anu, and Bel), India (Brahma, Vishnu, Shiva), and even China (Buddha, Dharma, Sangha). As for the immortality of the soul, Christians accepted it "not because Christ taught it, but because the belief was generally accepted in the Gentile world." The same held true of the idea that all evil, disease, and pain were due to sin; and that favor could be bought by prayer, penance, and sacrifice.[39]

After identifying Buddhism as the "religion of enlightenment," Carus's *The Dharma, Or, the Religion of Enlightenment: An Exposition of Buddhism* (1896) provided the reader with all manner of aphorisms, rules, poetry and meditations to explain and illustrate the Four Noble Truths, the Eightfold path to the emancipation from suffering, and the list of evils for persons to avoid. The book also offered explanations for the doctrine of the non-atman or the non-existence of the immutable self; the distinction between the soul-in-itself and the idea of the absolute self; the continuity in the evolution of life; the problem of transiency and permanence; the illusion of selfhood; and the state of Nirvana.[40] Perhaps most importantly, Carus laid out the basic tenets of Buddhism:

- Buddhism is the religion of deliverance from evil by enlightenment.
- Enlightenment means recognition of the truth affecting one's whole personality; it illumines the head, warms the heart, and guides the hand.
- The truth that imparts enlightenment can be gained only through energetic effort; it must be acquired by personal experience, through trials in the emotional life of the soul, and by a close investigation of the facts of existence.
- Enlightenment teaches that the law of cause and effect is irrefragable in the moral world not less than in the physical world, that every evil deed has its evil effects and every good deed its good effects.
- By enlightenment we learn that the main evil, indeed the sole absolute evil, is moral badness, and that its cause is selfhood.
- Selfhood consists in the notion that there is an independent and separate self, and that the welfare of self is the main purpose of existence.
- There is no self-in-itself, no atman in the sense of a separate ego-entity, the true self of a man is the combination of his whole personality, which is name and form, consisting mainly of the character of a man, his mind, his aspirations and modes of thought.
- Every being in its present existence is the exact product of all its deeds in former existences; and according to its deeds it will continue in future existences.
- Selfhood is an illusion, but the illusion is dispelled by enlightenment.
- Enlightenment recognizes the interconnection of all life, imparts an all-comprehensive kindness toward all living beings and a deep compassion with every creature that suffers.
- Enlightenment is more than knowledge, more than morality, more than goodness. It is wisdom, virtue, and an all-comprehensive love in one. It is truth manifesting itself in motor ideas as power. Enlightenment is perfect only when it dominates our thoughts, stimulates our sentiments, and regulates our conduct. Truth is like a lamp. It reveals the good law and points out the noble path of righteousness, leading to Nirvana.

- Nirvana is a state of mind in which the limitations of individuality disappear, and the eternity of truth is contemplated. It renders one's own individuality as objective as the individualities of others. Individual existence as a purpose ceases, and one's existence, one's self and soul, is identified with the truths of which it consists; and these truths are that something which would remain even though the whole world should break to pieces. In brief, Nirvana is the entire surrender of selfhood to truth. It is deliverance from evil and the highest bliss attainable.
- He who has attained to perfect enlightenment to be a teacher of mankind, is called a Buddha, which means the Enlightened One.
- Buddhists revere Gautama Siddhartha as the Buddha, for he for the first time most clearly pointed out the truth which proved an unspeakable blessing to many hundreds of millions of suffering beings.[41]

Buddhism's Christian Critics

Addressed principally to Christians, Carus intended his *Buddhism and Its Christian Critics* (1897) as a contribution to comparative religions but admitted at the outset that he wanted Christians more so than anyone else to "acquire an insight into the significance of Buddhist thought . . . at its best."[42] Recognizing that there was a greater rivalry between Christianity and Buddhism than between any other religion in that both had adopted science as a method of investigating the fields of psychology and philosophy, he felt it incumbent that they learn from each other as a way of aligning themselves with the practical demands of life. The world was in dire need of assimilating new truths, not dogmas. Only if Buddhism and Christianity chose this route would they most likely have the means and the capacity for growth. Christianity had conquered other religions by adopting the Logos philosophy of the Greeks and the ethics of struggle from the Teutons. It was when Christianity refused to assimilate new truths that its progress stopped.[43]

As a monist and Darwinist, Carus hoped that the rivalry between the two religions would result in a clarification of their respective belief systems and a cross-fertilization that might even result in their unity.

> Mankind is destined to have one religion, as it will have one moral ideal and one universal language, and the decision as to which religion will at last be universally accepted, cannot come about by accident. Science will spread, maybe, slowly but unfailingly, and the universal acceptance of a scientific world conception bodes the dawn of the Religion of Truth,—a religion based upon plain statements of fact unalloyed with myth or allegory. In the eventual conditions of religious life, there may be a difference of rituals and symbols, nay, even of names, according to taste, historical tradition, and individual preference, but in all essentials there will be one religion only, for there is only one truth, which remains one and the same among all nations, in all climes, and under all conditions. The law of the survival of the fittest holds good also in the domain of spiritual institutions. And let us remember that the greatest power lies not in numbers, not in wealth, not in political influence, but in truth. Whatever may be the fate of the various faiths of the world, we may be sure that the truth will prevail in the end.[44]

Above all, Carus wanted Christians to understand that Buddhism was a cosmopolitan religion whose "abstract simplicity fits all locks." Readily adaptable to almost any situation or condition, it offered comfort for the philosopher as well as the uneducated. It demanded no belief in miracles, nor the impossible, and assumed no authority except "the illumination of a right comprehension of the facts of existence." Buddha's conception of the world resonated with the theory of evolution as each soul structure, which constituted an individual's existence, functioned as the product of a chain of deeds gradually developed because of his or her karma.[45]

As Carus explained, Buddhism was popularly characterized as a religion without belief in either God or the human soul; without some form of future existence; quietistic in its ethics; and moving toward some form of final extinction into nothingness. These perceptions, he insisted, were clear distortions of the beliefs held by faithful Buddhists who not only believed in the equivalent of the Christian God (Sambhoga Kaya), but in a Trinity (Sambhoga Kaya, Kirmana Kaya, and Dharma Kaya) as well. The power and possibilities of Buddhism for its devotees remained undiminished despite attacks by Christian missionaries. In fact, he insisted that there was scarcely a scientist who would endorse the Christian belief of "a creation out of nothing" or adhere to the dualistic soul-conception "which assumes the existence of a psychic agent behind the facts of soul-life."[46]

The soul, identified by philosophers with the atman, the self, or the ego, was perceived as the metaphysical 'something' that encompassed man's sensations. It was the mysterious component in the individual which said, "I am this person." This "I" was the self, or atman. When Christians spoke of the soul, Buddhists spoke of the atman which represented the totality of one's existence including the bodily form, senses, activities, aspirations, and hopes. This position, explained Carus, harmonized with the views of Europe's most prominent psychologists. It was also in harmony with St. Paul, Thomas Aquinas, Meister Eckhart, Johannes Tauler, Ignatius Loyola, Friedrich August Tholuck, and others.[47]

Given the compilation of beliefs taught by Christian schools, Carus considered it natural for the Occidental mind to view Nirvana as a form of annihilation, or extinction of the soul, when it was actually the extinction of the illusion of self or the ego entity of all sinful traits. Nirvana was "the condition of enlightenment, or perfect understanding of truth." This explanation bore a close resemblance to the Christian idea of Heaven minus the Christian belief that each individual soul was preserved "as a separate and discrete entity." Except for the writings of the mystics like the thirteenth century German theologian Meister Eckhart, the concept of Christian resurrection included the retention of the ego, while the Buddhist explained it as the annihilation of the self's evil desires. Thus, the Buddhist viewed Nirvana as a state "not of death but eternal life, not annihilation but immortality, not destruction but indestructibility."[48]

In the years that followed, Carus found it necessary to clarify his position time and again regarding not only the connections he made between Christianity and Buddhism but his own personal beliefs. Was he a Christian or had he turned to Buddhism? Having grown up in a Christian society, the teachings of the Gospel had been part of his everyday life, colored his conversations, and stood as the foundation of his moral actions. Even if he refused to call himself a Christian in the sense of an active believer, his experiences from childhood onward derived from that worldview. In answer to a question from Dharmapala, Carus responded:

> If Christianity is nothing but the dogmatic Christianity of today, I would not hesitate to declare that I am not a Christian. But happily, for Christianity there is another Christianity which I may call either 'the moral spirit of Christ's teachings' or 'the possible Christianity of the future.' I am not prepared to give them up simply because I believe that Buddhism, that is, the Buddhism as I conceive it, is nearer to the truth than the creed Christianity of the churches, and I must add that Buddhism will have to learn of Christianity, as much as Christianity will have to learn Buddhism.[49]

Carus held a position that was simultaneously Kantian, Christian, and Buddhist, cherry-picking those elements of each that served his needs. "In a certain sense I am a Buddhist," he admitted, "for I adopt the main doctrines of Buddha as to the non-existence of the atman or ego-soul, and the irrationality of the belief in a creation of the world by a big ego-deity out of nothing." However, "should . . . the question arise whether I belong to one of the Buddhist sects, I would have to answer, 'No, I am not a Buddhist.'"[50] Still, Carus felt at home in the monistic teachings of Buddhism in that they rejected the doctrine of a separate soul. Its philosophy insisted on a unity of consciousness and the human form or self which alone was real. "Buddha propounded a consistent Monism in which he radically ignored all metaphysical assumptions and philosophical postulates, founding his religion on a consideration of the pure facts of experience."[51]

There is no indication that Carus embraced Buddhism as his personal faith. Having abandoned the orthodoxy of his father, he preferred to treat religion not as a personal belief system but as an object of scientific investigation with himself as its investigator. If pushed to decide, Buddhism stood at the top of his list of belief systems since he despaired of Christianity ever fulfilling its cosmic purpose as the religion of universal truth. Clinging to its mythology and failing to see any meaning deeper than its fictions, Christianity had not sufficiently matured to receive and accept the Truth.

* * *

Ultimately, Carus showed little concern for the prospect that Christianity and Buddhism, both religions of deliverance (i.e., man must die before he can be born into the real world), might have a common origin. To the degree that Buddhism became the religion of fulfillment in India, Christianity became the religion of fulfillment in the West, first in Palestine in western Asia, then northern Africa, before spreading over the Roman Empire and into northern Europe. Characterized by a spirit of universality, it became the normative basis for westernized ethics, truth, and ideals. Only secondarily were its dogmatic aspects of great importance. Besides, there was no idea that could not be traced to some pre-Christian period, whether Jewish, Greek, Egyptian, Babylonian, or unknown poets and prophets. Christianity represented "the fulfillment of the historical development of pre-Christian thought and, naturally enough, it appeared to the generations that lived in the third and fourth centuries as absolute truth, as the fullness of God's revelation, and the solution of the deepest problems of life."[52]

6
Land of Zen

> The basic idea of Zen is to come in touch with the inner workings of our being, and to do this in the most direct way possible without resorting to anything external or superadded.
>
> —D.T. SUZUKI, *An Introduction to Zen Buddhism* (1934)

Daisetsu Teitaro Suzuki, the most influential spokesperson of Zen thought in the twentieth century, was born in Kanazawa, Japan, in 1870, two years after the overthrow of the feudal shogunate that had ruled for over four hundred years. With the fall of feudal society, the Suzuki family lost their long-held standing as members of the samurai class. Impoverished and without a father, a physician who died when he was young, Suzuki came of age during the early years of the Meiji regime (1868–1912), a period of restless and uncertain transition into modernity. He began his student career at a junior college, learned English well enough to teach at a local high school, and continued his education first at Tokyo Semmon Gakko (Waseda University) and then at Tokyo Imperial University where he studied English literature. While there in the early 1890s, he commuted to Engakuji, the training monastery for Zen, a form of Buddhism in the Mahayana tradition resembling Christian mysticism that focuses on the purification of the faculties, the seeking of virtue, and union with the Buddha-mind; in other words, enlightenment and wisdom. There he studied under the mentorship of Imakita Kosen and later under the guidance of Abbot Shaku Soyen, an advocate for the New Buddhism (shin bukkyo). According to Palmer Rampell, the New Buddhists transformed their religion into a modern form of spirituality, winning over the younger generation of Western educated Japanese men "who were hailing either Christianity or materialist philosophy as the ideology of modernity."[1]

Emerson

During his studies at Tokyo Imperial University, Suzuki began a lifelong admiration of Emerson, Thoreau, and Transcendentalism which he considered the wellspring of American culture and the most Americanized representation of New Buddhism. Transcendentalism served as his touchstone for unlocking the full measure of man in the industrialized world. Both New Buddhism and Transcendentalism were the embodiment of man's spiritual strength and freedom in a time of change. Besides, the Transcendentalists had filtered elements of Oriental thought into the American mind, marking the beginnings of what would eventually expand into a treasure trove of Asian wisdom and philosophy. Symbolic of that relationship, Suzuki, who was never ordained a monk, would dedicate the first and second series of his *Essays in Zen Buddhism* (1927; 1933) to Emerson.[2]

As explained by Palmer Rampell, Suzuki's interest in Emerson, which extended over fifty years of his writing, began with his article "Zen Theory of Emerson" published in 1896 which found several key Zen concepts (spiritual truth as ineffable and intuitive, purification through meditation, and the annihilation or forgetfulness of self) embedded in Emerson's "Divinity School Address" (1838), "The Over-Soul" (1841), "Self-Reliance" (1841), and "Culture" (1860). Emerson possessed a mix of experiences and observations drawn from Socrates to Buddhism that provided for Japan what Unitarianism and Transcendentalism contributed to American thought and culture. In each there existed a respect for science, the manifestation of God in nature, an intuitive faith in humankind, a disavowal of traditional religions, and a pragmatic approach to daily life.[3] Ironically, at the same time Emerson was formulating the nation's most distinctive ideal of self-reliance and advocating non-Western literature to admiring readers, Suzuki, the unofficial ambassador of Zen Buddhism to the West, was introducing Emerson to the East.[4]

Years later, in his *Zen and Japanese Culture* (1959), Suzuki recalled how important Emerson had been in his comparison of Western and Eastern belief systems. In describing his early readings of Emerson, Suzuki called it "digging down into the recesses of my own thought."[5] Although Suzuki carried a stronger and more visual image of Zen in its relevancy to the modern world, he remained a lifelong admirer of Emerson, Thoreau, and Transcendentalism as the most Americanized representations of New Buddhism. All served as touchstones to unlocking the full measure of man in the industrialized world. Together, they represented the embodiment of man's spiritual strength and freedom in a time of change.[6]

La Salle

Suzuki's personal relationship with Carus began with the latter's interest in all things Oriental following the closing of the Parliament of Religions. In addition to serving as Soyen's translator and producing a Japanese translation (*Budda no fukuin*) of *The Gospel of Buddha*, he assisted Carus in his search for texts, especially those written in Chinese. When Carus had difficulty finding someone to translate Lao Tzu's *Tao Te Ching* into English, Soyen urged him to take Suzuki under his wing.[7] "He is an earnest student of philosophy and religion, and his ambition is to work for truth and humanity, not being anxious about worldly interests. He tells me that he has been so greatly inspired by your sound faith, which is perceptible in your various books, that he earnestly desires to go abroad and to study under your personal guidance. If you will be kind enough . . . to consent to take him under your patronage, he will willingly obey to do everything you may order him, as far as he can. . . . Though poor, he will be able to afford the expense of journey.[8] In August 1896, arrangements were been made to bring Suzuki to La Salle and employ him with the Open Court.

When Suzuki arrived in San Francisco in February 1897 on the steamship *China*, his plans for a quick journey east to La Salle was prevented due to the discovery of a case of smallpox on board the ship, causing the port authorities in San Francisco to quarantine its passengers on Angel Island in San Francisco Bay. During the fumigation process, many of Suzuki's belongings were destroyed. Carus tried to dispel his being disheartened by the experience, explaining that "in this way the people whom you are to meet need not be afraid of coming in contact with you." When released from quarantine, Carus sent him money to remain another week to make sure he did not carry any germs. While waiting for the quarantine to end, he encouraged Suzuki to use the time studying in the library, observing life in an American city, and attending different Christian churches to better understand their services.[9] Suzuki left San Francisco on March 9th, and on his arrival in Chicago, was put up in a hotel for several more days because one of the Carus children (Gustav) had contracted chicken pox. By the time he arrived in La Salle, Suzuki was physically exhausted from the experience.[10]

Writing to Soyen on March 29th, 1897, Carus informed him that Suzuki had arrived at last, explaining the unfortunate quarantine he had endured on account of the case of smallpox. "Mr. Suzuki is a modest and pleasant young man, and everybody who knows him is pleased with him. I expect that he will rapidly learn English and will, when he returns to Japan, be a valuable medium of knowledge for the Japanese. He is at present assisting me in my translation of the Tao-the-king, and I am glad to notice that he is well informed in the Chinese language. His assistance is very valuable to me."[11]

No one could have predicted that Suzuki would remain for eleven years at the Hegeler-Carus mansion in La Salle, preparing articles for publication, translating Chinese and

Japanese religious and philosophical texts into English, translating English works into Japanese, helping the family with household chores, and learning the basics of publishing. During those years, he worked on the publication of *Asvaghosha's Discourse on the Awakening of Faith in the Mahayana* (1900), *T'ai-Shang Kan-Yin P'ien: Treatise of the Exalted One on Response and Retribution* (1906), *Yin Chin Way: The Tract of the Quiet Way* (1906), *Amida-butsu* (1906), and his own *Outlines of Mahayana Buddhism* (1907), arguably Suzuki's most comprehensive examination of modern Buddhism. The book refuted many of the misguided opinions concerning the teachings of Mahayana Buddhism, including atman and its meaning within the context of rebirth or karma. Suzuki intended for the book to encourage the interest of scholars, especially those focusing on comparative religious studies, to expound on the differences between Buddhism's two great systems: Mahayanism and Hinayanism, otherwise known respectively as Northern and Southern Buddhism.[12]

Correspondence between Suzuki and M.A. Sacksteder, manager of the Open Court office in Chicago suggests that Suzuki was heavily involved in the day-to-day preparation of print copy, addressing engraving issues, and placing the correct accent marks on Chinese and Japanese script. It's also clear that Sacksteder found it difficult to communicate with Suzuki as each seemed to prefer a different system for organizing files, plates, and other apparatus.[13] There were also times when Carus showed his exasperation with Suzuki, such as the time he invited a young Japanese friend to La Salle without permission on the assumption that Carus would find him employment. "I do not know what to do with him," wrote Carus. "How can I look around to procure some kind of subsistence for a stranger of whose abilities I know nothing."[14]

Swedenborg

Suzuki was a member of the Hegeler-Carus household from 1897 to 1909 during which time he shared with the family his views on religion and philosophy; his interests in Emerson and Thoreau; and his growing fascination with William James, Charles Peirce, and the pragmatists. Yet, despite his work as an understudy for Carus's philosophy, Suzuki was drawn to the mystic Swedenborg, an inclination which one suspects represented an effort to step away from his nation's militant nationalism and seek more meditative form of Buddhism in its relationship to Japanese culture.[15]

Opinions differ on how Suzuki first learned of Swedenborg. One possibility is that he discovered the writings of the scientist-mystic in the aftermath of the Parliament of Religions which, although he did not attend, he served as a translator for Soyen's speeches which John Henry Barrows read before the delegates. Given this indirect involvement, it is also possible that he gained knowledge of Swedenborg from the fact that Charles Bonney, the chairman of the auxiliary committee to formulate a plan for a parliament of religions, was a Swedenborgian; that six members of the Church of the New Jerusalem presented papers before its plenary sessions; and that New Church delegates offered a well-attended symposium on the subject of Swedenborgianism in the Hall of Washington. Alternatively, he might have been introduced to Swedenborg through the lens of Emerson's *Representative Men* (1850), one of whom was the Swedish seer. Though Swedenborg was dismissed by many of his peers when he turned from his scientific investigations to mysticism, his ideas permeated the porous walls of the nation's metaphysical and occult traditions: Transcendentalism, Spiritualism, Perfectionism, Homeopathy, Theosophy, and New Thought. His influence was enough for Emerson to identify the first half of the nineteenth century the "age of Swedenborg."[16]

Others have speculated that Suzuki's interest in Swedenborg originated with his wife, Beatrice Erskine Lane, a graduate of Radcliffe whom he married in 1911. She had shown interest in a variety of religious traditions, including Christian Science, Theosophy, and the Baha'i faith. Still others have suggested the source was the English language *Buddhist Ray*

(1888–1894), edited by the Swedenborgian minister Herman Carl Vetterling. Vetterling was also known under the pseudonym of Philangi Dasa, author of *Swedenborg the Buddhist; Or, The Higher Swedenborgianism: Its Secret and Thibetan Origins* (1887) which was translated into Japanese in 1893.[17] Beneath the masthead of *Buddhist Ray* (1888–1894) was his commitment: "Devoted to Buddhism in General, and to the Buddhism in Swedenborg in Particular."[18] According to Vetterling, Swedenborg had actually been a Buddhist and had learned of its teachings intuitively from the Buddhist saints (adepts) in their secret location in the Himalayan mountains.[19]

According to Thomas Tweed, none of those explanations revealed the true source of Suzuki's interest in Swedenborg; instead, he pointed to Albert J. Edmunds's visit in 1903 to La Salle where he spent eight days with Carus and his staff. In his *Journal,* Edmunds remarked: "Suzuki felt the parting from me very much. Meantime, I have got him interested in Swedenborg . . . a mission well worth coming hither."[20] Suzuki would later confirm his debt to Edmunds whom he described as "Quaker, a Swedenborgian, and a Pali scholar, he . . . was the one who told me about Swedenborg." [21] In other words, it was Edmunds who was responsible for first suggesting that Suzuki look to Swedenborg as the best representative example of Buddhist thought in Western culture.

Edmunds, a British-American, had worked as a librarian at Haverford College (1887–89), the Philadelphia Library (1889–90), and the Historical Society of Pennsylvania (1891–1936). An aficionado of Buddhism, he spent much of his life comparing Buddhism and Christianity. His publications include *Buddhist and Christian Gospels* (1900), *Hymns of the Faith* (1902), *Buddhist and Christian Gospels Now Compared from the Originals* (1904), *Buddhist Texts in John* (1906), *A Dialogue between Two Saviors* (1908), and *Leaves from the Gospel of Mark* (1936), along with hundreds of poems, some of which are found in his *Fairmont Park and Other Poems* (1906). One of the early participants in the transnational exchanges between Japan and the United States, Edmunds wrote articles for the *Light of Dharma*

(1901–1907), a bi-monthly journal produced by the Pure Land Buddhist Mission temple in San Francisco.

Admired by Carus for his work with both Christianity and Buddhism, Edmunds enjoyed a lifetime of correspondence with scholars internationally who regarded his comparative studies, including work in Pali, Sanskrit, and Chinese to be among the best. Nurtured in a Quaker household, he had a natural inclination for Swedenborgianism, Theosophy, Spiritualism, séances, and other occult traditions. A member of the Oriental Society of Philadelphia, an honorary member of the International Buddhist Society of Rangoon, and translator of Buddhist writings from the Pali, he spent much of his time identifying uncanonical and canonical parallels among religions.

Leaving Oz

In 1909, Suzuki left La Salle, but before returning to Japan where he was offered a chair of English Literature at Peers' School in Tokyo, he spent time in London as a guest of the Swedenborg Society where he translated Swedenborg's *Heaven and Hell* (1910) into Japanese. Two years later he returned to England at the invitation of the Swedenborg Society to translate *The New Jerusalem and Its Heavenly Doctrine* (1914), *Divine Love and Wisdom* (1914) and *Divine Providence* (1915), followed by *Swedenborugu* (1915), a short examination of Swedenborg's life and thought, identifying the similarities between Buddhism and Swedenborgianism.

Perennially short of funds, Suzuki relied on Mary Carus to help him with his expenses. "Without your help, what could I have done? I appreciate your goodness most highly, let me assure you of this."[22] In another letter to Mary Carus he wrote: "In case everything fails I have nowhere to go. . . . I shall be left then in a most helpless condition, as all my resources have thus far entirely failed."[23] Suzuki remained on salary with the Open Court Publishing Company for several years after leaving La Salle. Prior to his visit to London as well as his travel to Germany and France, he was in the habit of seeking permission from Carus: "With your

Shaku Soyen (1860–1919), who brought Zen to Americans.

approval, may I have some more money before I undertake my continental trip?"[24] During his stay in London, Suzuki wrote to Hegeler, keeping him informed of his research as well as his ongoing expenses, much of the time explaining his dilemma of either living close by the British Museum and paying a higher price for lodging, or living further away and wasting time with travel. Suzuki photographed numerous manuscripts which he billed to Hegeler, one of which totaled $801.00.[25]

It concerned Carus that Suzuki continued to rely on the Open Court Company to cover his expenses. In 1910, he wrote Suzuki reminding him that he had already received over $2,400 from Hegeler but because his estate was currently tied up following his death, no further funds would be available. "When you left La Salle, you intended to enter the Japanese foreign service and I shall be glad if you would find it a satisfactory position. I deemed it in your own interest if you would continue to consider yourself in the employ of the Open Court Publishing Company which could render it easy for you to return to the U.S. The time has come for you to decide and I wish you would let me know soon. I have written you several times but never received a reply. Have these letters been lost? So far as I know, they were addressed to the same place as Mr. Hegeler's letters. . . . Hoping that I hear from you at your earliest convenience."[26]

In a letter to Suzuki dated March 27th, 1911, Carus commented on his own desire to visit the Orient before he got too old. In the event of a visit, he offered to discuss with Suzuki his possible return to the United States. "Perhaps you might procure a position in Chinese or Japanese either in Chicago or some other University which would be preferable to resuming your connection with the Open Court. . . . I am sorry to say that Professor [Friedrich] Hirth [at Columbia University] is opposed to Japanese teachers of Chinese, because he suspects them of falsifying the Chinese ideas. At any rate he mentioned that as an objection to my using your assistance in translations from the Chinese."[27] Nevertheless, as late as 1912–13, Carus and Suzuki were still hard at work translating and publishing books on Confucius, collecting poems for both *The Open Court* and *The Monist,* and preparing introductions and prefaces for second editions. Also, during this time, Suzuki edited *The Eastern Buddhist* which became an important bridge, along with *The Open Court* and *The Monist,* for introducing Buddhism to the West.[28]

After 1915, when Suzuki was forty-five years old, his connections with the Open Court Publishing Company ended. The same applied to his references to Swedenborg which diminished except for his article "Swedenborg's View of Heaven and 'Other Power'" published in 1924. As explained by David Loy, there is no reason to believe that he had changed his mind regarding the Swedish mystic for there remained in his writings any number of "profound similarities between what Swedenborg writes and what Buddhism teaches." The similarities included their rejection of the dualistic existence of the soul as defined by Cartesian self-consciousness. For both, the enlightened individual gives up the love and sense of self to be united with the whole, with doing good for the sake of others, of living a life of love. Then again, the Swedenborgian belief that God's influx or love was present in all being, is quite literally the same as the Mahayana expression of non-being. In both, there was no separation of God and man. "If God is the life or being in everything," explained Loy, "then it is just as true to say that nothing has any being of its own."[29]

On his return to Japan Suzuki took a position teaching English at the Peers School in Tokyo where he remained for twelve years. In 1921, he accepted a chair in Buddhist studies at Otani University in Kyoto where he remained until his retirement. While there, he founded the Eastern Buddhist Society focusing on Mahayana Buddhism and wrote some of his most important works on Zen which included *Essays in Zen Buddhism* (three volumes, 1927, 1933, 1934); *Studies in the Lankavatara Sutra* (1930); *In Index to the Lankayatara Sutra* (1933); *The Training of the Zen Buddhist Monk* (1934); *An Introduction to Zen Buddhism* (1934); *The Gandavyuha Sutra* (1934-36); *Manual of Zen*

Buddhism (1935); *Buddhist Philosophy and Its Effects on the Life and Thought of the Japanese People* (1936); *Japanese Buddhism* (1938); and *Zen Buddhism and Its Influence on Japanese Culture* (1938). He attended the World Congress of Faiths at the University of London in 1936 and, at age sixty-three, was conferred the Doctor of Letters. After his wife died in 1939, and as war encroached, Suzuki isolated himself from the outside world. During the war, he lived in Kamakura where he continued to study Zen, not just as an intellectual system, but as a practical way of living and as a source of reconciliation with the West in the postwar years.

By the end of the war, most if not all of Suzuki's books were out of print. In 1946, London's Buddhist Society worked with Suzuki on reprinting his former books and translating his newest manuscripts into English. These included *The Essence of Buddhism* (1947), *The Zen Doctrine of No-Mind* (1949), *A Miscellany on the Shin Teaching of Buddhism* (1949) and *Living by Zen* (1949). These, plus his *Essays in Zen Buddhism,* became the foundational texts on the principles of Zen and its reconstruction as a form of secular spirituality.

Columbia University

In 1950, at the age of eighty, following his help in launching the journal *Cultural East* and being elected a member of the Japan Academy of Sciences, Suzuki traveled to Hawaii where he took part in a conference "Philosophy, East and West." Soon afterwards, he was invited by the Rockefeller Foundation to give lectures at various American universities. For the most part, however, he remained at Columbia University in New York until 1958 where he gathered around him a broad group of students including Jack Kerouac, J.D. Salinger, John Cage, Martin Heidegger, Aldous Huxley, Carl Jung, Alan Watts, and Allen Ginsberg, all of whom endowed Zen with a character of their own.[30] It was then, too, that Suzuki published *Studies in Zen* (1955), *Mysticism: Christian and Buddhist* (1957), *Zen and Japanese Buddhism* (1958), *Zen and Japanese Culture* (1959), and with Erich

Fromm and Richard De Martino *Zen Buddhism and Psychoanalysis* (1960).[31]

In 1957, Suzuki returned to La Salle as the guest of honor and featured speaker at the Paul Carus Memorial Symposium held September 9th–12th, 1957. This event was planned by Edward H. Carus in his father's memory. The participants included professors of the history of religions and of comparative religions, plus friends and Carus family members. In his remembrances, Suzuki recalled that Carus was not so much interested in Sanskrit texts of Mahayana Buddhism or the Pali texts of the Theravada Buddhists but rather "he endeavored to grasp the spirit of Buddhism . . . . He was a pioneer in introducing Oriental ways of thought and feeling to the English-reading public."[32] One interesting comment Suzuki made at the symposium concerned the fact that he was now of a different opinion than both Carus and Hegeler regarding their belief that religion should be free from mythological elements. "I now think that a religion based solely on science is not enough," he explained. "There are certain 'mythological' elements in every one of us, which cannot be altogether lost in favor of science."[33]

Carus had arrived at the same opinion. His philosophy of science was quite conservative in that he found the old orthodoxies justified in many important ways while liberalism, in its effort to point out religion's contradictions, "often loses thereby the truth contained in religion." For that reason, he hoped that Christianity would drop its "belief in the letter and allow symbolical interpretation of their doctrines." As with his appreciation of Oriental art, he wished to keep the spirit found in the dogmas while foregoing their literal belief. "Art, not unlike religion, is a powerful factor in man's spiritual life," he explained. "There is no painting, no statue, no poem, no song, no symphony which has not back of it a sentiment of the All."[34]

Mystic Zen

Original or authentic Buddhism exists in the Pali scriptures, while Mahayana Buddhism is second generation with principles not about ancestral spirits but its applicability to modernity. Zen Buddhism is an altogether different story. It came to the West by way of Suzuki and is as distant from historical Buddhism as the theological Christ is from the historical Jesus. It offers an escape from the West's overemphasis on individualism and materialism as well as its adherence to a dualistic view of reality. Zen provides an alternative to traditional Buddhism as well as the liberal movement of Mahayana.[35]

The attraction of Zen lies in the fact that it elicits mystic immediacy, accepts the indivisibility of experience, sees experience as the sole reality, advocates the replacement of self-consciousness with a larger self, lives in the moment, and professes that life is wonderful even in the ordinary. Drawn to the Romantics, Transcendentalists, and the mystics Emanuel Swedenborg and Meister Eckhart, Zen is inexorably connected with Western style meditation. Suzuki considered the Dominican monk Meister Eckhart (1260–1328) as Zen's Christian counterpart since the goal for both was union with God or nothingness, in other words, Buddhahood. It was the mysticism of detachment when the individual retains nothing but is completely receptive to the Divine. Alan Watts compared it to the state of *satori*, that moment of heightened consciousness that defies both logic and reason; it represented a view of life that did not conform to any of the usual categories of Western thought.[36]

Initially, the Trappist contemplative Thomas Merton distinguished between Christianity and Zen, pointing to the former which derived from revelation, and the latter which he admitted to not fully understanding, which "seeks to penetrate the natural ontological ground of being."[37] All this changed, however, when Merton met Suzuki, after which he acknowledged the similarity between the "no mind" or "emptiness" of Zen and the "dark night" of St. John of the Cross.[38] For Merton, there was an exact correspondence between the two.[39]

When the Rev. John Wright Buckham of the Pacific Theological Seminary in Berkeley, California, wrote in *The*

Monist that science was nothing more than "disillusioned materialism" while mysticism represented a "return to truth," furnishing a process for attaining unity and certainty to the complexities of modern life with its myriad of conflicting interests, Carus dissented.[40] "If we accept the 'that' of existence," he responded, "we shall find that the world in all its concrete details is explicable—if not always in fact, on account of our lack of sufficient information, yet certainly in theory."[41]

Granted that science was not all of life since it was devoid of sentiment which was the source from which sprang mystic contemplations, nevertheless, sentiment disregarded logic, scorned criticism and rational analysis, ignored contradictions, revealed itself in paradoxes, and intoxicated individuals with flights of fancy. Mysticism represented "a short cut of sentiment to reach truth which under the circumstances may somehow be unattainable by the intellect." Carus admitted that truth was sometimes discovered in the writings of Swedenborg as well as in the German mystics Meister Eckhart of Strasbourg, Nikolaus of Basel, Henry Suso of Swabia, Johannes of Ruysbroek, Tauler of Strasbourg, Jacob Böhme, and Angelus Silesius. "They were guided not by a clear comprehension of the truth but by an instinct which made them feel what they could not yet understand." But there was always the danger that mysticism would become the source of superstitious practices, witch prosecutions, and heresy trials. "But even if mysticism remains antagonistic to scientific aspirations," concluded Carus, "we still recognize in it a force which if it happens to tend in the right direction, may very well serve as a surrogate for truth itself and will be of great service to . . . those who are incapable of thinking the truth with scientific exactness and must be taught in parables."[42] Nevertheless, he saw no need for mysticism in philosophy since the world was ultimately explicable. There was nothing that could not be understood and explained; nor were there problems "not yet ripe for discussion;" nor was the universe "too rich to be exhausted."[43]

* * *

For individuals like Carus, the spiritual crisis left in the wake of Darwin's theory of natural selection and the impact of the higher criticism made it difficult to build a moral code or a set of operating principles from the broken pieces of Christianity's discarded dogmas. No longer able to square the unfolding scientific discoveries with Christianity's rigid dogmatists, he found himself in the company of many of the scientific, literary and intellectual thinkers of the day who turned their personal anguish into an ethical necessity of finding a substitute set of standards in the secular world of science. In his solution, Carus chose not to reject religion but to reaffirm the Religion of Science which based humanity's hopes on spiritual enlightenment, a factor that eventually enamored him to the teachings of Buddhism. True religion and true science were intrinsically the same. Unlike Christianity whose myriad of denominations and sects stood divided on the power and importance of reason versus revelation, Carus recognized that New Buddhism insisted on the outcomes of scientific critique being synonymous with God's revelation. There was but one truth which science discovered and revealed in a world that was real, objective, and evolving.

7
The Three Amigos

Blessed is he who has found enlightenment. He conquers, although
he may be wounded; he is glorious and happy, although he may suffer;
he is strong, although he may break down under the burden of his work;
he is immortal, although he may die. The essence of his being is purity
and goodness.

—PAUL CARUS, *The Gospel of Buddha* (1894)

Chief among the outcomes of the World's Parliament of Religions was the expectation that it would create a movement dedicated to removing the prejudices that separated the religions of mankind. Even though notes of discord could be heard breaking against the general harmony of the seventeen-day event, the Parliament was thought by many to mark a new era of brotherhood and peace. Correspondence among its member delegates made frequent reference to reducing religious strife and persecution; securing the right to worship according to the dictates of conscience; and planning for future parliaments. Much of the enthusiasm for this optimism was due to recognition of the role evolution played in the progressive march of humanity. Praised for having taken religious thought to a level "never manifested before," Carus remarked that the old names of Catholic, Protestant, Anglican, Dissenter, Baptist, Methodist, Independent, Calvinist, and Armenian were losing their spell.[1] "How sane and healthy all this is!" he proclaimed. "We are now in sight of the goal, for we see that whatever becomes of the names, union will come by conserving and promoting all that is true and good in each. . . . Our present aim must be to get mutual tolerance which subsists already between the sections of Christendom." While rituals and symbols varied widely around the world, "the essence of religion can only be one and must remain one and the same among all nations, in all climes, and under all conditions."[2]

Tectonics

Indicative of the impact the Parliament had made on its participants, Carus and Hegeler returned to LaSalle with a renewed commitment to use the Open Court Publishing Company to further its work. They even considered the acquisition of property for a school ("Church of Science"), institute ("Hegeler Institute"), or college to teach the Science of Religion and the Religion of Science.[3] Given this euphoric view, neither Carus, Charles Carroll Bonney, nor John Henry Barrows could give up their belief that the seventeen days of speeches and discussions had made a lasting influence on religious sentiment worldwide and that a new age of cooperation had begun. Reflective of this optimism, the Parliament no sooner closed than a series of smaller congresses were arranged. These included a Mid-Winter Fair at San Francisco's Golden Gate Park in 1893-94; a Congress of Liberal Religious Societies which gathered at the Sinai Temple in Chicago in May 1894; and a series of summer programs begun by Sarah Farmer at Greenacre in Eliot, Maine, involving many of the Parliament's delegates as speakers.[4]

Even more significant was the New Year's Reunion on January 1, 1895, when over four thousand gathered at the Chicago

Auditorium Theatre on Michigan Avenue to celebrate the achievements of the World's Congress Auxiliary. During the celebration, Charles Bonney called for the creation of a World's Congress Extension and appointed Episcopal Bishop Samuel Fallows, president of the newly founded People's Institute of Chicago, as chair with the mandate to continue the work of the Auxiliary Congress. As explained by Carus, the Extension's purpose was "to promote harmonious personal relations and a mutual understanding between adherents of the various faiths, to awaken a living interest in religious problems, and above all to facilitate the attainment and actualization of religious truth." A local branch, called the Religious Parliament Extension of Chicago was also created with Dr. Frank M. Bristol of the Methodist Church of Evanston as chairman, Carus as secretary, and with additional support from an associate committee of women. With messages of encouragement from numerous well-wishers, Bonney expressed confidence that the work of the two organizations would be "an exemplification of Monism in religion."[5] As one of his first actions, Bonney mailed Barrow's two-volume history of *The World's Parliament of Religions* to Pope Leo XIII hoping to receive the Church's approval of any future parliaments.

Shortly after the January reunion celebration of the Auxiliary, a group of Protestant, Catholic, and Jewish clergy met in Bay City, Michigan, to discuss the ethical and moral ends in their respective beliefs. During their meeting, the members announced plans for a Pan-American Congress of Religion and Education to meet in Toronto in July, and that the first Dharma Mahotsava would convene at Ajmere in the Punjab in September 1895 to discuss God, soul, salvation, revelation, and mediatorship.[6] Interest was also expressed for creating a World's Religions Association and a possible federation of all denominations in North America whose goals would be to investigate and compare religious creeds in a spirit of brotherly love; accept that truth can be discovered and science is divine; and that "all formulations of truth as embodied in credos and confessions [should be] subject to revision and reformulation according to the needs of the time." Finally, there was a proposal to establish "Migratory Parliaments" that would meet regularly at different locations around the globe, including Jerusalem, the Holy City of three world religions, and in Japan where Shintoism, Confucianism, Buddhism, and Christianity lived side by side.[7]

The first meeting of the Religious Parliament Extension of Chicago was chaired by Merwin-Marie Snell, author of the article "Modern Theosophy in its Relation to Hinduism and Buddhism" in *The Biblical World,* and involved a serious discussion around the idea of establishing a religious union. Carus expressed his opinion that such an enterprise could only succeed if it protected the distinctive features of each religion. If the intent of the Extension was "to bring out the truth by comparison and investigation, it would perform a very useful and important work."[8] Establishing a union of all the different faiths was a concept not only possible, but necessary. "For all things are growing, all minds are broadening, and we learn that evolution not only affords us an explanation of the mysteries of the past but will also help us in solving the problems of the future." But such a union should not mean ceasing to be a Presbyterian or some other denominational member. Being a member of a "pan-religious union" should not prevent anyone from retaining their sectarian creed, nor should it prohibit anyone from sending out missionaries. Instead, it meant toleration, the love of truth, an enquiring mind willing to dig deeper into the mysteries of life and being charitable to other creeds.[9]

The New Normal

When Bishop Fallows declined to take the chairmanship of the World's Congress Extension, its activities were assumed by Bonney serving as president, Barrows assuming the role of vice president, and Carus offering to carry out the work of secretary. In his role as vice president, Barrows began a world lecture tour to discuss the accomplishments of the 1893 Parliament and encourage the continuation of the Parliament idea among the world's religious leaders. The tour, made possible by an endowment created by Mrs. Caroline E. Haskell to the University of Chicago, also supported a lectureship on comparative religions with Barrows as its first lecturer.[10]

In the years that followed, Bonney, Barrows, and Carus corresponded regularly to discuss how to further the goals of the Parliament, how to expand its activities nationally and internationally, and how to determine what locations were best suited for future meetings. Beneath these rather generalized objectives lay more ominous issues: how to discuss unity without threatening the individual denominations within Christianity; how to encourage the Pope and European Catholicism to continue their participation; how to minimize the growing hostility of Asia's religions to Christian missionary efforts; how to mediate between Asia's traditional religions and their westernized counterparts. Each of these issues basked in the glow of the Chicago success and the wish to continue the Parliament concept into the new century and beyond. Unspoken in the rhetorical flourish was the unpleasant reality that the original idea of the Parliament as well as its Extension was Protestant-motivated. Except for Carus, the private and not so private commun- ications among the three amigos perceived the West as home to the most evolved humans bringing truth and spiritual comfort to the remnants of the world's once great powers.[11]

The omens for truly ecumenical gatherings were not good. On receiving the draft program for the Toronto meeting, Bonney and Carus discovered that the event excluded participation of all non-western religions. To complicate matters, Vivekananda planned to participate even though the city's clergy refused his request. Their decision had been due to Vivekananda's intemperate remarks at the Parliament which had soured many western delegates to his views. Bonney suggested that he and Carus ought not to have anything to do with the monk's visit to Toronto as his presence would more than likely "stir up prejudice" and do harm to any future work of the Extension. "It is very unfortunate that some of our India friends have not adhered to the law of the Parliament that everyone should confine himself to a presentation of the good things of his own faith, and scrupulously abstain from any attacks on the religion of others," observed Bonney.[12] Carus responded with a similar opinion: "If we could rely on his tact there would be no objection to his being present in the audience . . . but of course we cannot do anything in the matter, and cannot even give him advice except to be prudent and to act wisely."[13]

Hoping, to avoid a diplomatic embarrassment, Carus eventually wrote Vivekananda apprising him of the feelings held towards him by those planning to attend the gathering in Toronto. "I hasten to reply that the clergymen of Toronto still insist on their protest. They have not only not made an allowance to you for your journey to Toronto, but in addition have refused to hear you. Should you intend to go to Toronto it would be an *entirely private affair* . . . ."[14] The Toronto event opened July 18th–25th, 1895, at the Horticultural Gardens Pavilion with an attendance of nearly a thousand, including Bonney. Given Carus's candid assessment, Vivekananda decided not to attend and instead joined Carus at a four-day Oak Island Christian Unity Conference where they both delivered speeches intended to bring the various faiths into closer alignment.

As time passed, even Carus expressed doubts about any future success of the Extension's activities. When, in 1896, Dr. Jenkin Lloyd Jones proposed to merge his publication *The New Unity* with *The Open Court,* thus making it the organ of the Liberal Congress of Religion, Carus demurred. When it was also suggested that *The Open Court* become the official organ of the Religious Parliament Extension, Carus feared it could change the character of the journal, causing a potential reduction in subscribers and a narrower cadre of contributors. He informed Bonney that he opposed the idea though the decision would ultimately lay in Hegeler's hands. Carus believed the changes possible *only* if agreement could be finalized on a Second Parliament of Religions.[15]

And there is where matters remained until Carus revised the masthead of *The Open Court* in 1897 from "A Weekly

Journal Devoted to the Religion of Science" to "A Monthly Magazine Devoted to the Science of Religion, the Religion of Science, and the Extension of the Religious Parliament Idea." The compromise language came from Bonney.[16] Hoping to clarify the future purpose and activities of the Extension, Carus sent out letters to former delegates in July 1897 that included a deluxe copy of the Secretary's Report titled *World's Parliament of Religions and the Religious Parliament Extension* and requested a response. "We wish especially to know whether in the circles of your activity the brotherly spirit among the different denominations has increased; whether people of different views now meet one another in greater kindness and show more respect for the convictions of others; and at the same time, whether the zeal for truth does or does not suffer from the broadening tendencies of the Parliament; and finally, how far religion can be said to be the gainer by the new spirit of brotherly exchange of thought that is now more and more pervading the world."[17]

In their replies, most of the former delegates sent highly supportive letters encouraging the extension idea and suggesting the creation of local parliaments in every country.[18] The replies led Carus to believe the parliament concept had many more friends than enemies. Dharmapala rejoiced at the idea. "On behalf of the Asiatic followers of the great teacher Gautama Buddha, I shall be glad to render all services consistent with the principles . . . embodied in . . . the completion of the great Congress held in Pataliputra twenty-one centuries ago, and disseminated all over the then known world by the order of the great Emperor Asoka."[19] Supportive letters also came from P. C. Mozoomdar in Calcutta; Jivarji Janstedj in Bombay; clergyman Josiah Strong, leader of the Social Gospel movement who predicted Buddhism would ultimately supplant Christianity as part of God's plan; Charles Eliot, president of Harvard; Congregational pastor Washington Gladden; British historian James Bryce; and theologian Lyman Abbott.[20]

On balance, however, the responses proved not as supportive as anticipated.[21] Writing from Pantheon Road,

Madras, the Reverend M. Phillips expressed his thanks for receiving the report, but after praising the planning committee for making every effort to represent the views of all Christian and non-Christian faiths, he concluded that the Parliament had "failed completely."

> The representatives of both Buddhism and Hinduism at the Parliament represented neither the one nor the other as they are, or as they even were, *but as they wish them to be!!* The Buddhism of Dharmapala has no place in history, and the Hinduism of Vivekananda is an exceedingly faint reflexion of that philosophical side of Hinduism called Vedantism. His papers . . . are altogether misleading . . . . I am surprised to see such a prominent place for his name in the Report. Surely Barrows must have told you that he was an imposter, a self-appointed delegate, and in no way recognized as a swami or Sannyasi by the Hindus. Indeed, the Hindus in the north were so disgusted with his assumptions that they forcibly ejected him from the temple as a defiled outcast! . . . I have spoken my plaint and I have done so in the *interest of the Parliament.*[22]

From Beirut, Syria, George E. Post confided that the "brotherly spirit" felt at the Parliament had not been welcomed in his part of the world. "You are probably aware that the government forbade its subjects to participate in our Parliament. I know of no paper which dared publish its proceedings. I believe that any effort to promote the objects of the extension would meet with immediate and vigorous repression by the strong hand of power."[23]

An especially interesting response came from Sri-Parthasarathy-Aiyangar, member of the Society for the Propagation of the Veda and Vedanta. Prepared in the form of a prayer, he responded:

> Meek Pres'dent Bonney well sums all men's *summum bonum* here.
> Peace-breaking Preacher Barrows' views must henceforth cease to appear.
> If proof of many a truth doth oft progress and e'en depend

On the *reduction-ad-absurdum* ground, it shouldn't offend.
That many a man, nay, man an *infant,* to damnation's doomed
By all souls' Sire, of His free choice, the Calvinists presumed;
So, Catholics shut heav'n 'gainst all who follow not the *Pope;*
Most Protestants say—"none who isn't of *Christ,* for heav'n
need hope;
Most Muslims send to hell, all who Mohammad do not own;
The man of God opes Heav'n to all who do not *God* disown.
His doctrine is: "In *God* we live and move and have our being;
Grown ripe by *God's* free grace. Gains heav'n, in time, *each*
living thing.
To lead a life that shall ne'er end, in blessedness that hath no
bounds.[24]

Lastly, Dr. Ernst Faber reported from Shanghai that news of the Parliament idea in China had been noticeably silent, even from those who attended its meetings in 1893. He then complained that the Pope, who had spoken favorably of the Parliament's outcome, refused to acknowledge Protestantism or its missions in those colonies under the domination of the Catholic Church.[25] Equally disappointing were responses from two well-known delegates. The first was Archbishop John Ireland of Minnesota who admitted to being unable to speak with regard to any future parliament.[26] The other came from President Elisha Benjamin Andrews of Brown University who wrote that the Parliament had made "no appreciable influence" on the people of Rhode Island. He reminded Carus that "many eminent men in New England (as well as elsewhere) consider this widening religious view not only as marking no advance but as a positively alarming sign of the times, heralding the approaching reign of Antichrist."[27] All of this put a damper on the once optimistic plans the three amigos had for the continuation of the Parliament concept. It seemed that the further removed from Chicago, the more remote the effects of the Parliament had been for anyone hoping to continue its activities. The true test of that hypothesis would be learned at the upcoming Paris Exposition of 1900.

Paris Woes

Given their usually optimistic disposition, Carus, Bonney, and Barrows hoped the upcoming Paris Exposition planned for 1900 would include a Congress of Religions program like that of the 1893 Parliament. In pursuing this idea, Barrow's world tour included a visit to Paris in 1895 where he conferred with proponents of the idea: M. Auguste Sabbatier, dean of the Protestant faculty at the University of Paris and editor of *Le Temps*; Zadok Kahn, chief rabbi of France; Protestant historian Charles Auguste Bonet-Maury; and Catholics Abbé Victor Charbonnel and Father Hyacinthe Loyson. The omens, however, were clear when the Archbishop of Paris vigorously opposed the Congress as did the Archbishop of Tours who wrote: "I do not think that the holding of the congress in question is possible in Paris. America is not France, neither the people nor the clergy are alike." Similarly, Pope Leo XIII wrote to Monsignor Francesco Satolli, the first Apostolic delegate to the United States, expressing doubt that the Church would participate in any European parliament.[28]

Carus's hope that the Chicago Parliament could be replicated at Paris changed over time. Initially, he supported the idea of its being held in a Catholic country and insisted that France was ideal due to it being a republic.[29] In a letter to Abbé Charbonnel, he reinforced this belief, explaining that by supporting the idea, France could demonstrate to the world that the Roman Catholic Church, which was often accused of being the most intolerant of all religions, could demonstrate its liberality by offering itself as the host religion. In the meantime, he offered himself and Bonney to assist in any possible manner.[30] However, writing several months later to dharmapala, Carus admitted that it remained unclear whether a Paris Congress could be conducted "in the same liberal spirit" as the one in Chicago.[31] His change of opinion stemmed from a vigorous anti-American party at the Vatican and what Bishop Ireland described as "many intrigues" within the European Catholic Church.[32]

In a letter to the French philosopher and mathematician Lucien Arréat at Versailles in May 1895, Carus expressed his concern that the catholicity required for a Parliament of Religions in France was becoming increasingly questionable given the "narrowness" of the European Catholic Church. He went on to identify three basic reasons: *First*, that France was Roman Catholic; *second*, that the Parisians were "religiously an indifferent people;" and *third*, that holding such a Parliament in a non-English speaking country would probably fail to draw a large audience. "English ought to be and remain the language of these aspirations, and to undertake anything in Paris would be a dead failure." Having again discussed the idea with Archbishop Ireland, Carus concluded that without the support of the Vatican, "the whole scheme had better be abandoned."[33]

Despite public expressions of support from the Parisian clergy for a Parliament of Religions, the Catholic hierarchy remained adamantly opposed to any repetition of the Chicago event. "There is no doubt," explained Carus in a letter to Bonney, "that you will not have his [Cardinal Richard, Archbishop of Paris] assistance in this meeting . . . and the situation of the clergy in Paris would be very difficult." He added that Arréat had advised abandoning the scheme altogether and plan instead for the next Parliament to meet in London.[34] Carus's advice proved accurate when, on August 12th, 1895, the Vatican delegate to the United States wrote the Holy See requesting a prohibitory pronouncement for Catholic involvement in any future interfaith congress similar to the 1893 Parliament. This was followed on September 18th with a letter from Pope Leo XIII advising that all future meetings between Catholics and non-Catholics would be discouraged. Instead, Catholics should hold their own meetings.[35]

Opposition continued to percolate as François Jauffret, Bishop of Bayonne insisted that holding an 1893-style Parliament would be a concession to "doctrinal skepticism" which now seemed to prevail among the middle classes. Furthermore, allowing it to take place on French soil would cause the Catholic population to conclude that they have been "led into error" by Catholic doctrine.[36] Given these concerns, Carus wrote William Pipe that "the intention is now, not to hold a Religious Parliament after the fashion of the Chicago Parliament but simply to hold a Congress of religious men, who come not as delegates, but on their own account, every one representing his own views and not the institution or church to which he belongs."[37]

The Paris Exposition opened in 1900, and instead of a Parliament of Religions following the pattern set by the Parliament that met in Chicago, the Exposition provided for an International Congress of the History of Religions organized by the Department of Religious Sciences at the Sorbonne under the presidency of M. Jean Réville. Presentations were limited to the study of past and present religions from a critical or scientific point of view, excluding any orations of a religious nature. The difference between the Chicago and Paris congresses lay in the insistence by the Paris managers that issues of creed were everywhere to be excluded from the program.

Thus, while the Parliament in Chicago had organized with notable representatives from the world's religions, no such opportunities were permitted by the planners of the French Exposition. Along with this difference came a decision by the Roman Catholic Church to refuse participation if the approach of its scholars was in any way reminiscent of the Chicago event.[38]

Disappointed with the outcome, Bonney sought an audience with Queen Victoria for the purpose of suggesting that a Second Religious Parliament be held at a future London Fair under her auspices. He based his reasoning on the fact that within the British empire, its Muslim and Hindu subjects vastly outnumbered Christians, and although England was a Christian nation, it could not be indifferent to its other religions. Besides, such a Parliament "can and must become the most powerful factor in the field of the missionary work for those higher forms of Christianity which through their agreement with truth constitute the conditions of our civilization; for truth will always maintain the field whenever and wherever it has a fair chance of a rigidly impartial comparison with error." The plan failed and a Second World Parliament of Religions did not materialize until 1993, convening at the Palmer House hotel in Chicago, a gathering that involved over eight thousand people representing the world's diversity of religious traditions.[39]

Despite their disappointment, the three amigos continued publicly to express their optimism. As staunch supporters of *The Open Court,* the Science of Religion, and the Religious Parliament Idea, they showed little reticence in their conviction that science and religious truth were bringing the different faiths into harmonious relation with each other. Having failed to elicit any response for a Parliament at a future London Exposition, they turned their attention to the next Exposition being planned for St. Louis in 1904. In anticipation of Catholic involvement much like it had been in Chicago, Carus sought a letter of support from Francisco Satolli, the Apostolic Delegate to the United States. His response proved devastating. "It is my conviction, which I frankly dare to express, that such a Parliament would only lead to skepticism and to naturalism. I must declare that no Catholic, whatever his condition or rank in the Church might be, should be allowed to take part or even sympathize with your work."[40]

The three amigos were not alone in their failure to keep the spirit of the Parliament alive. By 1898, the American Congress of Liberal Religious Societies and the Pan-American Congress of Religion and Education faced similar fates.[41] Another particularly disappointing failure was the collapse of the Greenacre movement in Maine, which had formed through the efforts of the religious pluralist Sarah Farmer in July 1894 as a summer program at the former Hotel Eliot with speakers of the caliber of Edward Everett Hale, Swami Vivekananda, Lewis G. Janes, Ralph Waldo Trine, Paul Carus, Annie Besant, W.E.B. Du Bois, Benjamin O. Flower. Topics discussed over its years of meetings included universal religion, Theosophy, Spiritualism, social evolution, natural selection, evolution and life, evolution of the God-Idea, individualism, and socialism. Carus took great interest in the program, delivering lectures on "Religion in Science," "Religion in Philosophy," and "Religion in Science and Philosophy."[42] Notwithstanding the program's many gifted speakers and generous subvention by Andrew Carnegie, the deterioration in Sarah Farmer's health led to the financial collapse of the summer program. It then fell into the hands of supporters of the Bahá'i faith whose fanaticism led to the exclusion of all other religions. One by one, the old Greenacreites dropped out, driven away by sectarianism, and Green Acre, newly named after the fortified coastal city of Acre in the Ottoman province of Syria, gave voice to a whole new source of spiritual revelation.[43]

* * *

Despite the best of intentions, the world was not ready for the ideals promoted by the three amigos. Remembering how the Asian and Protestant representatives lectured to enthusiastic audiences at the Parliament in 1893, the formidable Catholic Church as well as Protestant evangelicals had no intention of being twice burned.[44] As explained by Amy Kittelstrom, the Parliament represented "a momentary ripening of late Victorian idealism" amid the continuing war among scholars over science, the higher criticism, and biblical authority. The ripening, however, ended with the rise of fundamentalism, the conservativism of European Catholicism, and Pius X's encyclical *Pascendi Dominici Gregis* (1907) requiring all Catholic clergy and professors in theological seminaries to take oaths against modernist ideas. The Catholic hierarchy's flirtation with modernism ended and was now preparing to go on the attack. It would be a long time before the Catholic Church would show any willingness to participate in another interfaith gathering. Like the Man of La Mancha, the amigos learned too late that their vision of a Science of Religion and a Parliament of Religions was but a dream.[45]

8
The Unitary Whole

> Religion is not belief of any kind, it is not church membership, not mere devotion, not the performance of ritual, not the lip service of prayer, religion is part of our own being; it is the dominant idea of our soul, and it is characteristic of religion that it comprises the entire man, his sentiment, his will and his intellect. Religion is always a world-conception in which our relation to the All of life finds its determination.
>
> —PAUL CARUS, *The Dawn of a New Religious Era and Other Essays* (1899)

As a German-American positivist, although not in the same connotation as Comte or Spencer, Carus viewed monism as a unitary conception of the world where both spirit and matter were mere abstracts. Monism recognized the oneness of all existence with no differences of kind, no Creator or created, no supernatural and natural. God and the universe were one. Reality was indivisible even between the organic and inorganic as the former no doubt originated in the latter. Even the ego-centric consciousness of man was replaced by the unity of consciousness that was not a separate or separable something but part of the All-One. The universe constituted a unitary whole while man, whose personality or self-embraced body (living matter), soul (the psychic qualities of the organism), mind (intelligent portion of feelings), and spirit (combining feelings and intellectual functions), found harmony with the whole.[1] Man was not the sum total of matter but rather of form which consisted of those thought structures that embodied his aspirations, purposes, and will. "Man's life is like a tapestry adorned with divers patterns," wrote Carus. "The warp is the reality of facts while the woof is supplied by our spiritual comprehension, our thoughts and aspirations."[2]

William James

As evident in the previous chapters, Carus not only brought elements of Buddhist thought to the United States through his own writings and edited translations, he also facilitated others to do the same. By giving D.T. Suzuki access to the Open Court Publishing Company, Carus made Suzuki one of Carus's principal agents in this endeavor. Another was William James, one of the key spokespersons for the philosophy of pragmatism and religious pluralism who arrived at his understanding of Mahayana Buddhism from several sources, including D.T. Suzuki; Nishida Kitaro, the founder of the Kyoto School of philosophy; his neighbor Charles Layman, a Sanskrit scholar; the people and ideas drawn from own personal library; and editor Paul Carus with whom he had many interesting public and private conversations.[3]

Like Buddhism, the pragmatists showed a distrust for authority, were skeptics of abstract reasoning, and subordinated theory to the interaction of the organism with its environment. Their appeal was to experience minus any division of subject and object. Both accepted experience and an enhanced awareness as their grounding. Where they differed was in the principle of uses which, for the pragmatist, connected to a conscious teleology, while the Buddhist acted out his or her usefulness with greater detachment—finding life's worth in the simple act of living which becomes its own goal.[4]

James made numerous references to Buddhism in his *Varieties of Religious Experience*, noting that it was a system of thought which did not assume the existence of God as the Buddha himself stood in his place, a characteristic similar to the transcendental idealism of Emerson who "let God evaporate into abstract Ideality." Like Christianity, Buddhism was concerned with deliverance, meaning that "man must die to an unreal life before he can be born into the real life." Unlike mainstream Christianity, Buddhism existed without ritual sacrifices and instead substituted "renunciations of the inner self." Finally, in the matter of *judgment,* James leaned towards the Buddhist doctrine of Karma.[5]

James found Buddhism a congenial ally in his pursuit of curing sick souls. His explanation of "healthy-mindedness" led him inexorably to the belief that Buddhism offered a practical solution to human unhappiness.[6] Like pragmatism, it focused on the realm of human realities and did not retreat into more pleasing metaphors for the human condition. Instead it looked clearly into the human condition, avoiding the extremes of either asceticism or self-indulgence. It was the practical results that counted. This was the true test of 'the good.' The Buddha insisted: "Be lamps unto yourselves." Being "one's own refuge" was equivalent to saying that everyone who strove for enlightenment could find it by personal effort, a concept that did not resonate with Christians who required Jesus to redeem their fallen nature. Christ offered a hope outside the individual—an important difference between the two religions.[7] For James, morality rested not on divine authority but on the nature of man himself. Both, however, viewed the positive importance of good deeds, or, as Swedenborg emphasized in his doctrine of uses, every good deed was cosmically significant. Human progress did not depend upon prayers and rituals but builds on human nature. A religion without a god, it taught a rational faith not bound by creeds but knowledge, reason, compassion, mutual understanding, and experience.[8]

James's pluralistic universe included a god who was finite and limited to working with humanity to effect real changes. When the two worked together, the world became a better place. God was only real if he produced real effects.[9] As James described his philosophy to the French philosopher François Pillon:

> My philosophy is what I call a radical empiricism, a "thychism," which represents order as being gradually won and always in the making. It is theistic, but not essentially so. It rejects all doctrines of the Absolute. It is finitist; but it does not attribute to the question of the infinite, the great methodological importance of which you and Renouvier attribute to it. I feel that you may find my system too bottomless and romantic. I am sure that, be it in the end true or false, it is essential to the evolution of clearness in philosophical thought that someone should defend a pluralistic empiricism radically.[9]

Searching for Truth

There was an unmistakable kinship between James's philosophy of pragmatism as evidenced in his *Psychology* (1892) and *Essays in Radical Empiricism* (1912), and the Kyoto school of Zen Buddhism with its theory of truth, dedication to uses, a pluralistic universe, and emphasis on pure experience. James's pragmatism, a philosophy that emphasized consciousness and pure experience, intersected as well with the core functionalist elements of Buddhism.[10] The Buddha exemplified the type of wisdom that could be traced back to experience. For example, the Buddha's exhortation to examine one's experiences rather than rely on doctrine was an important connection to James and his attack on rationalism, specifically the distinction he made between mind and sense experience.

Still, there were differences. For Buddhists, the absolute was an achievable ideal, namely Nirvana. The pragmatists had no absolute. As Peirce explained, pragmatism was a theory of meaning, not Truth.[11] James clarified its meaning as well: "The 'absolutely' true, meaning what no farther experience will ever alter, is that ideal vanishing-point towards which we imagine that all our temporary truths will someday converge . . . . Meanwhile we have to live today by what truth we can get today and be ready tomorrow to call it falsehood."[12]

Carus's emphasis on forms became increasingly important in his later years while his aspirations for the advent of monistic philosophy grew ever more distant. For reality to be meaningful, he insisted on using these non-empirical categories which stood for "supreme reality." He equated truth with forms that were universal, pre-existent, absolute, immutable, and of intrinsic value regardless of the situation. They were the uniformities or laws that shaped the world.[13] Without objective criteria there could be no path to scientific truth. "Armed with his philosophy of forms," explained historian Donald Harvey Meyer, Carus "believed that truth was one [and] that science was the search for truth." Science became the source of new revelation, replacing older revelations with undisputable conclusions grounded in factual data.[14] Thus, when James remarked that "truth happens to an idea," referring to an attribute that might or might not occur, Carus took immediate issue, condemning it as a crass and unenlightened form of subjective empiricism. If, as James explained, truth was "whatever proves itself to be good in the way of belief, and good, too, for definite, assignable reasons," then what is it that makes a useful lie true?[15] Similarly, if "truth *happens* to an idea," how is it that an idea could be both true and untrue?[16] "Truth, thou art but one," insisted Carus. "Thou are one from eternity to eternity; and there is no second truth beside thee."[17] For this reason, Carus's rationalistic reductionism faced off with agnosticism, pragmatism and all other "isms" that proposed or settled for the uncertainty of knowledge. His adversaries included Peirce, Spencer, and James who, having inflated the powers of skepticism, devolved into moral relativism.

Carus's opposition to James's idea of truth was never so intense than in the area of ethics where he criticized pragmatic philosophy for becoming "the fashionable free thought of the day . . . closely connected with negativism and hedonism."[18] He condemned it as an expediency grounded in a temporary pleasure or happiness, neither of which was "sufficient to make a complete and worthy human life."[19] While materialism led to hedonism, and spiritualism led to asceticism, neither answered the search for truth.

> First, to inquire after truth.
> Second, to accept the truth.
> Third, to reject what is untrue.
> Fourth, to trust in truth.
> And fifth, to live the truth.[20]

There were no two kinds of truth, one religious and the other scientific; nor could truths conflict with one another. "There cannot be in religion any other method of ascertaining the truth than the method found in science. And if we renounce reason and science, we can have no ultimate criterion of truth."[21] Science was divine—a revelation of God. "In science he speaks to us. Science gives us information concerning the truth; and the truth reveals his will. . . . By surrendering science, you degrade man; you cut him off from the only reliable communication with God, and thus change religion into superstition."[22]

Carus insisted that truth was not an artifice made by man, but discoverable. It was rigid, not plastic, and "independent of our likes and dislikes." The truth of yesterday must be the truth of tomorrow. Ptolemaic astronomy was never true and would never be true even though it satisfied scientific enquiry at the time. If James was correct, the followers of Ptolemy need not have troubled themselves with the inconsistencies they found.[23] Carus rejected James's utilitarian approach to truth because it made something universal and objective into a relative and highly subjective "personal equation." Science stood or fell with the objectivity of truth. "If truth were mere opinion, if my truth might be different from your truth, even though all errors due to a difference of terminology were excluded, if both our truths in spite of being contradictory might be truths, truth would be subjective. It would appear different in different minds, and even in the same mind truth would be subject to change. Objective truth would be impossible." This Carus could not accept.[24]

The philosophy of the future, Carus insisted, should focus on the importance of memory as the soul-builder, science as the search instrument for objective truth, the unitary world-

The Hegeler family pose on the entrance staircase of their newly-built home in 1876. Today the Hegeler-Carus Mansion is a museum and national historic landmark, welcoming thousands of visitors from all over the world.

conception he called monism, and God as a "super-personality." Opposed to agnosticism which he called *nescience,* and pragmatism which had lost itself in pluralism and subjectivism, he turned to the works of Schiller and Goethe who he identified along with Plato as the "prophets of the philosophy of form."[25]

Following on the identification of a truth, it was the responsibility of philosophy to apply it to practical life, a discipline Carus called *pragmatology,* meaning the application of truths through sociology, education, political economy, religion, and ethics. In this new world conception, the philosophy of science become the single most important power in rendering visible the goals toward which mankind was moving. The test of progress was not as explained by Herbert Spencer, "passage from the homogeneous to a heterogeneous state," but the realization of truth.[26]

Assessment

While many of the publications on religious subjects by the Open Court Publishing Company appeared to be purely theoretical, Carus insisted that all had a practical purpose which was the reconstruction of religion based on modern science. Through its limited number of advertisements, the pages of *The Open Court* offered a selective menu that included a series of books published by Charles H. Kerr and Co. about religion with authors ranging from O.B. Frothingham, Francis Ellingwood Abbot, and John Fiske, to Theodore Parker and Asa Gray. Carus also offered his own series titled "Great Religions of the Human Race," "The Religion of Science Library," along with books by eminent mathematicians; books on Chinese religion, philosophy, language, literature, life and customs; plant breeding; hymns of the faith; and books by Frederick Starr on modern Mexican authors.[27]

Carus provided space in *The Open Court* for advertising *The Journal of Philosophy; Psychology and Scientific Methods; The Journal of Geography; The Living Age;* and *Bud-*

dhism: An Illustrated Quarterly Review. In addition, it offered special discounted subscriptions for those who combined purchases of *The Open Court* with *The Cosmopolitan*, *The Review of Reviews*, and *Woman's Home Companion.* Besides its books and journals, the publishing company sold illustrated portraits of Buddha, twenty eminent mathe- maticians, sixty-eight philosophers and psychologists. It even offered Japanese floral calendars.[28] Although Carus recognized that the free exchange of space between his journals and those of Theosophy would probably increase his circulation, he declined to do so, believing that the theosophical movement contained "so many crude elements which are most strongly represented in their leader that I prefer to keep out of it."[29] At the height of its popularity, *The Open Court* had approximately three thousand subscribers and *The Monist* about 750.[30] As the official repository for the Open Court Publishing Company and subsequently Carus Books, the Special Collections Research Center of Morris Library at Southern Illinois University Carbondale has made the full run of *The Open Court* magazine available at OpenSIUC via the Internet

<https://opensiuc.lib.siu.edu/ocj>

Carus's advocacy of monistic philosophy did not deter him from turning *The Open Court* and *The Monist* into lively platforms for debates on topics about which differences brewed between and among the world's philosophers. He gave the *Open Court* an eclectic look, mixing religion with biology, mathematics, politics, and metaphysics, while *The Monist,* begun in 1890, was devoted more directly to the philosophy of science. As editor, he had the enviable task of advancing any number of important issues at his discretion: scientific rationalism, skepticism, philology, anthropology, pragmatic theory, Darwinism, mathematics, Buddhism, and progressive evolution. Unlike most editors, Carus paid an honorarium to his authors for their articles. For a small select group like Thomas Rhys Davids, Max Müller, and Charles Peirce, he paid a higher honorarium.

Those authors who submitted articles for publication in *The Open Court* and *The Monist* included many of the world's leading intellectuals: evolutionary biologist George John Romanes; geologist and explorer John Wesley Powell; geologist Joseph Le Conte; philosopher and theologian Francis Ellingwood Abbot; French psychologist Alfred Binet; botanist, paleontologist and sociologist Lester Frank Ward; German biologist and philosopher Ernst Haeckel; Dutch botanist and geneticist Hugo de Vries; philosopher and psychologist John Dewey; philosopher and intellectual historian Arthur O. Lovejoy; essayist and playwright T.S. Eliot; Japanese Zen Buddhist D.T. Suzuki; and British philosopher and logician Bertrand Russell.

Among Carus's favorites were the Sanskrit scholar and philologist Friedrich Max Müller; the Austrian physician and philosopher Ernst Mach; and the truculent philosopher, logician, and mathematician Charles Saunders Peirce. Gracious and courteous to all, including William James, whose understanding of truth he vigorously opposed, he transformed the journals into forums of open discussion on some of philosophy's most contentious subjects.[31] As he explained to one author with whom he took strong exception, "I wish to state at once that I perused the greater part of the Ms. and found arguments with which I radically disagree, but they are stated vigorously and clearly. The arguments are not new but are exceedingly well presented and for that reason I wish to publish the article."[32]

Given Carus's own prodigious output and the generosity he showed towards scholars from multiple disciplines, it is surprising that he remained relatively obscure in their philosophical circles, referred condescendingly by some as an amateur philosopher and even a dilettante who offered a confused and not particularly helpful contributions to science, philosophy, and religion. Admired for the liberality of his magazines and his success in conveying to his international audience the breadth and depth of Eastern and Western thought, his own scholarly contributions were given a half-listening ear or otherwise ignored as the disciplines evolved into more specialized fields of study. As Harold Henderson explained, a new generation of thinkers first questioned and then rejected Carus's formal certainties in philosophy, physics, and even mathematics."[33] Taken for granted as a wannabe scholar, he faced increasing criticism from the very individuals he had nurtured. "The public to which he spoke," noted Donald Harvey Meyer, "was deaf to his voice" while intellectuals found him "too simple." Eventually his ideas regarding the unity of truth, cause and effect, and the preservation of matter and energy, were either written off as contradictory or dismissed as crudely formulated.[34]

Carus took no offence at negative reviews of his work provided they were fair and offered factual rebuttals to his work. "Praise and blame are redundant elements in reviews; they have, if any, a transient importance only. I do not look for either. I do not mind animosities, nor need I mind them especially as I can easily and effectively retaliate—although I make little use of it."[35] From the pragmatists and the relativity physicists who criticized objectivity and scientific truth, he faced challenges that began cordially and professionally but ended with indifference, as if Carus's questions were obsolete and no longer relevant to the discussion. Despite a lifetime of rubbing elbows with the likes of Ernst Mach, Charles Peirce, and D.T. Suzuki, Carus received less than charitable acknowledgement for his contributions. While grateful for access to his journals, the editor's stable of authors eventually turned on him. "It is the constant indoor life, the lack of acquaintance with the real needs of practical life, and the close confinement to a special mode of work," Carus observed, "that tends to make scholars one-sided, and if professional pride and personal vanity are added, a peculiar disease originates, which, in one word, we call *scholaromania.*"[36]

The discussions Carus initiated through his books and magazines were a reflection of his education. Trained in mathematics and in the classics by Indologist and scholar Hermann Grassmann, he demonstrated in his life's work the dynamic importance of the liberal arts by introducing subscribers of *The Open Court* and *The Monist* to multiple disciplines of study. With articles, book reviews, queries, announcements, and discussions that filled each issue, he made subscribers privy to conversations and debates among the world's leading scholars—both old and new—that turned on questions addressing the very meaning and purpose of life. In his thirty-two years as an author, publisher, and editor, he inspired those who read his books and magazines to reason and think critically in an ever-expanding world of information. By cultivating tolerance and an openness to the ideas of others, he gave generations of readers the tools to acquire a sense of themselves and of the world around them.

Fade Out

With the outbreak of the Great War, Carus displayed sentiments favorable to the Central Powers and was not shy in criticizing what he called the "sham neutrality" of the United States.[37] The war quickly became an obsession, and as the U.S. inched closer to participation, he weighted *The Open Court* with advertisements and reviews of books that were unabashedly critical of the Allied Powers. Similarly, he included articles critical of Russia, questioned America's judgment, recounted German contributions to the nation's achievements, and suggested that democracy had a greater chance of surviving if left to the Anglo-Saxon and Teutonic peoples than to the infusion of Slavs who posed a threat to Western civilization.[38] So striking had been the change in editorial policy that Roger Thomas wrote a letter to the *New York Tribune* accusing Carus of reversing *The Open Court*'s policy with his sympathy for the Central Powers.[39]

After the U.S. declared war on Germany in April 1917, the American public turned to its dark side as war-born fanaticism and outright xenophobia turned on German Americans, treating them as "hyphenated Americans" who had yet to assimilate into the reigning Anglo-American culture. Perceived as security threats, they faced a torrid of anti-German sentiment that resulted in the banning of German-language schools, the removal of German books from public libraries, and targeting individual German-Americans for being socialists. Fueled by this super-patriotism, state and local governments removed street signs that had German names; renamed sauerkraut as liberty cabbage and hamburgers as liberty steaks; and even banned German music from being played in some areas of the country.

The Carus family felt their share of this toxic atmosphere when the Department of Justice's Bureau of Investigation initiated surveillance against it as a result of 'reports' accusing them of possessing un-American literature and involved in subversive activities. Interviews were conducted of employees and members of the family seeking to verify the rumors. None were found to be true.[40]

For years, Mary Carus maintained a dual role by providing editorial assistance to her husband while carrying on her regular duties at the zinc plant. This even included the years when she served as president of the company. After her husband's death on February 11th, 1919, from a combination of strokes and Bright's Disease, she continued to manage the two journals until her own death in 1936. After forty-nine years of continuous operation, seventeen of which were in the hands of Mary Carus, the lively discussions, disagreements, and knotty speculations of its community of scholars came to an end when *The Open Court* and *The Monist* ceased publication.

Postscript

After the death of Mary Carus in 1936, under the leadership of Elizabeth Carus, daughter of Paul Carus, Open Court continued publishing with a reduced output, yet including such important works as the Carus Lectures Series, in cooperation with the American Philosophical Association, selecting leading American philosophers to deliver these prestigious lectures every two years.

In 1965 Paul Carus's grandson Blouke Carus founded a school textbook division and started to publish the *Open Court Correlated Language Arts Program* integrating, for the first time, all of the language arts: reading, classical children's literature, penmanship, grammar, usage, and a composition program, covering the primary grades and up to sixth grade. The program was frequently revised and finally completed in 1990. Open Court started developing *The Real Math Program* in 1980 and completed the K–6 mathematics program in 1995, just before the Open Court Textbook programs were sold to McGraw Hill in 1996.

The story of a small publisher including authentic children's literature and a powerful phonics method of teaching beginning reading plus integrating it all with a fully developed composition program is well described in Harold Henderson's book, *Let's Kill Dick and Jane*.

In the 1970s, the non-school-textbook part of Open Court began to be revived, and Open Court again began to make its mark in philosophical publishing. Beginning in 2000, Open Courrt had a major success with the new Popular Culture and Philosophy series, commencing with *Seinfeld and Philosophy* (2000), *The Simpsons and Philosophy* (2001), and *The Matrix and Philosophy* (2002).

Blouke's wife Marianne Carus founded *Cricket* magazine in 1973, and it soon became the leading children's magazine for good educational and artistic content. Later other magazines were added, including *Ladybug*, *Babybug*, *Muse*, *Click*, *Spider*, *Cicada*, *Ask*, *Cobblestone*, *Faces*, and *Dig*.

In 2011 Carus Publishing including Open Court and the *Cricket* magazine group were acquired by ePals, which later became CricketMedia. In 2019 CricketMedia decided to shut down all production of new Open Court titles, though continuing to sell the backlist.

Consequently, Blouke Carus decided to form a new company to carry on the historic mission of Open Court, and in 2021 Carus Books began to produce new titles under the imprints Open Universe and Carus Education. Carus Books publishes both trade and academic books, in philosophy, current affairs, popular culture, education, and related subjects.

Notes

Introduction

[1] Thomas A. Tweed, "American Occultism and Japanese Buddhism: Albert J. Edmunds, D.T. Suzuki, and Translocative History," *Japanese Journal of Religious Studies*, 32 (2005), 251.

[2] Thomas A. Tweed, "Night-Stand Buddhists and Other Creatures: Sympathizers, Adherents, and the Study of Religion," in Duncan Ryuken Williams and Christopher S. Queen, *American Buddhism: Methods and Findings in Recent Scholarship* (London: Curzon Press, 1999), 71-90. Peter N. Gregory, "Describing the Elephant: Buddhism in America," *Religion and American Culture: A Journal of Interpretation*, 11 (2001), 240.

[3] Gregory, "Describing the Elephant: Buddhism in America," 242, 244.

[4] Quoted in Frank Sewall, "A Narrative and Critical Account of the Parliament of Religions," in L.P. Mercer, ed., *The New Jerusalem in the World's Religious Congress of 1893* (Chicago: Western New-Church Union, 1894), 50.

[5] Gilbert Reid, "A Christian's Appreciation of Buddhism," *The Biblical World*, 47 (1916), 15–24.

[6] Martin Verhoeven, "The Dharma through Carus's Lens," in Paul Carus, *The Gospel of Buddha* (Chicago: Open Court Publishing Company, 2004), 56.

[7] Paul Carus, *Philosophy as a Science: A Synopsis of the Writings of Dr. Paul Carus* (Chicago: The Open Court Publishing Co., 1909), 26.

[8] Carus, *The Dawn of a New Religious Era and Other Essays* (Chicago: The Open Court Publishing Co., 1916), 117.

[9] Paul Carus, *God; An Enquiry into the Nature of Man's Highest Ideal and a Solution of the Problem from the Standpoint of Science* (Chicago: The Open Court Publishing Co., 1908), 52, 83.

[10] Percival Lowell, *Chöson: The Land of the Morning Calm. A Sketch of Korea* (Boston: Ticknor and Company, 1886), 107.

Chapter 1: Mingling the Waters

[1] Alan Hodder, "Asia in Emerson and Emerson in Asia," in Jean McClure Mudge, *Mr. Emerson's Revolution* (Cambridge: Open Book Publishers, 2015), 375. Read Philip C. Almond, *The British Discovery of Buddhism* (Cambridge: Cambridge University Press, 1990); Tomoko Masuzawa, *The Invention of World Religions* (Chicago: University of Chicago Press, 2005).

[2] Donald S. Lopez, "Foreword," in Paul Carus, *The Gospel of Buddha According to Old Records* (Chicago: Open Court, 2004), vii–viii.

[3] Read Carl T. Jackson, *The Oriental Religions and American Literature: Nineteenth-Century Explorations* (Westport: Greenwood Press, 1981).

[4] Nathan Schmidt, "Early Oriental Studies in Europe and the Work of the American Oriental Society, 1842–1922," *Journal of the American Oriental Society,* 43 (1923), 1–14. The American Oriental Society was preceded by the American Philosophical Society (1743), the American Academy of Arts and Sciences (1780), and the American Antiquarian Society (1812). The Society's *Journal*, issued quarterly, has been in publication since 1843. The oldest European Oriental Society was the French Société Asiatique founded in 1822, followed by the Royal Asiatic Society in 1823, and the Deutsche Morgenländische Gesellschaft in 1844.

[5] Hodder, "Asia in Emerson and Emerson in Asia," 375, 379–80. Read Philip C. Almond, "The Buddha in the West: From Myth to History," *Religion*, 16 (1986), 305–22; Edward E. Salisbury, "Memoir on the History of Buddhism," *Journal of the American Oriental Society*, 1 (1843–49), 81–135; Henry David Thoreau, ed., "The Preaching of the Buddha," *The Dial*, 4 (1844), 391–401; A Traveler, "Buddhist Superstition," *Southern Literary Messenger*, 25 (1857), 257–78; Arthur Christy, *The Orient in American Transcendentalism: A Study of Emerson, Thoreau, and Alcott* (New York: Octagon Books, 1978); Arthur Versluis, *American Transcendentalism and Asian Religions* (New York: Oxford University Press, 1993).

[6] See *The Dial* in <http://onlinebooks.library.upenn.edu/webbin/serial?id=thedial> (accessed December 1st, 2017);

<http://oll.libertyfund.org/titles/wilkins-the-bhagvat-geeta-or-dialogues-of-kreeshna-and-arjoon> (accessed December 1st, 2017).

[7] Thomas A. Tweed, "'The Seeming Anomaly of Buddhist Negation': American Encounters with Buddhist Distinctiveness, 1858–1877," *The Harvard Theological Review*, 83 (1990), 70–71. Read Victor Cousin, *Cours d'histoire de la philosophie* (2 vols.; Paris: Didier, Libraire-éditeur, 1840). Interest in Oriental studies carried over from the American Oriental Society to the American Philological Association (1869), the Archaeological Institute of America (1879), the Society for Biblical Literature and Exegesis (1880), and the American Historical Association (1884).

[8] Henry David Thoreau, *The Writings of Henry D. Thoreau, Journal Volume 3: 1848–1851*. John C. Broderick, ed., (Princeton: Princeton University Press, 1981), 62.

[9] Russell B. Goodman, "East-West Philosophy in Nineteenth-Century America: Emerson and Hinduism," *Journal of the History of Ideas*, 51 (1990), 625–45; Dale Riepe, "Emerson and Indian Philosophy," *Journal of the History of Ideas*, 28 (1967), 115–22.

[10] Thoreau, *The Writings of Henry David Thoreau. Journal Volume I, 1837–1846*, 266.

[11] Edgar A. Weir, Jr., "The Whiter Lotus: Asian Religions and Reform Movements in America, 1836–1933," (Ph.D. Dissertation, University of Nevada, Las Vegas, 2011), 16-17.

[12] Samuel Johnson, *Oriental Religions and their Relation to Universal Religion* (3 vols; Boston: Houghton, Mifflin, and Co., 1872–85).

[13] Read Arie Molendijk, *Friedrich Max Müller and the Sacred Books of the East* (Oxford: Oxford University Press, 2016); N.J. Girardot, "Max Müller's 'Sacred Books' and the Nineteenth-Century Production of the Comparative Science of Religions," *History of Religions*, 41 (2002), 213–50.

[14] Read Lee Irwin, *Reincarnation in America: An Esoteric History* (Lanham: Lexington Books, 2017), chapter 12.

[15] Edward Hungerford, "Buddhism and Christianity," *The New Englander*, 33 (1874), 278–79.

[16] Friedrich Max Müller, *Buddhist Pilgrims* (Chico: Scholars Pres, 1985), 243.

[17] Read Charles D.B. Mills, *The Indian Saint; Or, Buddha and Buddhism (Northampton: Journal and Free Press*, 1876); Felix Adler, "A Prophet of the People," *Atlantic Monthly*, 37 (1876), 683–84.

[18] Quoted in James Freeman Clarke, *Ten Great Religions. An Essay in Comparative Theology* (Boston: James R. Osgood and Co., 1871), 139. See also <https://en.wikipedia.org/wiki/Buddhist_influences_on_Christianity> (accessed January 11th, 2020).

[19] Richard Garbe, "Contributions of Buddhism to Christianity," *The Monist*, 21 (1911), 509–63.

[20] Clarke, *Ten Great Religions. An Essay in Comparative Theology*, 142–43.

[21] <https://newtopiamagazine.wordpress.com/2013/01/15/the-platonist-on-sunset-blvd> (accessed March 31st, 2017). Read Arthur Versluis, *The Esoteric Origins of the American Renaissance* (New York: Oxford University Press, 2001).

[22] Ethan Allen Hitchcock, *Remarks on Alchemy and the Alchemists* (Boston: Crosby, Nichols, and Co., 1857); Ethan Allen Hitchcock, *Swedenborg, a Hermetic Philosopher* (New York: D. Appleton and Co., 1858). See also <http://sueyounghistories.com/archives/2013/11/30/alexander-wilder-1823-1908> (accessed March 30th, 2017).

[23] Hitchcock, *Remarks on Alchemy and the Alchemists*, iv–ix, 45, 146, 225; I. Bernard Cohen, "Ethan Allen Hitchcock: Soldier—Humanitarian—Scholar, Discoverer of the "True Subject" of Hermetic Art," *Proceedings of the American Antiquarian Society,* 61 (1951), 29–139.

[24] "Salutatory," *The Platonist*, 2 (1884), 1.

[25] "The Platonist," *The Platonist*, 2 (1884), front matter. According to proponents of psychometry, every object receives and retains impressions of all that happens to it. Those impressions are indelible and can be reproduced in the mind as clearly as a picture.

[26] "Books and Periodicals," *The Platonist*, 1 (1881), 111. See also George Wyld, *Theosophy and the Higher Life* (London: Trubner and Co., 1881); and <https://newtopiamagazine.wordpress.com/2013/01/15/the-platonist-on-sunset-blvd> (accessed April 1st, 2017); Alfred Percy Sinnett, *The Occult World* (Boston: Houghton, Mifflin and Co., 1888 [1885]), 15–27.

[27] Alexander Wilder, "Entheasm," *The Platonist*, 1 (1881), 83.

[28] B.F. Underwood, "Concord School of Philosophy," *The Open Court*, 1 (1887), 355. As a teaching camp for Sunday-school teachers, it quickly expanded into concerts, theatre and lecturer series that attracted middle-class families and imparted an appreciation for education, religion, and the arts. Read Andrew C. Riser, *The Chautauqua Movement: Protestants, Progressives, and the Culture of Modern Liberalism* (New York: Columbia University Press, 2003).

[29] S.H. Emery, Jr. and F.B. Sanborn, "The Concord Summer School of Philosophy," *Journal of Speculative Philosophy*, 14 (1880), 251–53; F.B. Sanborn, ed., *The Genius and Character of Emerson: Lectures at the Concord School of Philosophy* (Boston: James R. Osgood and Co., 1885), ix–xxii.

[30] "The American Akadēmē," *The Platonist*, 2 (1884), 16.

[31] <https://newtopiamagazine.wordpress.com/2013/01/15/the-platonist-on-sunset-blvd> (accessed April 1, 2017).

[32] René Guénon, *Theosophy: History of a Pseudo-Religion* (Hillsdale: Sophia Perennis, 2004); Henry Steel Olcott, *Theosophy: Religion, and Occult Science* (London: Redway, 1885); Jeffrey D. Lavoie, The Theosophical Society: *The History of a Spiritualist Movement* (Boca Raton: BrownWalker Press, 2012); Robert Elwood, *Theosophy: A Modern Expression of the Wisdom of the Ages* (Wheaton: Quest Books, 2014). See also William James, *Varieties of Religious Experience* (New York: Longmans, Green, and Co., 1917 [1902]), 290.

[33] Alfred Percy Sinnett, *Esoteric Buddhism* (London: The Theosophical Publishing Society, 1907), xv, x–xi.

[34] H.P. Blavatsky, *Isis Unveiled: A Master-Key to the Mysteries of Ancient and Modern Science and Theology* (2 vols.; New York: J.W. Bouton, 1892), I, ix–x.

[35] Blavatsky, *Isis Unveiled*, Vol 1, xiv.

[36] Blavatsky, *Isis Unveiled*, Vol 1, xlv.

[37] Read Todd Jay Leonard, *Talking to the Other Side: A History of Modern Spiritualism* (New York: iUniverse Inc., 2005); Christine Ferguson, *Determined Spirits* (Edinburgh: Edinburgh University Press, 2012); Ann Braude, *Radical Spirits: Spiritualism and Women's Rights in Nineteenth-Century America* (Bloomington: Indiana University Press, 1989); Catherine L. Albanese, *A Republic of Mind and Spirit: A Cultural History of American Metaphysical Religion* (New Haven: Yale University Press, 2007); Emma Hardinge Britten, *Nineteenth Century Miracles: Spirits and Their Work in Every Country of the Earth* (New York: William Britten, 1884); Arthur Conan Doyle, *The History of Spiritualism* (2 vols.; New York: G.H. Doran, 1926); Frank Podmore, *Mediums in the Nineteenth Century* (2 vols.; New York: University Books, 1963).

[38] H.S. Olcott, "Spiritualism and Theosophy: Their Agreements and Disagreements," *The Theosophist*, 19 (1897), 101–105. Theosophists would later teach that it derived from a living person's mind by way of telepathy working through an astral body. See also Thierry Dodin and Heinz Räther, eds., *Imagining Tibet: Perceptions, Projections, and Fantasies* (Somerville: Wisdom Publications, 2001).

[39] Alfred Percy Sinnett, *The Occult World* (Boston: Houghton, Mifflin and Co., 1888 [1885]), 12–14, 32–33.

[40] Sinnett, *The Occult World*, 53, 176

[41] See A. Trevor Barker, ed., *The Mahatma Letters to A.P. Sinnett* (London: Rider and Co., 1926); G.A. Barborka, *The Mahatmas and Their Letters* (Madras: Theosophical Publishing House, 1973).

[42] Stephen Prothero, "Henry Steel Olcott and 'Protestant Buddhism'," *Journal of the American Academy of Religion*, 63 (1995), 286, 295.

[43] Read Stephen Prothero, *The White Buddhist: The Asian Odyssey of Henry Steel Olcott* (Bloomington: Indiana University Press, 1996).

[44] Prothero, "From Spiritualism to Theosophy: 'Uplifting' a Democratic Tradition," 208–210.

[55] Henry Steel Olcott, "Human Spirits and Elementaries," *Theosophist*, 28 (1907), 44.

[46] David L. McMahan, *The Making of Buddhist Modernism* (New York: Oxford University Press, 2008), 95, 98–101.

[47] Henry S. Olcott, *The Buddhist Catechism* (40th edition) (London: Theosophical Publishing Co., 1904), 1–3; 100. Joseph Rodes Buchanan, *Manual of Psychometry: The Dawn of a New Civilization* (Boston: Joseph R. Buchanan, 1885); A. Marques, "The Auras of Metals," *The Theosophist*, 20 (1899), 393–400; Karl Ludwig Friedrich Reichenbach, *Lettres Odiques-Magnetiques Du Chevalier de Reichenbach* (2nd ed.; Paris: Hachette Livre, 2012; c. 1897).

[48] Gary Lachman, *Madame Blavatsky: The Mother of Modern Spiritualism* (New York: Penguin, 2012).

[49] Dresser quoted in Wakoh Shannon Hickey, *Mind Cure: How Meditation Became Medicine* (New York: Oxford University Press, 2019), 69. Read also Henry C. Sheldon, *Theosophy and New Thought* (New York: The Abingdon Press, 1916); Henry Ridgely Evans, "Madame Blavatsky," *The Monist*, 14 (1900), 387.

[50] John S. Haller, Jr., *The History of New Thought: From Mind Cure to Positive Thinking and the Prosperity Gospel* (West Chester: Swedenborg Foundation Press, 2012), 209–213; Carl Jackson, "The New Thought Movement and the Nineteenth Century Discovery of Oriental Philosophy," *Journal of Popular Culture*, 9 (1975), 523–48.

[51] Robert C. Fuller, *Mesmerism and the American Cure of Souls* (Philadelphia: University of Pennsylvania Press, 1982); Glenn Mosley, *New Thought, Ancient Wisdom: The History and Future of the New Thought Movement* (Philadelphia: Templeton Foundation Press, 2006); Wakoh Shannon Hickey, *Mind Cure: How Meditation Became Medicine* (New York: Oxford University Press, 2019).

[52] "Seicho No Ie Movement," in <www.religious-information.com/seicho-no-ie.html> (accessed February 2nd, 2020).

[53] Quoted in Ernest Samuels, *Henry Adams: The Middle Years* (Cambridge: The Belknap Press of Harvard University, 1958), 135–36. See also Vern Wagner, "The Lotus of Henry Adams," *The New England Quarterly*, 27 (1954), 75–94.

[54] Read Van Wyck Brooks, *Fenollosa and His Circle, With Other Essays in Biography* (New York: E.P. Dutton, 1962); Lawrence W.

Chisolm, *Fenollosa: The Far East and American Culture.* (New Haven: Yale University Press, 1963); Foster Rhea Dulles, *Yankees and Samurai: America's Role in the Emergence of Modern Japan, 1791–1900* (New York: Harper and Row, 1965); and Robert Schwantes, *Japanese and Americans: A Century of Cultural Relations* (New York: Harper and Brothers, 1955).

Chapter 2: Apprentice Years

[1] Read Martin Baumann, "Culture Contact and Valuation: Early German Buddhists and the Creation of a 'Buddhism in Protestant Shape'," *Numen*, 44 (1997), 270–295; William Peiris, *The Western Contribution to Buddhism (Delhi: Motilal Banarsidass,* 1973), 251–55; Thomas A. Tweed, *The American Encounter with Buddhism 1844–1912: Victorian Culture and the Limits of Dissent* (Bloomington: Indiana University Press, 1992), 65–67; Paul Carus, "Goethe a Buddhist," *The Open Court*, X (1896), 4836-37; and Friedrich Wilhelm, "The German Response to Indian Culture," *Journal of the American Oriental Society*, 31 (1961), 395–405.

[2] Quoted from "Statement," in The Open Court Publishing Co. Records, Series 1, Correspondence, Sub-Series 5, Letterpress Books, Box 30, folder 37.

[3] Paul Carus, *Monism and Meliorism, A Philosophical Essay on Causality and Ethics* (New York: F.W. Christern, 1885), 5, 14–15; Paul Carus, "The Message of Monism to the World," *The Monist*, 4 (1890–91), 545; Paul Carus, "The Origin of Thought-Forms," *The Monist*, 2 (1888–89), 111.

[4] Carus, *Monism and Meliorism*, 5, 14–15; T.B. Wakeman, "Auguste Comte and Philosophy in America," *The Open Court*, 3 (1889–90), 1902.

[5] Carus, *Monism and Meliorism*, 7, 13, 15.

[6] Carus, *Monism and Meliorism*, 17–18, 46, 49.

[7] Carus, *Monism and Meliorism*, 71–72.

[8] Carus, *Monism and Meliorism*, 73.

[9] Carus, *Monism and Meliorism*, 74.

[10] Paul Carus, "In Memory of Mr. E.C. Hegeler," *The Open Court*, 24 (1910), 387–90.

[11] Carus, "In Memory of Mr. E.C. Hegeler," 387–90.

[12] B.F. Underwood to E.C. Hegeler, June 22nd, 1886, in "To the Readers of the Open Court," *The Open Court*, 1 (1887), 622. Underwood enlisted in the 15th Massachusetts Infantry and fought in the Battle of Ball's Bluff where he was wounded and captured. He was imprisoned in two Confederate prisons before being released. He then re-enlisted and served until the end of

the war. A Darwinist and friend of Robert Ingersoll, he wrote extensively on free thought.

[13] William H. Hay, "Paul Carus: A Case-Study of Philosophy on the Frontier," *Journal of the History of Ideas*, 17 (1956), 503–505.

[14] Nicholas L. Guardiano, "Monism and Meliorism: The Philosophical Origins of the Open Court," *European Journal of Pragmatism and American Philosophy*, 9 (2017), in <https://journals.openedition.org/ejpap/1072> (accessed December 30th, 2019); Edward C. Hegeler, "What the Monistic Religion is to Me," *The Open Court*, 1 (1887–88), 725.

[15] E.C. Hegeler to B.F. Underwood, December 3rd, 1886, in "To the Readers of the Open Court," *The Open Court*, 1 (1887), 627. It was Sara Underwood who suggested the title The Open Court.

[16] "Announcement," *The Open Court*, 1 (1887), 15.

[17] B.F. Underwood to E.C. Hegeler, December 7th, 1886, in "To the Readers of the Open Court," 628–29. Sara Underwood, the editor's wife, published the poem "I Do Not Know" in an early issue which expressed her agnosticism as a clear opposite of Hegeler's monism.

[18] Henderson, *Catalyst for Controversy*, 33–34, 37.

[19] "To the Readers of the Open Court," 636–38.

[20] Guardiano, <https://journals.openedition.org/ejpap/1072>.

[21] Henderson, *Catalyst for Controversy*, 41.

[22] B.F. Underwood to Hegeler, October 28th, 1887, in "To the Readers of the Open Court," 638.

[23] B.F. and S.A. Underwood, "The Editors' Farwell to the Readers of The Open Court," *The Open Court*, 1 (1887), 591.

[24] With the change in editor, *The Open Court* became a weekly and the title then changed to "A Weekly Journal devoted to the Religion of Science." This title remained until 1897 when *The Open Court* became a monthly. At that time, the titled changed again to "Devoted to the Science of Religion, the Religion of Science, and the Extension of the Religious Parliament Idea."

[25] Paul Carus, *The Dawn of a New Religious Era and Other Essays* (Chicago: The Open Court Publishing Company, 1916), 114.

[26] Carus, *The Dawn of a New Religious Era and Other Essays*, 117.

[27] Paul Carus, "Vocation," *The Open Court*, 3 (1890), 2027–28.

[28] Harold Henderson, *Catalyst for Controversy: Paul Carus of Open Court* (Carbondale: Southern Illinois University Press, 1993), 46.

[29] Carus, *The Dawn of a New Religious Era and Other Essays*, v–vi.

[30] Dr. Gustav Carus, "Christianity and Monism," *The Open Court*, 2 (1888), 1381.

[31] Paul Carus, "The Religious Character of Monism," *The Open Court*, 2 (1888), 1384. See correspondence in Open Court Publishing Company Records, Series 1, Correspondence, Box 2, folders 10–12.

[32] Paul Carus, *The Idea of God* (Chicago: The Open Court Publishing Company, 1896), 1, 26.

[33] Paul Carus, *God; An Enquiry into the Nature of Man's Highest Ideal and a Solution of the Problem from the Standpoint of Science* (Chicago: The Open Court Publishing Company, 1908), 4, 7.

[34] Carus, *God*, 17–18, 23–24, 35, 46.

[35] Carus, *God*, 84–85.

[36] Paul Carus, "God-Nature," *Open Court*, 28 (1914), 402; Meyer, "Carus and the Religion of Science," 601–602.

[37] Paul Carus, "Science as a Religious Revelation," *Open Court*, 7 (1893), 3810.

[38] Paul Carus, *Homilies of Science* (Chicago: The Open Court Publishing Company, 1892), v.

[39] Carus, *Homilies of Science*, vii.

[40] Carus, *Homilies of Science*, 1–3, 5, 12, 16–17.

[41] Carus, *Homilies of Science*, 21, 24.

[42] Carus, *Homilies of Science*, 17, 29.

[43] Carus, *The Dawn of a New Religious Era and Other Essays*, 74.

[44] Paul Carus, *Primer of Philosophy* (Chicago: The Open Court Publishing Company, 1893), iv, 2, 4–5, 6; Paul Carus, "Spencerian Agnosticism," *The Open Court*, 5 (1891), 2951; Paul Carus, "Agnosticism and Comte's Positivism," *The Open Court*, 3 (1889–90), 1589.

[45] Carus, *Primer of Philosophy,* 1, 2, 4.

[46] Paul Carus, *The Religion of Science* (2nd ed.; Chicago: Open Court Publishing Company, 1896 [1893]), iv–v; Paul Carus, "The God of Science," *The Monist*, 14 (1900), 458.

[47] Carus, *The Religion of Science*, 79–81.

[48] Carus, *The Religion of Science*, 7–8.

[49] Carus, *The Religion of Science*, 113.

[50] Carus, *The Religion of Science*, 35–43, 47–48, 51–52; Paul Carus, "The Immortality of the Soul," *The Open Court*, 19 (1905), 363.

[51] Carus, *The Religion of Science*, 55–62.

[52] Read Corvinus, "Religion and Science, the Reconciliation Mania of Dr. Paul Carus of Open Court Analysed and Refuted by Corvinus," *Freethought Magazine*, 13 (1895), 16–23; Henry Collin Minton, "A Review of Dr. Carus's 'Fundamental Problems' and 'The Surd of Metaphysics'," *The Monist*, 14 (1904), 452–58.

[53] Carus, *The Religion of Science*, 106, 110, 112–15.

[54] Carus, *The Dawn of a New Religious Era and Other Essays*, 20, 46, 122; Carus to Barrows, July 11, 1893, Open Court Publishing Co. Records, Series 1, Correspondence subseries 5, Letterpress Books, Box 29, folder 1.

[55] Donald Harvey Meyer, "Paul Carus and the Religion of Science," *American Quarterly*, 14 (1962), 599.

Chapter 3: Parliament of Religions

[1] The Columbian Exposition was preceded by an exhibition at the Crystal Palace in Hyde Park, London, in 1851, the Crystal Palace in New York in 1853, the Philadelphia Centennial in 1876, and the Paris Exhibition in 1889. Read Robert W. Rydell, *World of Fairs: The Century of Progress Expositions* (Chicago: University of Chicago Press, 1993); Robert W. Rydell, *Grand Illusions: Chicago's World's Fair of 1893* (Chicago: Chicago Historical Society, 1993).

[2] Robert W. Rydell, *All the World's a Fair: Visions of Empire at American International Expositions*, 1876–1916 (Chicago: University of Chicago Press, 1984), 68. The Auxiliary intended to include a Congress on Evolution within the Department of Science and Philosophy but delays forced the planning committee to transfer it to the Parliament of Religions as a way to give the world's religions the opportunity to reconcile the role of science with their respective beliefs. As Bonney explained, "the orthodox Christians may find in the doctrine of evolution not only a scientific explanation of their faith, but also the key that unlocks the great mystery of creation from monad to man." The subject matter for discussion included ethics, marriage, education, science, philosophy, evolution, music, labor, government, peace and war. At the meeting of evolutionists which met on September 27th–29th, the opening address was given by the chairman, Benjamin F. Underwood, former editor for *The Open Court*. This was followed by a series of presentations by individuals such as Herbert Spencer, Edward D. Cope, Edward S. Morse, Sara A. Underwood, Minot J. Savage, and others. See Programme of the World's Religious Congresses, The Open Court Publishing Company Records, Box 282, folder 3; "The Congress on Evolution," in Rossiter Johnson, ed., *A History of the World's Columbian Exposition* (4 vols.; New York: D. Appleton and Company, 1898), IV, 412.

[3] Henry Adams, *The Education of Henry Adams* (New York: Modern Library, 1918), 237. Read Rosemarie K. Bank, "Representing History: Reforming the Columbian Exposition," *Theatre Journal*, 54 (2002), 589–606.

[4] Read Arnold Lewis, *An Early Encounter with Tomorrow: Europeans, Chicago's Loop, and the World's Columbian Exposition* (Urbana: University of Illinois Press, 1997); Harold L. Platt, *The Electric City: Energy and the Growth of the Chicago Area*, 1880–1930 (Chicago: University of Chicago Press, 1991); John Michael Andrick, "A Modern Mecca of Psychic Forces: The Psychical Science Congress and the Culture of Progressive Occultism in *Fin-De-Siècle* Chicago, 1885–1900," (Ph.D. Dissertation, Urbana, Illinois: University of Illinois, 2016), 3; Lindon Simon, *Dark Light: Electricity and Anxiety from the Telegraph to the X-Ray* (Orlando: Harcourt,

Inc., 2004); Carolyn Marvin, *When Old Technologies were New: Thinking about Electric Communication in the Late Nineteenth Century* (New York: Oxford University Press, 1988); N. Vaschide, "Experimental Investigations of Telepathic Hallucinations," *The Monist*, 12 (1898), 273, 337.

[5] Charles Carroll Bonney, "The Religious Parliament Idea," *The Open Court*, 14 (1900), 513; Paul Carus, "Hon. C.C. Bonney, Inaugurator of the Parliament of Religions," *The Open Court*, 14 (1900), 4. What was originally called the Auxiliary Congress of Religions became the Parliament of Religions which convened in the Hall of Columbus with all the delegates in attendance. In addition to the Parliament, there were multiple Congresses representative of the different religions and denominations that met separately in the Hall of Washington and smaller meeting rooms to discuss their respective beliefs in greater detail. Read Richard H. Seager, " Pluralism and the American Mainstream: The View from the World's Parliament of Religions," *The Harvard Theological Review*, 82 (1989), 301–24. Read Alfred Lord Tennyson, *Death of Oenone, Akbar's Dream and Other Poems* (London: Macmillan and Co., 1892).

[6] Charles Bonney, "The World's Parliament of Religions," 5, Open Court Publishing Company Records, Box 280, folder 108. The three standard works recounting the Parliament and its speakers are John Henry Barrows, ed., *The World's Parliament of Religions: An Illustrated and Popular Story of the World's Parliament of Religions, Held in Chicago in Connection with the World's Columbian Exposition of 1893* (2 vols.; Chicago: Parliament Publishing Co., 1893); Walter R. Houghton, ed., *Neely's History of the Parliament of Religions at the World's Columbian Exposition* (Chicago: F.T. Neely, 1893); and J.W. Hanson, ed., *The World's Congress of Religions: The Addresses and Papers Delivered before the Parliament* (Chicago: W.B. Conkey, 1894).

[7] Charles Bonney, "The World's Parliament of Religions," p. 19.

[8] Read Carlos Hugo Parra, "Standing with Unfamiliar Company on Uncommon Ground: The Catholic Church and the Chicago Parliaments of Religions" (Ph.D. Dissertation, Toronto: University of Toronto, 2012); George W. Gilmore, "The Higher Criticism," *The Monist*, 14 (1900), 215.

[9] Paul Carus, *The Religion of Science* (Chicago: The Open Court Publishing Company, 1896), 26.

[10] Quoted in Carus, *The Religion of Science*, 21–22.

[11] Read James F. Clarke, *Ten Great Religions: An Essay in Comparative Theology* (Boston: James Osgood and Co., 1871).

[12] Quoted in Paul Carus, *The Dawn of a New Religious Era and Other Essays* (Chicago: The Open Court Publishing Company, 1916), vi.

[13] Carus, *The Dawn of a New Religious Era and Other Essays*, 17.

[14] Richard Hughes Segar, "Pluralism and the American Mainstream: The View from the World's Parliament of Religions," *Harvard Theological Review*, 82 (1989), 317.

[15] Carus, *The Dawn of a New Religious Era and Other Essays*, 6.

[16] Quoted in Paul Carus "The Dawn of a New Religious Era," *The Monist*, 4 (1894), 7–8.

[17] James E. Ketelaar, "Strategic Occidentalism: Meiji Buddhists at the World's Parliament of Religions," *Buddhist-Christian Studies*, 11 (1991), 45; Shokin Furuta, "Shaku Soyen: The Footsteps of a Modern Japanese Zen Master," *Philosophical Studies of Japan*, 15 (1967), 67–91.

[18] Hans Martin Kramer, *Shimaji Mokurai and the Reconception of Religion and the Secular in Modern Japan* (Honolulu: University of Hawaii Press, 2015), 88–113; Ketelaar, "Strategic Occidentalism: Meiji Buddhists at the World's Parliament of Religions," 40, 41–42.

[19] Ketelaar, "Strategic Occidentalism: Meiji Buddhists at the World's Parliament of Religions," 46.

[20] Zenshori Noguchi, "The Religion of the World," in Barrows, *The World's Parliament of Religions*, I, 442–43.

[21] Noguchi, "The Religion of the World," I, 442. Distributed by the Bukkyo Gakkuwai, a society whose purpose was the propagation of Buddhism, the books included S. Kuroda, *Outline of the Mahayana as Taught by Buddha* (Tokyo: Bukkyo Gakkukwai, 1893) Kuroda was the Superintendent of Education of the Jodo-Sect; *The Sutra of Forty-two Sections and Other Two Short Sutras* (Kyoto, Japan: Buddhist Propagation Society, 1892); S. Kato, *A Shin-Shiu Catechism* (Kato was from the Hongwanjiha of the Shinshiu Sect of Japan, published by the Buddhist Propagation Society of Kyoto, Japan in 1893); Rev. Prof. M. Tokunaga, *The Skeleton of a Philosophy of Religion* (translated by Zenshiro Noguchi in 1893); and Nissatsu Arai, *Outlines of the Doctrine of the Nichiren Sect* (Tokyo, Japan: Published by the Nichiren Sect, 1893). See Paul Carus, "The Parliament of Religions," 23, Open Court Publishing Co. Records, Box 280, folder 107.

[22] Howard L. Parsons, "Buddha and Buddhism: A New Appraisal," *Philosophy East and West*, 1 (1951), 15. Read Yoshiro Tamura, *Japanese Buddhism, A Cultural History* (Tokyo: Kosei Publishing Co., 2005); Sir Charles Eliot, *Japanese Buddhism* (London: Kegan Paul International, 2005).

[23] Kinza Riuge Hirai, "What Buddhism Teaches of Man's Relation to God, and Its Influence on Those Who Have Received It," in Hanson, *The World's Congress of Religions: The Addresses and Papers*, 395-99.

[24] Toki Horin, "Buddhism in Japan," in Barrows, *The World's Parliament of Religions*, I, 543–49.

[25] Toki Horin, "History of Buddhism and Its Sects in Japan," 226.

[26] Toki Horni, "What Buddhism Has Done for Japan," in Houghton, ed., *Neely's History of the Parliament of Religions and Religious Congresses at the World Columbian Exposition*, 779–81.

[27] Banryu Yatsubuchi, "Buddhism," in Barrows, *The World's Parliament of Religions*, I, 716–17.

[28] Judith Snodgrass, *Presenting Japanese Buddhism to the West: Orientalism, Occidentalism, and the Columbian Exposition* (Chapel Hill: University of North Carolina Press, 2003), chapters 5 and 6.

[29] Suzuki translated the lecture of Soyen into English and Natsume Soseki, a Japanese novelist, improved on the translation. See D.T. Suzuki, "A Glimpse of Paul Carus," in Joseph M. Kitagawa (ed.), *Modern Trends in World Religions: Paul Carus Memorial Symposium* (La Salle: The Open Court Publishing Company, 1959), x.

[30] Rt. Rev. Shaku Soyen, "The Law of Cause and Effect, as Taught by Buddha," in Barrows, *The World's Parliament of Religions*, II, 829–31.

[31] Soyen, "The Law of Cause and Effect, as Taught by Buddha," II, 830.

[32] Shaku Soyen, "Arbitration Instead of War," Walter R. Houghton, ed., *Neely's History of the Parliament of Religions and Religious Congresses at the World Columbian Exposition* (Chicago: F. Tennyson Neely, 1894), 797–98.

[33] H.R.H. Prince Chandradat Chudhadharn, "Buddhism as It Exists in Siam," in Barrows, *The World's Parliament of Religions*, I, 645–649. The four noble truths according to Buddha are (1) the existence of suffering; (2) the recognition of ignorance as the cause of suffering; (3) the extinction of suffering by the cessation of lust arising from ignorance; and (4) the eight paths that lead to the cessation of lust. The eight paths that constitute the way of salvation are (1) right understanding; (2) right resolutions; (3) right speech; (4) right acts; (5) right way of earning a living; (6) right efforts; (7) right meditation; and (8) right state of the mind.

[34] Rt. Rev. H. Sumangala, "Buddhism—Orthodox Southern," in Barrows, *The World's Parliament of Religions*, II, 894–97.

[35] Read David L. McMahan, *The Making of Buddhist Modernism* (Oxford: Oxford University Press, 2009); Stephen R. Prothero, *The White Buddhist: The Asian Odyssey of Henry Steel Olcott* (Bloomington: Indiana University Press, 1996).

[36] H. Dharmapala, "Good Wishes of Ceylon," in Houghton (ed.), *Neely's History of the Parliament of Religions and Religious Congresses at the World's Columbian Exposition*, 60.

[37] Quoted in R.S. Sugirtharaja, *The Bible and Asia: From the Pre-Christian Era to the Postcolonial Age* (Cambridge: Harvard University Press, 2013), 135–36.

[38] Dharmapala, "The World's Debt to Buddha," in Houghton, ed., *Neely's History of the Parliament of Religions and Religious Congresses at the World's Columbian Exposition*, 406–409.

[38] Lewis Pyle Mercer, *Review of the World's Religious Congresses of the World's Congress Auxiliary of the World's Columbia Exposition* (Chicago: Rand, McNally, and Company, 1893), 37.

[40] Amy Kittelstrom, "The International Social Turn: Unity and Brotherhood at the World's Parliament of Religions, Chicago, 1893," 243–74. At the Congress of Theosophists who assembled from September 15–17, Dharmapala spoke to the assembled guests as a Buddhist, not as a Theosophist. See American Section Headquarters, *The Theosophical Congress Held by the Theosophical Society at the Parliament of Religions* (New York: American Section Headquarters, 1893), 28.

[41] H. Dharmapala, "The World's Debt to Buddha," in J.W. Hanson, ed., *The World's Congress of Religions: The Addresses and Papers*, 382. Read Grant Allen, *Charles Darwin* (London: Longmans, Green, and Co., 1885).

[42] Dharmapala, "The World's Debt to Buddha," in Barrows, *The World's Parliament of Religions*, II, 878. Read George Abell, and Barry Singer, *Science and the Paranormal* (London: Junction Books, 1981); Kenneth Frazier, ed., *Paranormal Borderlands of Science* (Buffalo: Prometheus Books, 1982); Nicholas Rescher, *Peirce's Philosophy of Science* (Notre Dame: University of Notre Dame Press, 1978); Wilfrid Sellars, *Science, Perception, and Reality* (London: Routledge and Kegan Paul, 1963).

[43] Dharmapala, "Foreign Missionary Methods," in Houghton (ed.), *Neely's History of the Parliament of Religions and Religious Congresses at the World's Columbian Exposition*, 607–608.

[44] Dharmapala, "Buddhism and Christianity," in Houghton (ed.), *Neely's History of the Parliament of Religions and Religious Congresses at the World's Columbian Exposition*, 803–806.

[45] Judith Snodgrass, *Presenting Japanese Buddhism to the West: Orientalism, Occidentalism, and the Columbian Exposition* (Chapel Hill and London: The University of North Carolina Press, 2003), 85.

[46] Paul Carus, *The Philosophy of the Tool* (Chicago: The Open Court Publishing Company, 1893), 9–10, 16.

[47] Paul Carus, "Our Need of Philosophy," *The Open Court*, 7 (1893), 3783–86.

[48] Carus, *The Dawn of a New Religious Era and Other Essays*, 19–20, 24–25, 37.

[49] Carus, *The Dawn of a New Religious Era and Other Essays*,

89. Read also Samuel Johnson, *Oriental Religions and their Relation to Universal Religion* (Boston: Osgood, 1872).

[50] Carus, *The Dawn of a New Religious Era and Other Essays*, 22.

[51] Carus, *The Dawn of a New Religious Era and Other Essays*, 25, 26.

[52] Carus, *The Dawn of a New Religious Era and Other Essays*, 5, 6–7, 10, 81.

[53] Paul Carus, *Philosophy as a Science* (Chicago: The Open Court Publishing Co., 1909), 1–2, 5.

[54] F. Max Müller, "The Real Significance of the Parliament of Religions," *Arena*, 61 (1894), 1.

[55] John R. McRae, "Oriental Verities on the American Frontier: The 1893 World's Parliament of Religions and the Thought of Masao Abe," *Buddhist-Christian Studies*, 11 (1991), 28–30; Larry A. Fader, "Zen in the West: Historical and Philosophical Implications of the 1893 Parliament of Religions," *Eastern Buddhist*, 15 (1982), 122–45.

[56] Paul Carus, "The Dawn of a New Religious Era," *The Monist*, 4 (1894), 1, 16–17.

[57] Richard Hughes Seager, "Pluralism and the American Mainstream: The View from the World's Parliament of Religions," *Harvard Theological Review*, 82 (1989), 301–24. Read also Sydney Ahlstrom, *A Religious History of the American People* (New Haven: Yale University Press, 1972); Martin Marty, *Modern American Religion. Volume I, The Irony of It All, 1893–1919* (Chicago: University of Chicago Press, 1986); Paul Carter, *The Spiritual Crisis of the Gilded Age* (De Kalb: Northern Illinois University Press, 1971); Carl T. Jackson, *The Oriental Religions and American Thought: Nineteenth-Century Explorations* (Westport: Greenwood Press, 1981); Rick Fields, *How the Swans Came to the Lake: A Narrative History of Buddhism in America* (Boulder: Shambhala Publications, 1981); Catherine Albanese, *A Republic of Mind & Spirit: A Cultural History of American Metaphysical Religion* (New Haven: Yale University Press, 2007).

[58] Paul Carus, "The Parliament of Religions," pp 30–31, Open Court Publishing Company Records, Box 280, folder 107.

Chapter 4: The Wise Men

[1] Richard Hughes Segar, "Pluralism and the American Mainstream: The View from the World's Parliament of Religions," *Harvard Theological Review*, 82 (1989), 320.

[2] Quoted in Susan L. Dunston, *Emerson and Environmental Ethics* (Lanham: Lexington Books, 2018), 94; Protap Chunder Mozoomdar, "Emerson as Seen from India," in F.B. Sanborn, ed.,

The Genius and Character of Emerson: Lectures in the Concord School of Philosophy (Port Washington: Kennikat Press, 1971), 365–71.

[3] Protap Chunder Mozoomdar, *The Oriental Christ* (Boston: George H. Ellis, 1893 [1883]), 7, 9. Read Suresh Chunder Bose, *The Life of Protap Chunder Mozoomdar* (2 vols.; Calcutta: Nababidhan Trust, 1940).

[4] Mozoomdar, *The Oriental Christ*, 11. See also Sunrit Mullick, *The First Hindu Mission to America: The Pioneering Visits of Protap Chunder Mozoomdar* (New Delhi: Northern Book Center, 2010 [1883]).

[5] Mozoomdar, *The Oriental Christ*, 46.

[6] Mozoomdar, *The Oriental Christ,* 24, 27.

[7] Quoted in J.V. Nash, "India at the World's Parliament of Religions," *The Open Court*, 47 (1933), 224.

[8] Swami Vivekananda, *Complete Works of Swami Vivekananda* (9 vols.; Calcutta: Advaita Ashrama, 1977–84), IV, 95.

[9] Quoted in Paul Carus, "The Dawn of a New Religious Era," *The Monist*, 4 (1894), 8.

[10] Quoted in Carus, *The Dawn of a New Religious Era and Other Essays*, 7.

[11] *The Life of the Swami Vivekananda* (3 vols.; Mayavati, Almora: Published by the Swami Virajananda, 1914), II, 314–15.

[12] Read Swami Nikhilananda, *Vivekananda: A Biography* (Kolkata, India: Advaita Ashrama, 1964); Swami Vivekananda, *Complete Works of Swami Vivekananda*, <www.ramakrishna-vivekananda.info/vivekananda/volume1/vol1frame.htm> (accessed January 26th, 2020).

[13] David L. McMahan, "Modernity and the Early Discourse of Scientific Buddhism," *Journal of the American Academy of Religion*, 72 (2004), 898.

[14] "M. Dharmapala's Mission," *The Open Court*, X, (1896), 5071.

[15] The term "Protestant Buddhism" is credited to Gananath Obeyesekere at Princeton University. Read his *Buddhism Transformed: Religious Change in Sri Lanka* (with Richard Gombrich) (Princeton: Princeton University Press, 1988).

[16] Quoted in David L. McMahan, "Modernity and the Early Discourse of Scientific Buddhism," 907. Read also David L. MaMahan, *The Making of Buddhist Modernism* (Oxford: Oxford University Press, 2008), 98.

[17] Carus to Rt. Rev. W. Subhuti, September 26th, 1896, The Open Court Publishing Company Records, Series 1, Correspondence, Sub Series 5, Letterpress Books, Box 31, folder 18.

[18] Read N. Mottahedeh, ed., *Abdul'l-Baha's Journey West: The Course of Human Solidarity* (New York: Palgrave Macmillan, 2013).

[19] Anna Ballard, "Dharmapala, the Buddhist," *The Open Court*, X (1896), 5173–74.

[20] Paul Carus, "The Buddha Gaya Case," *The Open Court*, X (1896), 4957.

[21] Carus to Dharmapala, April 27th, 1896, in The Open Court Publishing Company, Series 1, Correspondence, Sub-Series 5, Letterpress Books, Box 30, folder 57. The meeting never took place because Suzuki did not arrive in La Salle for another year.

[22] Carus to C. T. Strauss, September 9th, 1896, in The Open Court Publishing Co. Records, Series 1, Correspondence, Sub Series 5, Letterpress Books, Box 31, folder 14.

[23] Carus to Prof. Charles R. Lanman, October 1st, 1896, in The Open Court Publishing Co. Records, Series 1, Correspondence, Sub-Series 5, Letterpress Books, Box 31, folder 19.

[24] Carus to Dharmapala, June 25th, 1897, in The Open Court Publishing Co. Records, Series 1, Correspondence, Sub Series 5, Letterpress Books, Box 32, folder 2.

[25] Carus to Dharmapala, February 11th, 1897, in The Open Court Publishing Co. Records, Series 1 Correspondence, Sub Series 5, Letterpress Books, Box 31, folder 52.

[26] Carus to Dharmapala, December 9th, 1896, in The Open Court Publishing Co. Records, Series 1, Correspondence, Sub-Series 5, Letterpress Books, Box 31, folder 34. Most of Dharmapala's collected works and letters are in *Return to Righteousness: A Collection of Speeches, Essays, and Letters of the Anagarika Dharmapala* (Colombo: Ministry of Eba and Cultural Affairs, 1965).

[27] Carus to H. Dharmapala, June 22nd, 1897, in The Open Court Publishing Co. Records, Series 1, Correspondence, Sub Series 5, Letterpress Books, Box 32, folder 1.

[28] Carus to Dharmapala, July 8th, 1897, in The Open Court Publishing Co. Records, Series 1, Correspondence, Sub Series 5, Letterpress Books, Box 32, folder 6.

[29] Carus to Dharmapala, September 15th, 1897, in The Open Court Publishing Co. Records, Series 1, Correspondence, Sub Series 5, Letterpress Books, Box 32, folder 19.

[30] Carus to the Rev. P.A. Jinavaravansa, July 8, 1897, in The Open Court Publishing Co. Records, Series 1, Correspondence, Sub Series 5, Letterpress Books, Box 32, folders 5–6.

[31] Paul Carus, "The Parliament of Religions," 27, Open Court Publishing Co. Records, Box 280, folder 107.

[32] Quoted in Martin J. Verhoeven, "Introduction: The Dharma Through Carus's Lens," in Paul Carus, *The Gospel of Buddha: According to Old Records* (Chicago: Open Court Publishing Co., 2004), 43.

[33] Martin J. Verhoeven, "Americanizing the Buddha: Paul Carus and the Transformation of Asian Thought," in *The Faces of Buddhism in America*, eds. Charles S. Prebish and Kenneth K. Tanaka (Berkeley: University of California Press, 1998), 207.

[34] Shaku Soyen to Carus, December 16th, 1893, in Open Court Publishing Co. Records, Series 1, Correspondence, Box 2, folder 6.

[35] Carus to the Rt. Rev. Shaku Soyen, January 23, 1896, in Open Court Publishing Co. Records, Series 1, Correspondence, Sub-Section 5, Letterpress Books, Box 30, folder 63; Rev. John Henry Barrows, "A Controversy on Buddhism," *The Open Court*, 11 (1897), 46.

[36] Quoted in David L. McMahan, "Modernity and the Early Discourse of Scientific Buddhism," *Journal of the American Academy of Religion*, 72 (2004), 902; "Controversy on Buddhism Between the R. Rev. Shaku Soyen and the Rev. Dr. John Henry Barrows," *The Open Court*, 19 (1905), 43; 46.

[37] Shaku Soyen, *Sermons of a Buddhist Abbot* (Chicago: Open Court Publishing Company, 1906; web edition published by Global Grey, 2013), 71–72.

[38] The letter was reproduced in *The Open Court* in January 1897

[39] Soyen, *Sermons of a Buddhist Abbot*, 7, 14–20.

[40] Soyen, *Sermons of a Buddhist Abbot*, 45–50.

[41] Daisetz Teitaro Suzuki, "Translator's Preface," in Soyen, *Sermons of a Buddhist Abbot*, 1–2. The book was later retitled *Zen for Americans* (New York: Barnes and Noble, 1993).

[42] Soyen, *Sermons of a Buddhist Abbot*, 202–03, 211.

[43] John R. McRae, "Oriental Verities on the American Frontier: The 1893 World's Parliament of Religions and the Thought of Masao Abe," *Buddhist-Christian Studies,* 11 (1991), 28–30.

Chapter 5: Open Sesame

[1] Martin J. Verhoeven, "Introduction," in Paul Carus, *The Gospel of Buddha According to Old Records* (Chicago: Open Court, 2004), 3.

[2] David L. McMahan, "Modernity and the Early Discourse of Scientific Buddhism," *Journal of the American Academy of Religion*, 72 (2004), 914.

[3] Paul Carus, "Brahmanism and Buddhism, or, the Religion of Postulates and the Religion of Facts," *The Open Court*, 10 (1896), 4853.

[4] Quoted in Jackson, "The Meeting of East and West: The Case of Paul Carus," 82.

[5] Carus, "Buddhism and the Religion of Science," 4845.

[6] Carus to Walter H. Page, Esq., December 1st, 1893, Open Court Publishing Co. Records, Series 1, Correspondence, Sub Series 5, Letterpress Books, Box 29, folder 17.

[7] J.G.R. Forlong, "Through What Historical Channels did Buddhism Influence Early Christianity?" *The Open Court*, 1 (1887), 382–84; 416–18; 439–41.

[8] Quoted in Paul Carus, *Karma: A Story of Buddhist Ethics* (Chicago: Open Court Publishing Co., 1917), iv, 21.

[9] Carus, *The Dawn of a New Religious Era and Other Essays*, 31–32.

[10] Harold Henderson, *Catalyst for Controversy* (Carbondale: Southern Illinois University Press, 1993), 89.

[11] Suzuki note in file dated June 1952 on the eve of departure for Japan, The Open Court Publishing Co., Box 47, folder 44.1.

[12] Verhoeven, "Introduction," 7.

[13] Max Müller, *Chips from a German Workshop. Vol. I* (New York: Scribner, Armstrong, and Co., 1874), 221.

[14] Müller, *Chips from a German Workshop. Vol. I*, 243, 247.

[15] Carus to Soyen, January 10th, 1894, Open Court Publishing Co. Records, Series 1, Correspondence, Sub-series 5, Letterpress Books, Box 29, folder 22. See also Judith Snodgrass, "The Deployment of Western Philosophy in the Meiji Buddhist Revival," *Eastern Buddhist*, 30 (1997), 173–98.

[16] Paul Carus, *The Gospel of Buddha* (Chicago: Open Court Publishing Company, 1915), x. Read Notto R. Thelle, *Buddhism and Christianity in Japan: From Conflict to Dialogue, 1854–1899* (Honolulu: University of Hawaii Press, 1987).

[17] Verhoeven, "Introduction," 17–18.

[18] Verhoeven, "Introduction," 2.

[19] Shaku Soyen to Carus, March 25, 1894 in Open Court Publishing Co. Records, Series 1, Correspondence, Box 2, folder 7; Shaku Soyen to Carus, May 17th, 1894, in Open Court Publishing Co. Kakachi O'Hara. Records, Series 1, Correspondence, Box 2, folder 8.

[20] "A Japanese Translation of 'The Gospel of Buddha,'" *The Open Court*, 9 (1894), 4405. See also Judith Snodgrass, "'Budda no Fukuin': The Deployment of Paul Carus's 'Gospel of Buddha' in Meiji Japan," *Japanese Journal of Religious Studies*, 25 (1998), 326.

[21] Carus to Col. R.G. Ingersoll, July 2nd, 1895, in The Open Court Publishing Co. Records, Series 1, Correspondence, Sub-series 5, Letterpress Books, Box 30, folder 23; Carl T. Jackson, "The Meeting of East and West: The Case of Paul Carus," *Journal of the History of Ideas*, 29 (1968), 85. A Chinese version was made by Mr. Kakachi O'Hara of Otzu; a German edition by E.F.L. Gauss; a French translation by Dr. L. de Milloue; a Spanish by Dr. Federigo Rodriguez; and Dutch by Felix Orth. See Kakachi O'Hara to Carus, August 18th, 1894, in Open Court Publishing Co. Records, Series 1, Correspondence, Box 2, folder 9; Kakachi O'Hara to Carus, August 18th, 1894, in Open Court Publishing Co. Records, Series 1,

Correspondence, Box 2, folder 9; Carus to O'Hara, September 19th, 1895, in The Open Court Publishing Co. Records, Series 1, Correspondence, Sub-Series 5, Letterpress Books, Box 30, folder 36.

[22] Paul Carus, *The Gospel of Buddha* (Chicago: Open Court Publishing Company, 1915), v–vi.

[23] Thomas A. Tweed, *The American Encounter with Buddhism 1844–1912: Victorian Culture and the Limits of Dissent* (Bloomington: Indiana University Press, 1992), 65.

[24] Blouke Carus, "Preface," in Paul Carus, *The Gospel of Buddha According to Old Records* (Chicago: Open Court, 2004), xii.

[25] Bonney to Carus, Aril 29, 1895 in Open Court Publishing Co. Records, Series 1, Correspondence, Box 2, folder 12.

[26] George S. Goodspeed, "Review," *The Biblical World*, 4 (1894), 475–76.

[27] Joseph Estlin Carpenter, "Review," *New World*, 4 (1895), 157–58.

[28] George W. Gilmore, "Review," *The Biblical World*, 11 (1898), 284–86. Read Thomas Rhys Davids, *The Hibbert Lectures, 1881. Lectures on the Origin and Growth of Religion as Illustrated by Some Points in the History of Indian Buddhism* (London: Williams and Norgate, 1881); Thomas Rhys Davids, *American Lectures on the History of Religions. First Series. Buddhism Its History and Literature* (New York: G.P. Putnam's Sons, 1907 [1896]).

[29] E. Washburn Hopkins, "Review," *New World*, 7 (1898), 571–73.

[30] Judith Snodgrass, "'Budda no Fukuin': The Deployment of Paul Carus's 'Gospel of Buddha' in Meiji Japan," *Japanese Journal of Religious Studies*, 25 (1998), 322.

[31] Snodgrass, "'Budda no Fukuin'," 319–44.

[32] Paul Carus, "Buddhism and Christianity," *The Monist*, 5 (1894), 67, 83–85, 86–87.

[33] Thomas Rhys Davids, *Buddhist Birth Stories* (London: Routledge, 2000 [1880]), xliii.

[34] Rudolf Seydel, *Das Evangelium von Jesu in seinen Verhältnissen zu Buddhasage und Buddha-Lehre (Leipzig: Breitkopf und Härtel*, 1882); Rudolf Seydel, *Die Buddha-Legende und das Leben Jesu nach den Evangelien Erneute Prüfung ihres gegenseitigen Verhältnisses* (Weimar: E. Felber, 1897); Otto Pfleiderer, *The Early Christian Conception of Christ and Its Significance and Value in the History of Religion* (New York: Putnam, 1905 [1903]); Bergh van Eysinga, *Indische Einflüsse auf evangelische Erzählungen* (Göttingen: Vandenhoeck und Ruprecht, 1909); Albert J. Edmunds, *Buddhist and Christian Gospels* (Philadelphia: Innes, 1909).

[35] Albert J. Edmunds, "Buddhist Loans to Christianity," *The Monist*, 22 (1912), 136–37; Albert J. Edmunds, "A Buddhist Genesis," *The Monist*, 14 (1900), 207, 472.

[36] Carus, *Buddhism and Its Christian Critics* (Chicago: Open Court Publishing Co., 1897), 165–236; Paul Carus, "The Philosophical Basis of Christianity in Its Relation to Buddhism," *The Monist*, 8 (1894), 273; Paul Carus, "Buddhism and Christianity," *The Monist*, 5 (1891), 65; 8 (1894), 273.

[37] Carus, *The Gospel of Buddha*, xii–xv.

[38] Carus, "Buddhism and Christianity," 89, 93, 97–98, 100.

[39] Paul Carus, "Christianity as the Pleroma," *The Monist*, 14 (1903), 140–41.

[40] Paul Carus, *The Dharma, Or the Religion of Enlightenment* (rev. Chicago: Open Court Publishing Co., 1918 [1896]), iii, 6–7.

[41] Carus, *The Dharma of the Religion of Enlightenment*, 96–98.

[42] Paul Carus, *Buddhism and Its Christian Critics* (Chicago: The Open Court Publishing Company, 1897), 5.

[43] Carus, *Buddhism and Its Christian Critics*, 9.

[44] Carus, *Buddhism and Its Christian Critics*, 10–11.

[45] Carus, *Buddhism and Its Christian Critics*, 26–27, 83; Paul Carus, "Karma and Nirvana," *The Monist*, 4 (1890–91), 417.

[46] Carus, *Buddhism and Its Christian Critics*, 128, 131.

[47] Carus, *Buddhism and Its Christian Critics*, 142, 144–45.

[48] Carus, *Buddhism and Its Christian Critics*, 146, 150, 163.

[49] Carus to H. Dharmapala, February 26, 1896, in The Open Court Publishing Co. Records, Series 1, Correspondence, Sub-Series 5, Letterpress Books, Box 30, folder 71.

[50] Paul Carus, "Words and Their Meaning," *The Open Court*, 8 (1894), 4236.

[51] Paul Carus, "Brahmanism and Buddhism, or, the Religion of Postulates and the Religion of Facts," *The Open Court*, 10 (1896), 4853.

[52] Paul Carus, "Christianity as the Pleroma," *The Monist*, 14 (1903), 122–23.

Chapter 6: Land of Zen

[1] Palmer Rampell, "Laws that Refuse to be Stated: The Post-Sectarian Spiritualities of Emerson, Thoreau, and D.T. Suzuki," *The New England Quarterly*, 84 (2011), 629. This explains why Soyen eventually encouraged Suzuki to study under Carus as a means of gaining further insight into Western thought and culture. What better place than the publishing home of the *Open Court* and *Monist* magazines and their stable of international writers?

[2] Read Arthur Christy, *The Orient in American Transcendentalism: A Study of Emerson, Thoreau, and Alcott* (New York: Octagon Books, 1978 [1968])); Frederick Ives Carpenter, *Emerson and Asia* (New York: Haskell House, 1968).

[3] Rampell, "Laws that Refuse to be Stated: The Post-Sectarian Spiritualities of Emerson, Thoreau, and D.T. Suzuki," 623, 630–31.

[4] Thomas A. Tweed, "'The Seeming Anomaly of Buddhist Negation': American Encounters with Buddhist Distinctiveness, 1858–1877," 70–71.

[5] D.T. Suzuki, *Zen and Japanese Culture* (Princeton: Princeton University Press, 1959), 343–44.

[6] Rampell, "Laws that Refuse to Be Stated: The Post-Sectarian Spiritualities of Emerson, Thoreau, and D. T. Suzuki," 621–54.

[7] [Suzuki fragments, circa 1957], in Open Court Publishing Co. Records, Box 420, folder 21.

[8] Soyen to Carus, December 1st, 1895, in Open Court Publishing Co. Records, Series 1, Correspondence, Box 2, folder 15.

[9] Carus to Suzuki, February 26th, 1897, in Open Court Publishing Co. Records, Series 1, Correspondence, Sub Series 5, Letterpress Books, Box 31, folder 57.

[10] Carus to Mr. Sacksteder, March 6th, 1897, in The Open Court Publishing Co. Records, Series 1, Correspondence, Sub Series 5, Letterpress Books, Box 31, folder 62.

[11] Carus to Soyen, March 29th, 1897, in The Open Court Publishing Co. Records, Series 1, Correspondence, Sub Series 5, Letterpress Books, Box 31, folder 68.

[12] D.T. Suzuki, *Outlines of Mahayana Buddhism* (London: Luzac and Co., 1907), v–vii.

[13] [miscellaneous letters] Open Court Publishing Co. Records, Box 47, folder 44.

[14] Carus to Suzuki, September 13th, 1897, in The Open Court Publishing Co. Records, Series 1, Correspondence, Sub Series 5, Letterpress Books, Box 32, folder 18.

[15] Tomoe Moriya, "Social Ethics of 'New Buddhists' at the Turn of the Twentieth Century: A Comparative Study of Suzuki Daisetsu and Inoue Shuten," *Japanese Journal of Religious Studies*, 32 (2005), 283–304.

[16] Harold Bloom, ed., *The American Renaissance* (New York: Chelsea House, 2004), 42. Also read John S. Haller, Jr., *The History of New Thought* (West Chester: The Swedenborg Foundation Press, 2012).

[17] Thomas A. Tweed, "American Occultism and Japanese Buddhism: Albert J. Edmunds, D.T. Suzuki, and Translocative History," *Japanese Journal of Religious Studies*, 32 (2005), 255.

[18] Philangi Dasa's *Swedenborg the Buddhist* portrayed a dream conversation among several individuals—Swedenborg, a Buddhist monk, a Brahmin, a Parsi, a Chinese, an Aztec, an Icelander, and a woman—who recounted their respective religious beliefs in a form of Socratic dialogue that ultimately revealed that Swedenborg was to

all intents a Buddhist. See Herman Carl Vetterling, *Swedenborg the Buddhist; Or, the Higher Swedenborgianism, Its Secrets and Thibetan Origin* (Los Angeles: The Buddhist Swedenborgian Brotherhood, 1887).

[19] "Dicta of Swedenborg," *The Buddhist Ray*, 1 (1884), 1. There remains the question of whether Swedenborg ever became knowledgeable of the Buddhism of Mongolia and Tibet. In one instance he speaks of the "Great Tartary." "I have spoken with spirits and angels who came from there, and they said that they possess a Word and have from ancient times; and that their divine worship is performed according to this Word, which consists of pure correspondences . . . . They said that they worship Jehovah, some as an invisible, and some as a visible God. Moreover they said that they do not permit foreigners to come among them, except the Chinese, with whom they cultivate peace, because the emperor of China is from their country . . . . Seek for it in China, and perhaps you will find it there among the Tartars" (*Apocalypse Revealed*, §11).

[20] Quoted from Edmunds's Journal, dated July 18th, 1903, in Thomas A. Tweed, "American Occultism and Japanese Buddhism: Albert J. Edmunds, D. T. Suzuki, and Translocative History," *Japanese Journal of Religious Studies*, 32 (2005), 258.

[21] Quoted in Tweed, "American Occultism and Japanese Buddhism: Albert J. Edmunds, D.T. Suzuki, and Translocative History," 258.

[22] Suzuki to Mary Carus, December 24th, 1907, in Open Court Publishing Co. Records, Box 47, folder 44.

[23] Suzuki to Mary Carus, December 17th, 1907, in Open Court Publishing Co. Records, Box 47, folder 44.

[24] Suzuki to Hegeler, June 3rd, 1909, Open Court Publishing Co. Records, Box 47, folder 44.1.

[25] Hegeler to Suzuki, December 18th, 1909, in Open Court Publishing Co. Records, Box 47, folder 44.

[26] Paul Carus to Suzuki, June 26th, 1910, in Open Court Publishing Co., Box 47, folder 44.1.

[27] Carus to Suzuki, March 27th, 1911, in Open Court Publishing Co. Records, Box 47, folder 44.1.

[28] D.T. Suzuki "Introduction: A Glimpse of Paul Carus," in Joseph M. Kitagawa (ed.), *Modern Trends in World Religions: Paul Carus Memorial Symposium* (La Salle: Open Court, 1959), ix–xi.

[29] David Loy, "The Dharma of Emanuel Swedenborg: A Buddhist Perspective," *Buddhist-Christian Studies*, 16 (1996), 14, 18–19, 20.

[30] Read Rick Fields, *How the Swans Came to the Lake: A Narrative History of Buddhism in America* (Boston: Shambhala Publications, 1992).

[31] After D.T. Suzuki, the leading exponent of Zen to the West was the Buddhist-Christian dialogue of Masao Abe who had trained at

Kyoto University before studying at Union Theological Seminary and Columbia University. As pointed out by John R. McRae, "his ideas should not be taken to represent all of Buddhism, because they are so deeply informed by European and American intellectual categories." See John R. McRae, "Oriental Verities on the American Frontier: The 1893 World's Parliament of Religions and the Thought of Masao Abe," *Buddhist-Christian Studies*, 11 (1991), 8.

[32] D.T. Suzuki, "A Glimpse of Paul Carus," in Joseph M. Kitagawa, ed., *Modern Trends in World Religions: Paul Carus Memorial Symposium* (La Salle: The Open Court Publishing Co., 1959), ix, xiv.6

[33] Suzuki, "A Glimpse of Paul Carus," x.

[34] Carus, *The Philosophy of Form* (Chicago: The Open Court Publishing Co., 1911), 39, 43.

[35] But Zen also had its detractors. According to Dale Riepe, any examination of it will find it to be "an irrational, illogical, egoistical, cynical, anti-social, and self-righteous form of private fanaticism having little to do with the Buddhism of much of China, and less with the Buddhism of India." In a nutshell, Zen is "simply madness decked out as super-sense." It was a war with the world because that world did not conform to Zen's needs which preferred passivity, peace, subjectivity, and inwardness to science and the work syndrome. See Dale Riepe, "Discussion: Zen and the Scientific Outlook," *Philosophy of Science*, 31 (1964), 71, 73.

[36] Alan W. Watts, *The Way of Zen*: (New York: Pantheon, 1957), 17. See also Alan W. Watts, *The Spirit of Zen: A Way of Life, Work, and Art in the Far East*. New York: Grove Press, 1960 [1958].

[37] Thomas Merton, *Zen and the Birds of Appetite* (New York: New Directions Publishing Corp., 1968), 45, 61.

[38] Thomas Merton, *Mystics and Zen Masters* (New York: Farrar, Strauss and Giroux, 1967), 242.

[39] William F. Healy, "Thomas Merton's Evaluation of Zen," *Angelicum* 52 (1975), 397. Critics of Merton insisted that the experience of the former is a "matter of grace" which is "essentially beyond the experience of Zen." One represented aesthetic or natural contemplation while the other was an "intuitive gaze on God." See Healy, "Thomas Merton's Evaluation of Zen," 400.

[40] John Wright Buckham, "Return to the Truth in Mysticism," *The Monist*, 18 (1908), 67–74; "The New Mysticism," *The Homiletic Review*, 46 (1913), 8–13; John Wright Buckham, *Mysticism and Modern Life* (New York: The Abingdon Press, 1915).

[41] Paul Carus, "Mysticism," *The Monist*, 18 (1908), 78–79.

[42] Carus, "Mysticism," 82, 83, 110.

[43] Carus, "Mysticism," 79, 82.

Chapter 7: The Three Amigos

[1] Paul Carus, *The Dawn of a New Religious Era and Other Essays* (Chicago: Open Court Publishing Company, 1899), 10; Paul Carus, "The World's Religious Parliament Extension," *The Monist*, 5 (1891), 345.

[2] Paul Carus, "The World's Religious Parliament Extension," in *The World's Parliament of Religions and the Religious Parliament Extension* (Chicago: R.R. Donnelley and Sons Co., 1896), 36, 38.

[3] "Hegeler Institute," [c1893] *Open Court Publishing Co. Records*, Series 2, Box 63, folder 98.

[4] Paul Carus, "The American Congress of Liberal Religious Societies," *The Open Court*, 9 (1895), 4531.

[5] Paul Carus, "The World's Religious Parliament Extension," *The Monist*, 5 (1895), 345; "The Parliament of Religions," *Review of Reviews*, 11 (1895), 695.

[6] Pandit G. Krishna Sastri, *Life and Work of an Indian Saint: Being the Autobiography of Swami Sivaganacharya, a Great Social Reformer and Religious Teacher* (Mylapore, Madras: Vedic Mission, 1912), 66–68.

[7] Bonney to Carus, June 22, 1895 in Open Court Publishing Co. Records, Series 1, Correspondence, Box 2, folder 13; Carus to Caswell Ellis, Esq., February 3, 1894, Open Court Publishing Co. Records, Series 1, Correspondence, Sub-series 5, Letterpress Books, Box 29, folder 25; Carus to Isaac Keeler, Esq., September 11th, 1895, in The Open Court Publishing Co. Records, Series 1, Correspondence, Sub-Series 5, Letterpress Books, Box 30, folder 35; "The Progress of World's Congress Extension," p. 1, Open Court Publishing Co. Records, Box 280, folder 109.

[8] "Minutes of the Local Committee for the Establishment of a World's Religious League," Open Court Publishing Co. Records, Box 281, folder 2. See also Merwin-Marie Snell, "Modern Theosophy in its Relation to Hinduism and Buddhism," *The Biblical World*, 5 (1895), 200–05.

[9] Paul Carus, "Is a Religious Union Possible?" [draft speech], Open Court Publishing Co. Records, Box 280, folder 112.

[10] Gustave Carus, "The Religious Parliament Idea," *The Open Court*, 47 (1933), 348.

[11] "A Continuation of the Religious Parliament," The Open Court Publishing Co. Records, Series 1, Correspondence, Sub-Series 5, Letterpress Books, Box 31, folder 30.

[12] Bonney to Carus, June 13th, 1895 in Open Court Publishing Co. Records, Series 1, Correspondence, Box 2, folder 13.

[13] Carus to Bonney, July 5th, 1895. Open Court Publishing Co. Records, Series 1, Correspondence, Sub-series 5, Letterpress Books, Box 30, folder 23.

[14] Carus to Swami Vivekananda, July 5th, 1895, in Open Court Publishing Co. Records, Series 1, Correspondence, Sub-series 5, Letterpress Books, Box 30, folder 23.

[15] Carus to Bonney, December 8th, 1896, in The Open Court Publishing Co. Records, Series 1, Correspondence, Sub-Series 5, Letterpress Books, Box 31, folder 34.

[16] Paul Carus, *The Dawn of a New Era and Other Essays* (Chicago: The Open Court Publishing Co., 1899), 10, 17.

[17] Circulatory letter sent by Paul Carus as Secretary to the Religious Parliament Extension, July 10th, 1897, in Open Court Publishing Co. Records, Box 281, folder 1.

[18] Benjamin Arnett, Secretary of Bishop's Council, African, Methodist, Episcopal Church, to Carus, March 12, 1894, in Open Court Publishing Co. Records, Series 1, Correspondence, Box 2, folder 7.

[19] H. Dharmapala to Carus, April 10th, 1894 in Open Court Publishing Co. Records, Series 1, Correspondence, Box 2, folder 7.

[20] [letters to the editor supporting the World's Parliament of Religions Extension], Open Court Publishing Co. Records, Box 280, folder 113.

[21] Paul Carus, "Responses," Open Court Publishing Co. Records, Box 281, folder 1.

[22] M. Phillips to Paul Carus, September 8th, 1897, in Open Court Publishing Co. Records, Box 281, folder 1.

[23] George E. Post to Paul Carus, August 15th, 1897 in Open Court Publishing Co. Records, Box 281, folder 1. See also Henry H. Jessup to Paul Carus, November 4th, 1897, in Open Court Publishing Co. Records, Box 281, folder 1.

[24] Pamphlet, "Universal Religion Formulated: in reply to a letter which is printed on the back of this leaf, and which, along with a report, printed in book form, was received from Paul Carus," in Open Court Publishing Company Records, Box 281, folder 1.

[25] Letter from Ernst Faber to Paul Carus, September 14th, 1897, Open Court Publishing Co. Records, Box 281, folder 1.

[26] John Ireland to Paul Carus, July 16th, 1897, in Open Court Publishing Co. Records, Box 281, folder 1.

[27] Elisha Benjamin Andrews to Paul Carus, July 16th, 1897, Open Court Publishing Co. Records, Box 281, folder 1.

[28] Carlos Hugo Parra, "Standing with Unfamiliar Company on Uncommon Ground: The Catholic Church and the Chicago Parliaments of Religions," (Ph.D. Dissertation, Toronto: University of Toronto, 2012), 30.

[29] Carus to Abbé V. Charbonnel, November 26th, 1895, in The Open Court Publishing Co. Records, Series 1, Correspondence, Sub-series 5, Letterpress Books, Box 30, folder 49.

[30] Carus to Abbé Victor Charbonnel, May 20th, 1896, in The Open Court Publishing Co. Records, Series 1, Correspondence, Sub Series 5, Letterbox Books, Box 30, folder 61.

[31] Carus to Dharmapala, November 21st, 1895, in The Open Court Publishing Co. Records, Series 1, Correspondence, Sub-Series 5, Letterpress Books, Box 30, folder 48.

[32] Carus to Bonney, October 28th, 1895, in The Open Court Publishing Co. Records, Series 1, Correspondence, Sub-Series 5, Letterpress Books, Box 30, folder 44.

[33] Carus to L. Arréat, Esq., May 27th, 1895, in the Open Court Publishing Co. Records, Series 1, Correspondence, Box 2, folder 12; Paul Carus, "The Reason Why Abbé Charbonnel Failed," *The Open Court*, 12 (1898), 300; Victor Charbonnel, "An Explanation in Reply to 'The Reason Why Abbé Charbonnel Failed,'" *The Open Court*, 13 (1899), 36.

[34] Carus to Bonney, June 23, 1895 in Open Court Publishing Co. Records, Correspondence, Sub-series 5, Letterpress Books, Box 30, folder 21. See Lucian Arréat, "Religion in France," *The Monist*, 13 (1899), 235.

[35] Parra, "Standing with Unfamiliar Company on Uncommon Ground: The Catholic Church and the Chicago Parliaments of Religions," 79.

[36] "European Opinions on the Second Parliament of Religions," *The Open Court*, X (1896), 4807–4810.

[37] Carus to William Pipe, May 18th, 1897 in The Open Court Publishing Co. Records, Series 1, Correspondence, Sub Series 5, Letterpress Books, Box 31, folder 79.

[38] The Congress's planning committee established eight sections: (1) religions of non-civilized peoples and of pre-Columbian America; (2) religions of the extreme Orient; (3) religions of Egypt; (4) Semitic religions; (5) religions of India and Persia; (6) religions of Greece and Rome; (7) religions of the Germans, Celts, Slavs, and pre-historical archeology of Europe; and (8) history of Christianity. Read Jean Réville, "The International Congress of the History of Religions, September 3rd–9th, 1900," *The Open Court*, 14 (1900), 271–76; Lucien Arréat, "Congress of the History of Religions and the Congress of Bourges," *The Open Court*, 14 (1900), 700.

[339] Resolution passed at a meeting of the Officers of the Religious Parliament Extension, undated, in Open Court Publishing Co. Records, Box 281, folder 2.

[40] Quoted in Parra, "Standing with Unfamiliar Company on Uncommon Ground: The Catholic Church and the Chicago Parliaments of Religions," 84.

[41] Carl T. Jackson, "The Meeting of East and West: The Case of Paul Carus," *Journal of the History of Ideas*, 29 (1968), 86.

[42] Carus to Miss Sarah J. Farmer, June 21th, 1897 in The Open Court Publishing Co. Records, Series 1, Correspondence, Sub Series 5, Letterpress Books, Box 32, folder 1.

[43] Robert P. Richardson, "The Rise and Fall of the Parliament of Religions at Greenacre," *The Open Court*, 45 (1931), 129–166.

[44] Winston L. King, "Eastern Religions: A New Interest and Influence," *Annals of the American Academy of Political and Social Science*, 387 (1970), 66–76.

[45] Amy Kittelstrom, "The International Social Turn: Unity and Brotherhood at the World's Parliament of Religions, Chicago, 1893," *Religion and American Culture; A Journal of Interpretation* 19 (2009), 244.

Chapter 8: The Unitary Whole

[1] Carus, *The Philosophy of Form*, 19, 25, 28.

[2] Carus, *The Philosophy of Form*, 34.

[3] Dale Riepe, "The Indian Influence in American Philosophy: Emerson to Moore," *Philosophy East and West*, 17 (1967), 125–137. See also William James, *The Varieties of Religious Experience* (New York: The Modern Library, n.d.); Josiah Royce, *Spirit of Modern Philosophy* (Boston: Houghton Mifflin and Co., 1899); Josiah Royce, *The World and the Individual* (New York: Macmillan Co., 1904); Kurt Leidecker, *Josiah Royce and Indian Thought* (New York: Kailas Press, 1931); Irving Babbitt, *The Dhammapada* (New York: Oxford University Press, 1936); Read David Scott, "William James and Buddhism: American Pragmatism and the Orient," *Religion*, 30 (2000), 1–20; Van Meter Ames, *Zen and American Thought* (Honolulu: University of Hawaii Press, 1982); Arthur Christy, *The Orient in American Transcendentalism* (New York: Columbia University Press, 1932).

[4] Van Meter Ames, "Zen and Pragmatism," *Philosophy East and West*, 4 (1954), 19–33.

[5] William James, *Varieties of Religious Experience* (New York: Longmans, Green and Co., 1917 [1902]), 31–32.

[6] Read Dale Riepe, "A Note on William James and Indian Philosophy," *Philosophy and Phenomenological Research*, 28 (1968), 587–90.

[7] Read Bonnie Thurston, "A Christian's Appreciation of the Buddha," *Buddhist-Christian Studies*, 19 (1999), 121–28.

[8] Clarence H. Hamilton, "Buddhism Resurgent," *The Journal of Religion*, 17 (1937), 30–36.

[9] Randolph Crump Miller, "William James and the American Scene," *American Journal of Theology and Philosophy*, 15 (1994), 3–14.

[10] Henry James, ed., *The Letters of William James* (2 vols.; Boston: The Atlantic Monthly Press, 1920), II, 203–04.

[11] Read David Dilworth, "The Initial Formations of 'Pure Experience' in Nishida Kitaro and William James," *Monumenta Nipponica*, 24 (1969), 93–111; Miranda Shaw, "William James and Yogacara Philosophy: A Comparative Inquiry," *Philosophy East and West*, 37 (1987), 223–44.

[12] Joseph John, "David Kalupahana on William James and the Development of Early Buddhism," *William James Studies*, 10 (2013), 1–10.

[13] William James, "Pragmatism, (1909)" in *Pragmatism and Other Writings* (New York: Penguin Books, 2000), 98.

[14] Paul Carus, *The Surd of Metaphysics* (Chicago: Open Court Publishing Co., 1908), 165; Paul Carus, "Truth," *Monist*, 20 (1910), 507.

[15] Donald Harvey Meyer, "Paul Carus and the Religion of Science," *American Quarterly*, 14 (1962), 601.

[16] Donald H. Bishop, "The Carus-James Controversy," *Journal of the History of Ideas*, 35 (1974), 510–11.

[17] William James, *Pragmatism* (New York: Longmans, Green and Co., 1907), 76.

[18] James, *Pragmatism*, 201.

[19] Carus, *Homilies of Science*, 58.

[20] Carus, *Fundamental Problems*, 5–6.

[21] Paul Carus, *The Ethical Problem* (Chicago: Open Court Publishing Co., 1910), xii.

[22] Carus, *The Religion of Science*, 8.

[23] Carus, *The Dawn of a New Religious Era and Other Essays*, 28.

[24] Carus, *The Dawn of a New Religious Era and Other Essays*, 25–26.

[25] Paul Carus, "Pragmatism," *The Monist*, 18 (1908), 329, 345–46.

[26] Read Paul Carus, *Truth on Trial, An Exposition of the Nature of Truth* (Chicago: Open Court Publishing Co., 1911), 46, 51.

[27] Carus, *The Philosophy of Form*, 1–3, 5, 13.

[28] The Series included books on Animism, Pantheism, Judaism, Islam, Buddhism, Hinduism, the religions of ancient Israel, Mexico, Rome, Japan, Persia, and Peru; the Psychology of Religion, and others.

[29] "Notes" *The Open Court*, X (1896), 5141.

[30] Carus to Miss Marie Howland, January 4th, 1896, in Open Court Publishing Co. Records, Series 1, Correspondence, Sub Series 5, Box 31, folder 40, p. 302.

[31] Henderson, *Catalyst for Controversy*, 41; Constance Myers, "Paul Carus and the Open Court: The History of a Journal," *American Studies*, 5 (1964), 57–68.

[32] Carl T. Jackson, "The Meeting of East and West: The Case of Paul Carus," *Journal of the History of Ideas*, 29 (1968), 75.

[33] Carus to John M Pryce, Esq., New York, in Open Court Publishing Co. Records, Series 1, Correspondence, Sub-series 5, Letterpress Books, Box 29, folder 7, p. 135.

[34] Harold Henderson, *Catalyst for Controversy* (Carbondale: Southern Illinois University Press, 1993), 144.

[35] Donald Harvey Meyer, "Carus and the Religion of Science," *Journal of the History of Ideas*, 29 (1968), 606.

[36] Carus to Professor C.L. Herrick, Denison University, November 1st, 1893, Open Court Publishing Co. Records, Series 1, Correspondence, sub-series 5, Letterpress, Box 29, folder 14, p. 272.

[37] Paul Carus, "Scholaromania," *The Open Court*, 9 (1895), 4435.

[38] Paul Carus, "Made in America" [editorial], *The Open Court*, 29 (1915), 503–505.

[39] Paul Carus, "Anglo-Saxon and Teuton," *The Open Court*, 31 (1917), 117; Arminius, "Beilliss-Trial Government, The Russian Autocracy and Its Dupes," *Ibid.*, 65; Paul Carus, "British Failure," *Ibid.*, 124; Paul Carus, "An Italian War Hero," *Ibid.*, 439; Paul Carus, "Pro-Ally Literature," *Ibid.*, 690; Paul Carus, "Slave and Goth," *Ibid.*, 569; Albert Gehring, "German Contributions to our National Achievement," *Ibid.*, 109; Joseph W. Pennypacker, "An American Judgment of Germany's Cause," *Ibid.*, 89; Riccardo Cipriani, "Letters of an Italian Officer to his Sister in America," *Ibid.*, 414.

[40] Roger Thomas, "Letter to Editor," *New York Tribune*, September 17th, 1917.

[41] J.P. Kantor, "Obituary," *The Journal of Philosophy, Psychology, and Scientific Methods*, 16 (1919), 223–24; David Eugene Smith, "Mary Hegeler Carus, 1861–1936," *The American Mathematical Monthly*, 44 (1937), 280–83.

Bibliography

Books

Abe, Masao, ed. *A Zen Life: D.T. Suzuki Remembered.* New York: Weatherhill, 1986.

Abell, George, and Barry Singer. *Science and the Paranormal.* London: Junction Books, 1981.

Adams, Henry. *The Education of Henry Adams.* New York: Modern Library, 1918.

———. *Letters of Henry Adams. (1858-1891).* Edited by Worthington Chauncey Ford, Boston: Houghton Mifflin, 1930.

Ahlstrom, Sidney. *A Religious History of the American People.* New Haven: Yale University Press, 1972.

Albanese, Catherine. *American: Religion and Religions.* Belmont: Wadsworth, 1981.

———. *A Republic of Mind and Spirit: A Cultural History of American Metaphysical Religion.* New Haven: Yale University Press, 2007.

Allen, Grant. *Charles Darwin.* London: Longmans, Green and Co., 1885.

Almond. Philip C. *The British Discovery of Buddhism.* Cambridge: Cambridge University Press, 1990.

American Section Headquarters. *The Theosophical Congress Held by the Theosophical Society at the Parliament of Religions.* New York; American Section Headquarters, 1893.

Ames, Van Meter. *Zen and American Thought.* Honolulu: University of Hawaii Press, 1982.

Ando, Shoei. *Zen and American Transcendentalism.* Tokyo: Hokuseido Press, 1970.

Andrick, John Michael. *A Modern Mecca of Psychic Forces: The Psychical Science Congress and the Culture of Progressive Occultism in Fin-de Siècle Chicago, 1885–1900.* Ph.D. Dissertation, Urbana: University of Illinois, 2016.

Bibliography

Arai, Nissatsu. *Outlines of the Doctrine of the Nichiren Sect.* Tokyo: Nihiren Sect, 1893.

Arnold, Sir Edwin. *The Light of Asia, or The Great Renunciation (Mahabhinishkramana), Being the Life and Teaching of Gautama.* Los Angeles: The Theosophical Company, 1879, 1977.

Ashvagosha, Patriarch. *The Awakening of Faith in the Mahayana Doctrine—The New Buddhism.* Shanghai: Christian Literature Society, 1907.

Babbitt, Edwin Dwight. *Religion as Revealed by the Material and Spiritual Universe.* New York: Babbitt and Co., 1881.

———. *The Dhammapada.* New York: New Directions Publishing, 1936.

Barborka, G. A. *The Mahatmas and Their Letters.* Madras; Theosophical Publishing House, 1973.

Barbour, Ian G. *Religion and Science. Historical and Contemporary Issues.* San Francisco: HarperSanFranscisco, 1997.

Barker, A. Trevor, ed. *The Mahatma Letters to A.P. Sinnett.* London: Rider and Co., 1926.

Barrows, John Henry, ed. *The World's Parliament of Religions: An Illustrated and Popular Story of the World's First Parliament of Religions, Held in Chicago in Connection with the Columbian Exposition of 1893.* 2 vols.; Chicago: Parliament Publishing Company, 1893.

Batchelor, Stephen. *The Awakening of the West: The Encounter of Buddhism and Western Culture.* Berkeley: Parallax Press, 1997.

Bellah, Robert, and Richard Madsen, William Sullivan, Ann Swidler, and Steven M. Tipton. *Habits of the Heart: Individualism and Commitment in American Life.* Berkeley: University of California Press, 1985.

Bigelow, W.S. *Buddhism and Immortality. The Ingersoll Lecture 1908.* Boston: Houghton Mifflin, 1908.

Bisland, Elizabeth. *The Life and Letters of Lafcadio Hearn.* Boston: Houghton Mifflin, 1906.

Blavatsky, H.P. *Isis Unveiled: A Master-Key to the Mysteries of Ancient and Modern Science and Theology.* 2 vols., New York: J.W. Bouton, 1892 [1877].

———. *The Secret Doctrine.* 2 vols., London, England: The Theosophical Publishing Co., 1888.

———. *The Key to Theosophy.* London: Theosophical Publishing Company, 1889.

Bloom, Harold, ed. *The American Renaissance.* New York: Chelsea House, 2004.

Bond, George D. *The Buddhist Revival in Sri Lanka: Religious Tradition, Reinterpretation, and Response.* Columbia: University of South Carolina Press, 1988.

Bose, Churesh Chunder. *The Life of Protap Chunder Mozoomdar.* 2 vols.; Calcutta: Nababidhan Trust, 1940.

Boucher, Sandy. *Turning the Wheel: American Women Creating the New Buddhism.* Boston: Beacon Press, 1993.

Braude, Ann. *Radical Spirits: Spiritualism and Women's Rights in Nineteenth-Century America.* Bloomington: Indiana University Press, 1989.

Brazier, David. *The New Buddhism.* New York: Palgrave, 2001.

Britten, Emma Hardinge. *Nineteenth Century Miracles: Spirits and Their Work in Every Country of the Earth.* New York: William Britten, 1884.

Brooks, Van Wyck. *Fenollosa and His Circle, With Other Essays in Biography.* New York: E.P. Dutton, 1962.

Brownson, Orestes Augustus. *New Views of Christianity, Society, and the Church.* Boston: James Munroe and Company, 1836.

Buchanan, Joseph Rodes. *Manual of Psychometry: The Dawn of a New Civilization.* Boston: Joseph R. Buchanan, 1885.

Buckham, John Wright. *Mysticism and Modern Life.* New York: Abingdon Press, 1915.

The Buddha. *The Sutra of Forty-two Sections and Two Other Short Sutras.* Kyoto: Buddhist Propagation Society, 1892.

Buddhadasa, Bhikkhu. *Christianity and God.* Bangkok: Sinclair Thompson, Memorial Lecture, 1967.

Burg, David F. *Chicago's White City of 1893.* Lexington: University Press of Kentucky, 1976.

Burke, Marie Louise. *Swami Vivekananda in the West: New Discoveries. The World Teacher.* Calcutta: Advaita Ashrama, 1985.

Burnouf, Eugène. *Introduction a l'Histoire du Buddhisme indien.* Paris: Imprimerie Royal, 1844.

Butler, Alison. *Victorian Occultism and the Making of Modern Magic.* Houndmills: Palgrave Macmillan, 2011.

Cafaro, Philip. *Thoreau's Living Ethics: Walden and the Pursuit of Virtue.* Athens: University of Georgia Press, 2004.

Cameron, Kenneth Walter. *Emerson's Transcendentalism and British Swedenborgism.* Hartford: Transcendental Books, 1984.

Canavarro, Marie deSaiza. *Insight into the Far East.* Los Angeles: Wetzel Publishing Company, 1925.

Carpenter, Frederic Ives. *Emerson and Asia.* New York: Haskell House, 1968.

Carter. Paul. *The Spiritual Crisis of the Gilded Age.* De Kalb: Northern Illinois University Press, 1971.

Carus, Paul. *Amitabha: A Story of Buddhist Theology.* Chicago: Open Court Publishing Co., 1906

———. *Buddhism and Its Christian Critics.* Chicago: Open Court, 1897.

———. *Buddhist Hymns: Versified Translations from the Dhammapada and Various Other Sources. Adapted to Modern Music*. Chicago: The Open Court Publishing Company, 1911.
———. *The Dawn of a New Religious Era and Other Essays.* Chicago: Open Court, 1916.
———. *The Dharma, Or, the Religion of Enlightenment, An Exposition of Buddhism.* Chicago: Open Court Publishing Co., 1918.
———. *The Ethical Problem.* Chicago: Open Court Publishing Co., 1910.
———. *Fundamental Problems: The Method of Philosophy as a Systematic Arrangement of Knowledge*. Preface to the First Edition. Kila: Kessinger Publishing, 2004.
———. *God; An Enquiry into the Nature of Man's Highest Ideal and a Solution of the Problem from the Standpoint of Science.* Chicago: The Open Court Publishing Co., 1908.
———. *Godward: A Record of Religious Progress.* Chicago: Open Court Publishing Co., 1898.
———. *The Gospel of Buddha.* Chicago: Open Court, 1904.
———. *The Gospel of Buddhism, Compiled from Ancient Records.* Chicago: Open Court, 1915.
———. *The Gospel of Buddha According to Old Records.* Chicago: Open Court, 2004.
———. *Homilies of Science.* Chicago: Open Court, 1892.
———. *The Idea of God.* Chicago: The Open Court Publishing Co., 1886.
———. *Karma: A Story of Buddhist Ethics*. Chicago: Open Court Publishing, 1917 [1894].
———. Letters to and from D.T. Suzuki, Anagarika Dharmapala, Shaku Soyen, Zitsuzen Ashitsu and others at the Paul Carus Collection/Morris Library, Southern Illinois University, Carbondale.
———. *Monism and Meliorism. A Philosophical Essay on Causality and Ethics.* New York: F.W. Christern, 1885.
———. *Philosophy as a Science: A Synopsis of the Writings of Dr. Paul Carus.* Chicago: Open Court, 1909.
———. *The Philosophy of Form.* Chicago: The Open Court Publishing Co., 1911.
———. *The Philosophy of the Tool.* Chicago: The Open Court Publishing Co., 1893.
———. *The Pleroma. An Essay on the Origin of Christianity*. Chicago: The Open Court Publishing Co., 1893.
———. *Primer of Philosophy.* Chicago: The Open Court Publishing Co., 1893.
———. *The Religion of Science.* Chicago: Open Court, 1893; 1896.
———. *The Soul of Man.* Chicago: Open Court Publishing Co., 1891.

———. *The Surd of Metaphysics.* Chicago: Open Court Publishing Co., 1908.

———. *Truth on Trial, An Exposition of the Nature of Truth.* Chicago: Open Court Publishing Co., 1911.

———. *Whence and Whither? An Inquiry into the Nature of the Soul, Its Origin and Destiny.* Chicago: Open Court Publishing Company, 1903.

Chari, V.K. *Whitman in the Light of Vedantic Mysticism: An Interpretation.* Lincoln: University of Nebraska Press, 1965.

Chisholm, Lawrence. *Fenollosa: The Far East and American Culture.* New Haven: Yale University Press, 1963.

Christy, Arthur E. *The Orient in American Transcendentalism: A Study of Emerson, Thoreau, and Alcott.* New York: Octagon Books, 1978 [1968].

Clarke, James Freeman. *Ten Great Religions: An Essay in Comparative Theology.* Boston: Osgood and Co., 1871.

Clarke, John. *Oriental Enlightenment: The Encounter Between Asian and Western Thought.* London: Routledge, 1997.

Clayton, Mary Kupiec. *Emerson's Emergence: Self and Society in the Transformation of New England, 1800–1845.* Chapel Hill: University of North Carolina Press, 1989.

Cobb, John. *Beyond Dialogue. Towards a Mutual Transformation of Christianity and Buddhism.* Philadelphia: Fortress Press, 1987.

Cohen, Paul A. *Discovering History in China; American Historical Writing on the Recent Chinese Past.* New York: Columbia University Press, 1997.

Conway, Moncure. *My Pilgrimage to the Wise Men of the East.* Boston and New York: Houghton, Mifflin, and Company, 1906.

Copleston, Frederick. *Religion and One. Philosophies East and West.* London: Search Press, 1982.

Cotkin, George. *William James: Public Philosopher.* Baltimore: Johns Hopkins University Press, 1990.

Cousin, Victor. *Cours d'histoire de la philosophie.* 2 vols. Paris: Didier, Libraire-éditeur, 1840.

Crunden, Robert M. *A Brief History of American Culture.* New York: Paragon House, 1994.

Cunningham, A. *The Bhilsa Topes, or Buddhist Monuments of Central India.* London, 1854.

Dewey, John. *Art as Experience.* New York: Putnam's, 1934.

Dhar, Sailendra Nath. *A Comprehensive Biography of Swami Vivekananda.* Madras: Vivekananda Prakashan Kendra, 1975.

Dharmapala, Angarika. *Return to Righteousness: A Collection of Speeches, Essays and Letters of the Anagarika Dharmapala.* Colombo: Government Press, 1965.

Dodin, Thierry, and Heinz Räther, eds. *Imagining Tibet: Perceptions, Projections, and Fantasies.* Somerville: Wisdom Publications, 2001.

Doyle, Arthur Conan. *The History of Spiritualism.* 2 vols. New York: G.H. Doran, 1926.

Dulles, Foster Rhea. *Yankees and Samurai: America's Role in the Emergence of Modern Japan, 1791–1900.* New York: Harper and Row, 1965.

Dumoulin, Heinrich. *Christianity Meets Buddhism.* La Salle: Open Court, 1974.

———. *Zen Buddhism in the Twentieth Century.* New York: Weatherhill, 1992.

Dunston, Susan L. *Emerson and Environmental Ethics.* Lanham: Lexington Books, 2018.

Edmunds, Albert J. *Buddhist and Christian Gospels.* Philadelphia: Innes, 1909.

Eliot, Charles. *Hinduism and Buddhism.* 2 vols. London: Edward Arnold, 1921.

Elwood, Robert. *Theosophy: A Modern Expression of the Wisdom of the Ages.* Wheaton: Quest Books, 2014.

Emerson, Ralph Waldo. *The Complete Works of Ralph Waldo Emerson.* Boston and New York: Houghton, Mifflin and Company, 1903–1904.

———. *Emerson's Essays: First and Second Series.* New York: Thomas Y. Crowell, 1926.

———. *Indian Superstition. Edited with a Dissertation on Emerson's Orientalism at Harvard by Kenneth Walker Cameron.* Hanover: The Friends of Dartmouth Library, 1954.

———. *Selected Writings of Ralph Waldo Emerson.* New York: Signet Classic, 2003.

———. *The Spiritual Emerson: Essential Writing.* Edited by David M. Robinson. Boston: Beacon Press, 2003.

Eliot, Charles. *Hinduism and Buddhism.* 2 vols.; London: Edward Arnold, 1921.

———. *Japanese Buddhism.* London: Kegan Paul International, 2005.

Elliott, G.R. *Humanism and Imagination.* Chapel Hill: The University of North Carolina Press, 1938.

Ellwood, Robert S. *Alternative Altars: Unconventional and Eastern Spirituality in America.* Chicago: University of Chicago Press, 1979.

———. *The Eagle and the Rising Sun: Americans and the New Religions of Japan.* Philadelphia: Westminster, 1974.

Eysinga, Bergh van. *Indische Einflusse auf evangelische Erzählungen.* Göttingen: Vandenhoeck und Ruprecht, 1909.

Fenollosa, Ernest. *Epochs of Chinese and Japanese Art*. Edited by Mary Fenollosa. 2 vols. London: Heinemann, 1912. Revised edition, New York: Stokes, 1921.

Ferguson, Christine. *Determined Spirits.* Edinburgh: Edinburgh University Press, 2012.

Fields, Rick. *How the Swans Came to the Lake: A Narrative History of Buddhism in America.* Boston: Shambala Publications, 1992 [1981].

Foner, Eric. *Who Owns History? Rethinking the Past in a Changing World.* New York: Hill and Wang, 2002.

Ford, Marcus. *William James's Philosophy.* Amherst: University of Massachusetts Press, 1982.

Frothingham, Octavius Brooks. *Transcendentalism in New England: A History.* New York: G.P. Putnam, 1876.

Fuller, Robert C. *Mesmerism and the American Cure of Souls.* Philadelphia: University of Pennsylvania Press, 1982.

———. *Spiritual, but Not Religious: Understanding Unchurched America.* New York: Oxford University Press, 2001.

Gandhi, Mahatma. *The Gandhi Reader: A Sourcebook of His Life and Writings*. Edited by Homer A. Jack. New York: Grove Press, 1994.

Gombrich, Richard, and Gananath Obeyesekere. *Buddhism Transformed: Religious Change in Sri Lanka.* Princeton: Princeton University Press, 1988.

Guénon, René. *Theosophy: History of a Pseudo-Religion.* Hillsdale: Sophia Perennis, 2004.

Gura, Philip F. *American Transcendentalism: A History.* New York: Hill and Wang, 2007.

Halbfass, Wilhelm. *India and Europe: An Essay in Understanding.* Albany: State University of New York Press, 1988.

Haller, Jr., John S. *The History of New Thought: From Mind Cure to Positive Thinking and the Prosperity Gospel.* West Chester: Swedenborg Foundation Press, 2012.

Hamilton, Charles H. *Buddhism: A Religion of Infinite Compassion.* New York: The Liberal Arts Press, 1952,

Hanson, J.W., ed. *The World's Congress of Religions: Addresses and Papers Delivered Before the Parliament.* Chicago: W.B. Conkey, 1894.

Harding, John S. *Mahayana Phoenix: Japan's Buddhists at the 1893 World's Parliament of Religions.* New York: Peter Lang, 2008.

Hardy, R. Spence. *A Manual of Buddhism in Its Modern Development.* London, 1850.

Hayward, Jeremy W. *Shifting Worlds, Changing Minds: Where the Sciences and Buddhism Meet.* Boston: Shambhala, 1999.

Hearn, Lafcadio. *Lafcadio Hearn's Japan: An Anthology of His Writings on the Country and Its People*. Edited and with and introduction by Donald Richie. Tokyo, Japan: Tuttle, 1997.

———. *Lafcadio Hearn: Japan's Great Interpreter: A New Anthology of His Writings: 1894–1904.* Edited by Louis Allen and Jean Wilson. New York: Routledge, 1992.

———. *The Writings of Lafcadio Hearn.* Boston and New York, Houghton Mifflin Company, 1922.

Helmstadter, Richard J., and Bernard Lightman, eds. *Victorian Faith in Crisis: Essays on Continuity and Change in Nineteenth-Century Religious Belief.* Stanford: Stanford University Press, 1991.

Henderson, Harold. *Catalyst for Controversy: Paul Carus of Open Court.* Carbondale: Southern Illinois University Press, 1993.

———. 2006, *Let's Kill Dick and Jane: How the Open Court Publishing Company Fought the Culture of American Education*. St. Augustine's Press.

Hesig, James W., and John C. Maraldo, eds. *Rude Awakenings: Zen, the Kyoto School, and the Question of Nationalism.* Honolulu: University of Hawaii Press, 1994.

Hickey, Wakoh Shannon. *Mind Cure: How Meditation Became Medicine.* New York: Oxford University Press, 2019.

Hitchcock, Ethan Allen. *Remarks on Alchemy and the Alchemists.* Boston: Crosby, Nichols, and Co., 1857.

———. *Swedenborg, a Hermetic Philosopher.* New York: Appleton and Co., 1858.

Holland, David F. *Sacred Borders: Continuing Revelation and Canonical Restraint in Early America.* New York: Oxford University Press, 2011.

Holmes, Oliver Wendell. *Ralph Waldo Emerson John Lothrop Motley, Two Memoirs*. Boston and New York: Houghton, Mifflin, and Company, 1892.

Houghton, Walter R., ed. *Neely's History of the Parliament of Religions at the World's Columbian Exposition.* Chicago: F.T. Neely, 1893.

Howe, Irving. *The American Newness: Culture and Politics in the Age of Emerson.* Cambridge: Harvard University Press, 1986.

Hubbell, G.G. *Fact and Fancy in Spiritualism, Theosophy, and Physical Research*. Cincinnati: The Robert Clarke Company, 1901.

Hughes, E.R., ed. *The Individual in East and West.* London: Oxford University Press, 1937.

Hutchinson, William R. *The Modernist Impulse in American Protestantism.* Cambridge: Harvard University Press, 1976.

Huxley, Thomas. *Evolution and Ethics.* London: Pilot Press, 1947.

Inada, Jenneth, and Nolan Jacobson, eds. *Buddhism and North American Thinkers.* Delhi: Sri Satguru Publications, 1991.

Inden, Ronald. *Imagining India.* Oxford: Blackwell, 1990.
Irwin, Lee. *Reincarnation in America: An Esoteric History.* Lanham: Lexington Books, 2017.
Jackson, Carl T. *The Oriental Religions and American Thought: Nineteenth Century Explorations.* Westport: Greenwood Publishing Co. 1981.
———. *Vedanta for the West: The Ramakrishna Movement in the United States.* Bloomington: Indiana University Press, 1994.
Jacobson, Nolan. *The Heart of Buddhist Philosophy.* Carbondale: Southern Illinois University Press, 1985.
Jaffe, Richard M. *Seeking Sakyamuni: South Asia in the Formation of Modern Japanese Buddhism.* Chicago: University of Chicago Press, 2019.
James, William. *The Letters of William James,* 2 vols. Boston: The Atlantic Monthly Press, 1920.
———. *Pragmatism.* New York: Longmans, Green, and Co., 1907.
———. *Pragmatism and Other Writings.* New York: Penguin Books, 2000.
———. *The Varieties of Religious Experience. The Gifford Lectures in 1901–1902.* New York: Longmans, Green, and Co., 1917 [1902].
Johnson, Rossiter, ed. *A History of the World's Columbian Exposition.* 4 vols.. New York: D. Appleton and Co., 1898.
Johnson, Samuel. *Oriental Religions and Their Relation to Universal Religion.* 3 vols. Boston: Houghton, Mifflin, and Co., 1872–85.
Jordan, Louis Henry. *Comparative Religion: Its Genesis and Growth.* Edinburgh: T. and T. Clark, 1905.
Kasulis, Thomas. *Zen Action, Zen Person.* Honolulu: University of Hawaii Press, 1981.
Kishimoto, Hideo, ed. *Religion. Volume 2. Japanese Thought in the Meiji Era.* Tokyo: Obunsha, 1956.
Kant, Immanuel. *Critique of Pure Reason.* New York: St. Martin's Press, 1965.
Kato, S. *A Shin-Shiu Catechism.* Kyoto, Japan: Buddhist Propagation Society of Kyoto, 1893.
Kerr, Howard, and Charles L. Crow, eds. *The Occult in America: New Historical Perspectives.* Urbana: University of Illinois Press, 1986.
King, Richard. *Orientalism and Religion: Postcolonial Theory and the 'Mystic East'.* London: Routledge, 1999.
Kitagawa, Joseph, ed. *Modern Trends in World Religions—Paul Carus Memorial Symposium.* La Salle: Open Court, 1959.
———. *The 1893 World's Parliament of Religions and Its Legacy.* Chicago: University of Chicago, Divinity School, 1984.
Knight, David. *The Age of Science. The Scientific World-view in the Nineteenth Century.* Oxford: Basil Blackwell Ltd., 1986.

Konovitz, Milton R. and Gail Kennedy, eds. *The American Pragmatists.* Cleveland: The World Publishing Co., 1960.

Koeppen, Karl F. Von. *Die Religion des Buddha*. Berlin, 1857.

Krämer, Hans Martin. *Shimaji Mokurai and the Reconception of Religion and the Secular in Modern Japan.* Honolulu: University of Hawaii Press, 2015.

Kubose, Gyomay. *American Buddhism. A New Direction.* Chicago: The Dharma House, 1976.

Kuroda, Shinto. *Outlines of the Mahayana as Taught by Buddha.* Tokyo: Bukkyo Gakkukwai, 1893.

Lachman, Gary. *Madame Blavatsky: The Mother of Modern Spiritualism.* New York: Penguin, 2012.

Lavoie, Jeffrey D. *The Theosophical Society: The History of a Spiritualist Movement.* Boca Raton: BrownWalker Press, 2012.

Laycock, Steven. *Mind as a Mirror and the Mirroring of Mind: Buddhist Reflections on Western Phenomenology.* New York: State University of New York Press, 1994.

Layman, Emma McCloy. *Buddhism in America.* Chicago: Nelson Hall, 1976.

Lears, T.J. Jackson. *No Place of Grace: Anti-modernism and the Transformation of American Culture, 1880–1920.* New York: Pantheon Books, 1983.

Leidecker, Kurt F. *Forward to Buddhism and Science.* Delhi: Motilal Banarsidas, 1984.

Leonard, Todd Jay. *Talking to the Other Side: A History of Modern Spiritualism.* New York: iUniverse Inc, 2005.

Levine, Lawrence W. *The Opening of the American Mind: Canons, Culture, and History.* Boston: Beacon Press, 1996.

Levinson, Henry. *The Religious Investigations of William James.* Chapel Hill: University of North Carolina Press, 1981.

Lewis, Arnold. *An Early Encounter with Tomorrow: Europeans, Chicago's Loop, and the World's Columbian Exposition.* Urbana: University of Illinois Press, 1997.

The Life of the Swami Vivekananda. 3 vols. Mayavati, Almora: Swami Virajananda, 1914.

Lowell, A. Lawrence. *Biography of Percival Lowell.* New York: Macmillan, 1935.

Lowell, Percival. *Chöson: The Land of the Morning Calm. A Sketch of Korea.* Boston: Ticknor and Co., 1886.

———. *Occult Japan or The Way of the Gods. An Esoteric Study of Japanese Personality and Posses*sion. Boston: Houghton Mifflin, 1894.

———. *The Soul of the Far East.* Boston: Houghton Mifflin, 1888.

Lysaker, John T. *Emerson and Self-Culture.* Bloomington: Indiana University Press, 2008.

MacLoughlin, William Gerald. *Revivals, Awakenings, and Reform: An Essay on Religion and Social Change in America, 1607-1977.* Chicago, IL: University of Chicago Press, 1978.

McMahan, David L. *Empty Vision: Metaphor and Visionary Imagery in Mah y na Buddhism.* New York: RoutledgeCurzon, 2002.

———. *The Making of Buddhist Modernism.* Oxford: Oxford University Press, 2008.

McNally, Dennis. *Desolate Angel: Jack Kerouac, the Beat Generation, and America.* Cambridge: Da Capo Press, 2003.

Marvin, Carolyn. *When Old Technologies were New: Thinking About Electric Communication in the Late Nineteenth Century.* New York: Oxford University Press, 1988.

Marty, Martin E. *Modern American Religion, Vol. 1: The Irony of It All.* Chicago: University of Chicago Press, 1986.

Masuzawa, Tomoko. *The Invention of World Religions.* Chicago: University of Chicago Press, 2005.

Mercer, Lewis Pyle, ed. *The New Jerusalem in the World's Religious Congress of 1893.* Chicago: Western New-Church Union, 1894.

———. *Review of the World's Religious Congresses of the World's Congress Auxiliary of the World's Columbia Exposition.* Chicago: Rand, McNally, and Co., 1893.

Merton, Thomas. *Mystics and Zen Masters.* New York: Farrar, Strauss and Giroux, 1967.

———. *Zen and the Birds of Appetite.* New York: New Directions Publishing Corp, 1968.

Mills, Charles D.B. *The Indian Saint: Or, Buddha and Buddhism.* Northampton: Journal and Free Press, 1876.

Miner, Earl. *The Japanese Tradition in British and American Literature.* Princeton: Princeton University Press, 1958.

Molendijk, Arie. *Fredrich Max Müller and the Sacred Books of the East.* Oxford: Oxford University Press, 2016.

Moore, C.A., ed. *Essays in East-West Philosophy: An Attempt at World Philosophical Synthesis.* Honolulu: University of Hawaii Press, 1951.

Moore, Robert Laurence. *In Search of White Crows: Spiritualism, Parapsychology, and American Culture.* New York: Oxford University Press, 1977.

Moraldo, Heinrich and John Moraldo. *The Cultural, Political, and Religious Significance of Buddhism in the Modern World.* New York: Macmillan, 1976.

Morreale, Don. *The Complete Guide to Buddhist America.* Boston: Shambhala, 1998.

Mosley, Glenn. *New Thought, Ancient Wisdom: The History and Future of the New Thought Movement.* Philadelphia: Templeton Foundation Press, 2006.

Mottahedeh, N., ed. *'Abdul'l-Baha's Journey West: The Course of Human Solidarity.* New York: Palgrave Macmillan, 2013.

Mozoomdar, P.C. *The Oriental Christ.* Boston: George Ellis, 1892 [1883].

Mudge, Jean McClure. *Mr. Emerson's Revolution*. Cambridge: Open Book Publishers, 2015.

Müller, Friedrich Max. *Buddhist Pilgrims.* Chico: Scholars Press, 1985.

———. *Chips from a German Workshop. Vol. 1.* New York: Scribner, Armstrong, and Co., 1874.

———. *Essay on Comparative Mythology.* London: G. Routledge, 1909 [1856].

———. *Introduction to the Science of Religion.* London: Longmans, Green, 1873.

———, ed. *Sacred Books of the East.* 51 vols.; Oxford: Clarendon Press, 1879–1910.

Mullick, Sunrit. *The First Hindu Mission to America: The Pioneering Visits of Protap Chunder Mozoomdar.* New Delhi: Northern Book Center, 2010 [1883].

Murano, Kuran. *What American Buddhist Pioneers Think*. Los Angeles: 1939.

Murphet, Howard. *When Daylight Comes: A Biography of Helena Petrovna Blavatsky*. Wheaton: The Theosophical Publishing House, 1975.

Nash, Henry S. *The History of the Higher Criticism of the New Testament.* New York: The Macmillan Co., 1901.

Nikhilananda, Swami. *Vivekananda: A Biography.* Kolkata: Advaita Ashrama, 1964.

Nisbett, Richard E. *The Geography of Thought: How Asians and Westerners Think Differently . . . and Why*. New York: Free Press, 2003.

Northrop, F.S.C. *The Meeting of East and West. An Inquiry Concerning World Understanding.* New York: The Macmillan Co., 1950.

Notovitch, Nicolas. *The Unknown Life of Jesus Christ.* Chicago: Indo-American Book Company, 1916 [1894].

Numerich, Paul. *Old Wisdom in the New World: Americanization in Two Immigrant Teravada Buddhist Temples.* 1996.

Obeyesekere, Gananath, and Richard Gombrich. *Buddhism Transformed: Religious Change in Sri Lanka.* Princeton: Princeton University Press, 1988.

Olcott, Henry Steel. *Applied Theosophy and Other Essays.* Adyar, India: Theosophical Publishing House, 1975.

———. *A Buddhist Catechism.* Madras: Graves, Cookson, and Co., 1886.

———. *The Buddhist Catechism.* London: Theosophical Publishing Co., 1904.

———. *A Collection of Lectures on Theosophy and Archaic Religions, Delivered in India and Ceylon by Colonel H.S. Olcott, President of the Theosophical Society.* Madras: A Theyagar Rajier, 1883.

———. *The Golden Rules of Buddhism.* Adyar, India: Theosophical Publishing House, 1887.

———. *Theosophy: Religion, and Occult Science.* London: Redway, 1885.

———. *Inside the Occult: The True Story of Madame H.P. Blavatsky.* (Original Title, *Old Diary Leaves*). Philadelphia: Runing Press, 1975.

Oldenberg, Hermann. *Ancient India: Its Language and Religions.* Chicago: Open Court Publishing Co., 1898.

Oppenheim, Janet. *The Other World: Spiritualism and Psychical Research in England, 1850–1914.* Cambridge: Cambridge University Press, 1985.

Parra, Carols Hugo. *Standing with Unfamiliar Company on Uncommon Ground: The Catholic Church and the Chicago Parliaments of Religions.* Ph.D. Dissertation, Toronto: University of Toronto, 2012.

Peiris, William. *Edwin Arnold, A Brief Account of His Life and Contribution to Buddhism.* Kandy: Buddhist Publication Society, 1970.

———. *The Western Contribution to Buddhism.* Delhi: Motilal Banarsidass, 1973.

Persons, Stow. *Free Religion: An American Faith.* New Haven: Yale University Press, 1947.

Pfleiderer, Otto. *The Early Christian Conception of Christ and Its Significance and Value in the History of Religion.* New York: Putnam, 1905 [1903].

Platt, Harold L. *The Electric City: Energy and the Growth of the Chicago Area, 1880–1930.* Chicago. University of Chicago Press, 1991.

Podmore, Frank. *Mediums of the 19th Century.* 2 vols. New York: University Books, 1963.

Pratt, James B. *The Pilgrimage of Buddhism.* New York: Macmillan, 1928.

Prebish, Charles S. *American Buddhism.* North Scituate: Duxbury Press, 1979.

———. *Luminous Passage: The Practice and Study of Buddhism in America.* Berkeley: University of California Press, 1990.

Prebish, Charles S., and Kenneth K. Tanaka, eds. *The Faces of Buddhism in America.* Berkeley: University of California Press, 1998.

Proceedings of the First American Congress of Liberal Religious Societies. Chicago: Bloch and Newman, 1894.

Prothero, Stephen. *The White Buddhist: The Asian Odyssey of Henry Steel Olcott.* Bloomington: Indiana University Press, 1996.

Queen, Christopher S., ed. *Engaged Buddhism in the West.* Boston: Wisdom Publications, 2000.

Rajasekharaiah, T.R. *The Roots of Whitman's Grass: Eastern Sources of Walt Whitman's Poetry.* Rutherford: Fairleigh Dickenson University Press, 1971.

Rayapati, J.P. Rao. *Interest in Vedanta: Pre-Emersonian Interest in Vedic Literature and Vedantic Philosophy*. New York: Asia Publishing House, 1973.

Reichenbach, Karl Ludwig Friedrich. *Lettres Odiques-Magnetiques Du chevalier de Reichenbach.* 2nd ed. Paris: Hachette Livre, 2022; c. 1897.

Rescher, Nicholas. *Peirce's Philosophy of Science.* Notre Dame: University of Notre Dame Press, 1978.

Rhys Davids, Thomas. *American Lectures on the History of Religions. First Series. Buddhism Its History and Literature.* New York: G.P. Putnam's Sons, 1907 [1896].

———. *Buddhist Birth Stories.* London: Routledge, 2000.

———. *The Hibbert Lectures, 1881. Lectures on the Origin and Growth of Religion as Illustrated by Some Points in the History of Indian Buddhism.* London: Williams and Norgate, 1881.

Richardson, Robert D., Jr. *Emerson: The Mind on Fire*. Berkeley: University of California Press, 1995.

Riser, Andrew C. *The Chautauqua Movement: Protestants, Progressives, and the Culture of Modern Liberalism.* New York: Columbia University Press, 2003.

Rorty, Richard. *Objectivity Relativism and Truth: Philosophical Papers*. Cambridge: Cambridge University Press, 1999.

Rydell, Robert. *All the World's a Fair: Visions of Empire at American International Exhibitions, 1876–1916.* Chicago: University of Chicago Press, 1984.

———. *Grand Illusions: Chicago's World's Fair of 1893.* Chicago: University of Chicago Press, 1993.

———. *World of Fairs: The Century of Progress Expositions.* Chicago: University of Chicago Press, 1993.

Saint-Hilaire, J. Barthelemy. *Le Bouddha et sa Religion.* Paris, 1860.

Samuel, Geoffrey, and Jay Johnston. *Religion and the Subtle Body in Asia and the West: Between Mind and Body.* New York: Routledge, 2013.

Samuels, Ernest. *Henry Adams: The Middle Years*. Cambridge: The Belknap Press of Harvard University, 1958.

Sanborn, F.B., ed. *The Genius and Character of Emerson: Lectures at the Concord School of Philosophy.* Port Washington: Kennikat Press, 1971 [1885].

Sangarakshita, Bhikshu. *Anagarika Dharmapala. A Biographical Sketch*. Kandy: Buddhist Publication Society, 1964.

Sansom, G.B. *The Western World and Japan. A Study in the Interaction of European and Asiatic Cultures*. New York: Vintage, 1973.

Santayana, George. *The Genteel Tradition: Nine Essays*. Edited and with an Introductory by Douglas L Wilson. Cambridge: Harvard University Press, 1967.

Sastri, Pandit G. Krishna. *Life and Work of an Indian Saint: Being the Autobiography of Swami Sivaganacharya, a Great Social Reformer and Religious Teacher.* Mylapore, Madras: Vedic Mission, 1912.

Schlagintweit, Emil. *Buddhism in Thibet.* London, 1863.

Schwantes, Robert. *Japanese and Americans: A Century of Cultural Relations.* New York: Harper and Brothers, 1955.

Seager, Richard Hughes. *Buddhism in America.* New York: Columbia University Press, 1999.

———. *The World's Parliament of Religions: The East / West Encounter, Chicago, 1893.* Bloomington: Indiana University Press, 1995.

Sellars, Wilfrid. *Science, Perception, and Reality.* London: Routledge and Kegan Paul, 1963.

Seydel, Rudolf. *Die Buddha-Legende und das Leben Jesu nach den Evangelien Erneute Prüfung ihres gegenseitigen Verhältnisses.* Weirmar: E. Felber, 1897.

———. *Das Evangelium von Jesu in seinen Verhältnissen zu Buddhasage und Buddha-Lehre.* Leipzig: Breitkopf und Härtel, 1882.

Sheldon, Henry C. *Theosophy and New Thought.* New York: the Abingdon Press, 1916.

Sheridan, James Francis. *Paul Carus: A Study of the Thought and Work.* Ph.D. dissertation, University of Illinois, 1957.

Sherman, Paul. *The Shores of America: Thoreau's Inward Exploration.* Urbana: University of Illinois Press, 1958.

Simon, Lindon. *Dark Light: Electricity and Anxiety from the Telegraph to the X-Ray.* Orlando: Harcourt, Inc., 2004.

Sinnett, Alfred Percy. *Esoteric Buddhism.* London: The Theosophical Publishing Society, 1907.

———. *The Occult World.* Boston: Houghton, Mifflin and Co., 1888 [1885].

Snodgrass, Judith. *Presenting Japanese Buddhism to the West. Orientalism, Occidentalism, and the Columbian Exposition.* Chapel Hill: The University of North Carolina Press, 2003.

Soyen, Shaku. *Sermons of a Buddhist Abbot: Addresses on Religious Subjects.* Chicago: The Open Court Publishing Company, 1906.

———. *Zen for Americans: Including the Sutra of Forty-two Chapters.* New York: Barnes and Noble Books, 1993 [1913].
Strauss, David. *Percival Lowell: The Culture and Science of a Boston Brahmin.* Cambridge: Harvard University Press, 2001.
Styers, Randall. *Making Magic: Religion, Magic, and Science in the Modern World.* Oxford: Oxford University Press, 2004.
Sugirtharaja, R.S. *The Bible and Asia: From the Pre-Christian Era to the Postcolonial Age.* Cambridge: Harvard University Press, 2013.
Suzuki, D.T. *A Brief History of Chinese Philosophy.* London: Probsthain, 1914.
———. *Essays in Zen Buddhism.* First Series, 1927; Second Series, 1933; Third Series, 1934.
———. *Manuel of Zen Buddhism.* Kyoto: The Eastern Buddhist Society, 1935.
———. *Swedenborg: Buddha of the North.* West Chester: Swedenborg Foundation, 1996.
———. *The Zen Doctrine of No-Mind.* London: Ryder, 1949.
———. *Zen and Japanese Culture.* London: Routledge and Kegan Paul, 1959.
Swedenborg, Emmanuel. *Apocalypse Revealed*
———. *Arcana Coelestia*
———. *Divine Love and Wisdom.*
———. *Divine Providence*
———. *Heaven and Hell*
———. *True Christian Religion.*
Tamura, Yoshiro. *Japanese Buddhism, a Cultural History.* Tokyo: Kosei Publishing Co., 2005.
Taylor, Eugene. *William James on Exceptional Mental States: The 1896 Lowell Lectures.* New York: Charles Scribner's Sons, 1982.
———. *William James on Consciousness Beyond the Margin.* Princeton: Princeton University, 1996.
———. *Shadow Culture: Psychology and Spirituality in America.* Washington, D.C.: Counterpoint, 1999.
Tennyson, Alfred Lord. *Death of Oenone, Akbar's Dream and Other Poems.* London: Macmillan and Co., 1892.
Thelle, Notto R. *Buddhism and Christianity in Japan: From Conflict to Dialogue, 1854–1899.* Honolulu: University of Hawaii Press, 1987.
Thomas, Edward J. *The History of Buddhist Thought.* London: Kegan Paul, 1933.
Thomas, Wendell. *Hinduism Invades America.* New York: Beacon Press, 1930.
Thoreau, Henry D. *The Transmigration of the Seven Brahmins: A Translation from the Harivansa of Langlois by Henry David Thoreau.* Edited from Manuscript, with an introduction and notes by Arthur Christy. New York: William Edwin Rudge, 1932

———. *Walden; Or, Life in the Woods*. Mineola: Dover Publications, 1854, 1995.

———. *The Writings of Henry David Thoreau*. 20 vols. Edited by Bradford Torrey and Francis H. Allen, New York: AMS Press, 1968.

———. *The Writings of Henry D. Thoreau, Journal Volume 3: 1848–1851*. John C. Broderick, ed. Princeton: Princeton University Press, 1981.

Tweed, Thomas A. *The American Encounter with Buddhism, 1844–1912: Victorian Culture and the Limits of Dissent*. Bloomington: Indiana University Press, 1992.

Versluis, Arthur. *American Transcendentalism and Asian Religions*. New York: Oxford University Press, 1993.

———. *The Esoteric Origins of the American Renaissance*. New York: Oxford University Press, 2001.

Vetterling, Herman Carl. *Swedenborg the Buddhist; Or, The Higher Swedenborgianism, Its Secrets and Thibetan Origin*. Los Angeles: The Buddhist Swedenborgian Brotherhood, 1887.

Veysey, Laurence R. *The Communal Experience: Anarchist and Mystical Communities in Twentieth-Century America*. Chicago: The University of Chicago Press, 1978.

Vivekananda, Swami. *Complete Works of Swami Vivekananda*. 9 vols.; Calcutta: Advaita Ashrama, 1977–84.

Wachmeister, Constance. *Reminiscences of H.P. Blavatsky and the Secret Doctrine*. Wheaton: The Theosophical Publishing House, 1976.

Wallace, B. Alan, and Arnold P. Lutzker, eds. *Buddhism and Science: Breaking New Ground*. New York: Columbia University Press, 2003.

Watts, Alan W. *The Spirit of Zen; A Way of Life, Work, and Art in the Far East*. New York: Grove Press, 1960 [1958].

———. *The Way of Zen*. New York: Pantheon, 1957.

Welbon, Guy. *The Buddhist Nirvana and Its Western Interpreters*. Chicago: University of Chicago Press, 1968.

Williams, Duncan Ryuken, and Christopher S. Queen, eds. *American Buddhism: Methods and Findings in Recent Scholarship*. London: Curzon Press, 1999.

Williams, Paul. *Mahayana Buddhism*. London: Routledge and Kegan Paul, 1990.

Wilson, Leigh. *Modernism and Magic: Experiments with Spiritualism, Theosophy, and the Occult*. Edinburgh: Edinburgh University Press, 2013.

Wright, Brooks. *Interpreter of Buddhism to the West: Sir Edwin Arnold*. New York: Bookman Association, 1957.

Wyld, George. *Theosophy and the Higher Life*. London: Trübner and Co., 1881.

Journals

American Journal of Theology and Philosophy
The American Mathematical Monthly
American Quarterly
American Studies
Angelicum
Annals of the American Academy of Political and Social Science
Arena
Atlantic Monthly
The Biblical World
Buddhist-Christian Studies
The Buddhist Ray
The Congregationalist
The Dial
Eastern Buddhist
European Journal of Pragmatism and American Philosophy
Freethought Magazine
Harvard Theological Revie
The Homiletic Review
Isis
Japanese Journal of Religious Studies
Journal of American History
The Journal of Philosophy, Psychology, and Scientific Methods
Journal of Popular Culture
Journal of Religion
Journal of Religious Ethics
Journal of Speculative Philosophy
Journal of the American Academy of Religion
Journal of the American Oriental Society
Journal of the History of Ideas
Monist (The)
Monumenta Nipponica
New England Quarterly
The New Englander
New World
Numen
The Open Court
The Platonist
Philosophical Studies of Japan
Philosophy and Phenomenological Research
Philosophy East and West
Philosophy of Science
Proceedings of the American Antiquarian Society
Religion

Religion and American Culture: A Journal of Interpretation
Review of Reviews
Science
Southern Literary Messenger
Theatre Journal
Theosophist (The)
Transactions of the Charles S. Peirce Society
William James Studies

Karma

A Story of Buddhist Ethics

Paul Carus

Commit no evil, but do good
And let thy heart be pure

That is the gist of Buddhahood,
The Lore that will endure.

—*The Dhammapada*, 183

Publisher's Advertisement (1903)

All are needed by each one:
Nothing is fair or good alone.
—EMERSON

Soon after the first appearance of Karma in the columns of *The Open Court*, several applications to translate the story were received, and the requests granted. Some of these have appeared, others may still be expected. A few translations were made without the author's knowledge. A German edition was published by The Open Court Publishing Co. Altogether one Japanese, one Urdu, three German, and two French renderings are at present in the author's possession. It is possible that the story also exists in Icelandic, Tamil, Singhalese, and Siamese versions. (An Icelandic translation has been made by the Rev. Matthias Jochumson of Akureyri, Iceland, but we do not know whether it has appeared in book form.

A Russian translation was made by Count Leo Tolstoy, who recommends the story to his countrymen and sums up his opinion as follows:

> This tale has greatly pleased me both by its artlessness and its profundity. The truth, much slurred in these days, that evil can be avoided and good achieved by personal effort only and that there exists no other means of attaining this end, has here been shown forth with striking clearness. The explanation is felicitous in that it proves that individual happiness is never genuine save when it is bound up with the happiness of all our fellows. From the very moment when the brigand on escaping from Hell thought only of his own happiness, his happiness ceased and he fell back again into his former doom.
>
> This Buddhistic tale seems to shed light on a new side of the two fundamental truths revealed by Christianity : that life exists only in the renunciation of one's personality—'he that loseth his life shall find it' (Matt. x. 39), and, that the good of men is only in their union with God, and through God with

> one another—'As thou art in me and I in thee, that they also may be one in us' (John xvii. 21).
>
> I have read this tale to children and they liked it. And amongst grown-up people its reading always gave rise to conversation about the gravest problems of life. And, to my mind, this is the very best recommendation.

From the Russian the story *Karma* was translated, together with several other sketches, by E. Halpérine-Kaminsky, and the work was published under Tolstoy's name at Paris by the *Société d'éditions littéraires et artistiques* (Librairie Paul Ollendorf, 50 Chausée d'Antin, 1900). Either from Tolstoy's Russian version or from the French translation, an abbreviated German translation was made by an author who signs himself "y," and this appeared in the Berliner Evangelisches Sonntagblatt, May 2, 1897 (No. 18, pp. 140–41). Here, too, the story goes under Tolstoy's name.

While the evangelical Sunday paper reproduces *Karma* as a story that inculcates Christian principles, the late Professor Ludwig Büchner, famous as the author of the leading materialistic work, Force and Matter (*Kraft und Stoff*) translated *Karma* from the English under the impression that he had before him some mysterious ancient Buddhist document, for he calls it "an Indian tale from the English of the P.C." Apparently he mistook the signature *P.C.*, over which the story first appeared, for an abbreviated title of some forgotten *P*âli *C*odex or *P*undit *C*ollection, and at any rate, a *P*agan *C*uriosity. It appeared in *Ethische Kultur*, the organ of the German Ethical Societies, Berlin, June 1 and 8, 1895 (Vol. III, Nos. 22 and 23).

Having appeared under Tolstoy's name in French and in German, the story continued in its further migrations to sail under the famous Russian author's name. An enterprising American periodical entitled *The International Magazine* published an English translation in Chicago, and it is curious that the office of this journal was in the very same block with that of The Open Court Publishing Company. So the story had completed its rounds through Russia, Germany, and France, and had returned to its home in the far West.

Since the story had gained currency under Tolstoy's name, the author (having previously had correspondence with him) wrote to Posnia, and Tolstoy replied expressing his regret at the misunderstanding saying of *Karma*:

> It was only through your letter that I learned it had been circulated under my name, and I deeply regret, not only that such a falsehood was allowed to pass unchallenged, but also the fact that it really was a falsehood, for I should be very happy were I the author of this tale. It is one of the best products of national wisdom and ought to be bequeathed to all mankind, like the Odyssey, the History of Joseph, and Shakyamuni.

Karma appeared first in book form in Japanese, where The Open Court Publishing Company brought out Hasegawa's three successive editions on crêpe paper, illustrated in colors by Kwason Suzuki. In the present edition the Japanese illustrations, which were retouched by Eduard Biedermann, are reproduced in black and white, and we hope that the artistic garb will do much to make the little tale attractive.

The Open Court Publishing Company

Dêvala's Rice Cart

Long, long ago in the days of early Buddhism, India was in a most prosperous condition. The Aryan inhabitants of the country were highly civilised, and the great cities were centres of industry, commerce, and learning

It was in those olden times that Pandu, a wealthy jeweller of the Brahman caste, travelled in a carriage to Bârânasî, which is now called Benares. He was bent on some lucrative banking business, and a slave who attended to the horses accompanied him.

The jeweller was apparently in a hurry to reach his destination, and as the day was exceedingly pleasant, since a heavy thunderstorm had cooled the atmosphere, the horses sped along rapidly.

While proceeding on their journey the travellers overtook a samana, as the Buddhist monks were called, and the jeweller, observing the venerable appearance of the holy man, thought to himself: "This samana looks noble and saintly. Companionship with good men brings luck; should he also be going to Bârânasî, I will invite him to ride with me in my carriage."

Having saluted the samana the jeweller explained whither he was driving and at what inn he intended to stay in Bârânasî. Learning that the samana, whose name was Nârada, also was travelling to Bârânasî, he asked him to accept a seat in his carriage. I am obliged to you for your kindness," said the samana to the Brahman, "for I am quite worn out by the long journey. As I have no possessions in this world, I cannot repay you in money ; but it may happen that I can reward you with some spiritual treasure out of the wealth of the information I have received while following Shakyamuni, the Blessed One, the Great Buddha, the Teacher of gods and men."

They travelled together in the carriage and Pandu listened with pleasure to the instructive discourse of Nârada. After about an hour's journey, they arrived at a place where the road had been rendered almost impassable by a washout caused by the recent rain, and a farmer's cart heavily laden with rice prevented further progress. The loss of a linchpin had caused one of the wheels to come off, and Dêvala, the owner of the cart, was busily engaged in repairing the damage. He, too was on his way to Bârânasî to sell his rice, and was anxious to reach the city before the dawn of the next morning. If he was delayed a day or two longer, the rice merchants might have left town or bought all the stock they needed.

When the jeweller saw that he could not proceed on his way unless the farmer's cart was removed, he began to grow angry and ordered Mahâduta, his slave, to push the cart aside, so that his carriage could pass by. The farmer remonstrated because, being so near the slope of the road, it would jeopardise his cargo; but the Brahman would not listen to the farmer and bade his servant overturn the rice-cart and push it aside. Mahâduta, an unusually strong man, who seemed to take delight in the injury of others, obeyed before the samana could interfere. The rice was thrown on the wayside, and the farmer's plight was worse than before.

The poor farmer began to scold, but when the big, burly Mahâduta raised his fist threateningly, he ceased his remonstrances and only growled his curses in a low undertone.

When Pandu was about to continue his journey the samana jumped out of the carriage and said: "Excuse me, sir, for leaving you here. I am under obligations for your kindness in giving me an hour's ride in your carriage. I was tired when you picked me up on the road, but now, thanks to your courtesy, I am rested, and recognising in this farmer an incarnation of one of your ancestors, I cannot repay your kindness better than by assisting him in his troubles."

The Brahman jeweller looked at the samana in amazement: "That farmer, you say, is an incarnation of one of my ancestors? That is impossible !"

"I know," replied the samana, that you are not aware of the numerous important relations which tie your fate to that of the farmer; but sometimes the smartest men are spiritually blind. So I regret that you harm your own interests, and I shall try to protect you against the wounds which you are about to inflict upon yourself."

The wealthy merchant was not accustomed to being reprimanded, and feeling that the words of the samana, although uttered with great kindness, contained a stinging reproach, bade his servant drive on without further delay.

The Jeweller's Purse

The samana saluted Dêvala, the farmer, and began to help him repair his cart and load up the rice, part of which had been thrown out. The work proceeded quickly and Dêvala thought: "This samana must be a holy man; invisible devas seem to assist him. I will ask him how I deserved ill treatment at the hands of the proud Brahman." And he said: "Venerable sir, can you tell me why I suffer an injustice from a man to whom I have never done any harm?"

And the samana said: "My dear friend, you do not suffer an injustice, but only receive in your present state of existence the same treatment which you visited upon the jeweller in a former life. You reap what you have sown, and your fate is the product of your deeds. Your very existence, such as it is now, is but the Karma of your past lives."

"What is my Karma?" asked the farmer.

"A man's Karma," replied the samana, "consists of all the deeds both good and evil that he has done in his present and in any prior existence. Your life is a system of many activities which have originated in the natural process of evolution, and have been transferred from generation to generation. The entire being of every one of us is an accumulation of inherited functions which are modified by new experiences and deeds. Thus we are what we have done. Our 'Karma' constitutes our nature. We are our own creators."

"That maybe as you say," rejoined Dêvala, "but what have I to do with that overbearing Brahman?"

The samana replied: "You are in character quite similar to the Brahman, and the Karma that has shaped your destiny differs but little from his. If I am not mistaken in reading your thoughts, I should say that you would, even to-day, have done the same unto the jeweller if he had been in your place, and if you had such a strong slave at your command as he has, able to deal with you at his pleasure."

The farmer confessed, that if he had had the power, he would have felt little compunction in treating another man, who had happened to impede his way, as he had been treated by the Brahman, but thinking of the retribution attendant upon unkind deeds, he resolved to be in the future more considerate with his fellow-beings.

The rice was loaded and together they pursued their journey to Bârânasî, when suddenly the horse jumped aside. "A snake, a snake!" shouted the farmer ; hut the samana looked closely at the object at which the horse shuddered, jumped out of the cart, and saw that it was a purse full of gold, and the idea struck him: "This money can belong to no one but the wealthy jeweller."

Nârada took the purse and found that it contained a goodly sum of gold pieces. Then he said to the farmer: "Now is the time for you to teach the proud jeweller a lesson, and it will redound to your well-being both in this and in future lives. No revenge is sweeter than the. requital of hatred with deeds of good will. I will give you this purse, and when you come to Bârânasî drive up to the inn which I shall point out to you; ask for Pandu, the Brahman, and deliver to him his gold. He will excuse himself for the rudeness with which he treated you, but tell him that you have forgiven him and wish him success in all his undertakings. For, let me tell you, the more successful he is, the better you will prosper ; your fate depends in many respects upon his fate. Should the jeweller demand any explanation, send him to the vihâra where he will find me ready to assist him with advice in case he may feel the need of it."

Business in Benares

To corner the market of the necessities of life is not a modern invention. The Old Testament contains the story of Joseph, the poor Hebrew youth who became minister of state, and succeeded with unscrupulous but clever business tricks in cornering the wheat market, so as to force the starved people to sell all their property, their privileges, and even their lives, to Pharaoh. And we read in the Jâtaka Tales that one of the royal treasurers of Kasi, which is the old name of Bârânasî, made his first great success in life by cornering the grass market of the metropolis on the day of the arrival of a horse dealer with five hundred horses.

When Pandu the jeweller arrived at Bârânasî, it so happened that a bold speculator had brought about a corner in rice, and Mallika, a rich banker and a business friend of Pandu, was in great distress. On meeting the jeweller he said: "I am a ruined man and can do no business with you unless I can buy a cart of the best rice for the king's table. I have a rival banker in Bârânasî who, learning that I had made a contract with the royal treasurer to deliver the rice to-morrow morning, and being desirous to bring about my destruction, has bought up all the rice in Bârânasî. The royal treasurer must have received a bribe, for he will not release me from my contract, and to-morrow I shall be a ruined man unless Krishna will send an angel from heaven to help me."

While Mallika was still lamenting the poverty to which his rival would reduce him, Pandu missed his purse. Searching his carriage without being able to find it, he suspected his slave Mahaduta; and calling the police, accused him of theft, and had him bound and cruelly tortured to extort a confession.

The slave in his agonies cried: "I am innocent, let me go, for I cannot stand this pain; I am quite innocent, at least of this crime, and suffer now for other sins. Oh, that I could beg the farmer's pardon whom, for the sake of my master, I wronged without any cause! This torture, I believe, is a punishment for my rudeness."

While the officer was still applying the lash to the back of the slave, the farmer arrived at the inn and, to the great astonishment of all concerned, delivered the purse. The slave was at once released from the hands of his torturer. But being dissatisfied with his master, he secretly left and joined a band of robbers in the mountains, who made him their chief on account of his great strength and courage.

When Mallika heard that the farmer had the best rice to sell, fit for delivery to the royal table, he at once bought the whole cartload for treble the price that the farmer had ever received. Pandu, however, glad at heart to have his money restored, rewarded the honest finder, and hastened at once to the vihara to receive further explanation from Nârada, the samana.

Nârada said: "I might give you an explanation, but knowing that you are unable to understand a spiritual truth, I prefer to remain silent. Yet I shall give you some advice: Treat every man whom you meet as your own self; serve him as you would demand to be served yourself; for our Karma travels; it walks apace though, and the journey is often long. But be it good or evil, finally it will come home to us. Therefore it is said:

Slowly but surely deeds

Home to the doer creep.

Of kindness sow thy seeds,

And bliss as harvest reap.

"Give me, O samana, the explanation," said the jeweller, "and I shall thereby be better able to follow your advice."

The samana said: "Listen then, I will give you the key to the mystery. If you do not understand it, have faith in what I say. Self is an illusion, and he whose mind is bent upon following self, follows a will-o'-the-wisp which leads him into the quagmire of sin. The illusion of self is like dust in your eye that blinds your sight and prevents you from recognising the close relations that obtain between yourself and your fellows, which are even closer than the relations that obtain among the various organs of your body. You must learn to trace the identity of your self in the souls of other beings. Ignorance is the source of sin. There are few who know the truth. Let this motto be your talisman:

Who injureth others
Himself hurteth sore;
Who others assisteth
Himself helpeth more.
Let th' illusion of self
From your mind disappear,
And you'll find the way sure;
The path will be clear.

"To him whose vision is dimmed by the dust of the world, the spiritual life appears to be cut up into innumerable selves. Thus he will be puzzled in many ways concerning the nature of rebirth, and will be incapable of understanding the import of an all-comprehensive loving-kindness toward all living beings."

The jeweller replied : "Your words, O venerable sir, have a deep significance and I shall bear them in mind. I extended a small kindness which caused me no expense whatever, to a poor samana on my way to Baranasi, and lo! how propitious has been the result! I am deeply in your debt, for without you I should not only have lost my purse, but would have been prevented from doing business in Baranasi which greatly increases my wealth, while if it had been left undone it might have reduced me to a state of wretched poverty. In addition, your thoughtfulness and the arrival of the farmer's rice-cart preserved the prosperity of my friend Mallika, the banker. If all men saw the truth of your maxims, how much better the world would be! Evils would be lessened, and public welfare enhanced."

The samana replied: "Among all the religions there is none like that of the Buddha. It is glorious in the beginning, glorious in the middle, and glorious in the end. It is glorious in the letter and glorious in the spirit. It is the religion of loving-kindness that rids man of the narrowness of egotism and elevates him above his petty self to the bliss of enlightenment which manifests itself in righteousness."

Pandu nodded assent and said: "As I am anxious to let the truth of the Buddha be understood, I shall found a vihâra at my native place, Kaushambî, and invite you to visit me, so that I may dedicate the place to the brotherhood of Buddha's disciples."

Among the Robbers

Years passed on and Pandu's vihâra at A Kaushambî became a place in which wise samanas used to stay and it was renowned as a centre of enlightenment for the people of the town.

At that time the king of a neighboring country had heard of the beauty of Pandu's jewelry, and he sent his treasurer to order a royal diadem to be wrought in pure gold and set with the most precious stones of India. Pandu gladly accepted the order and executed a crown of the most exquisite design. When he had finished the work, he started for the residence of the king, and as he expected to transact other profitable business, took with him a great store of gold pieces.

The caravan carrying his goods was protected by a strong escort of armed men, but when they reached the mountains they were attacked by a band of robbers led by Mabdduta, who beat them and took away all the jewelry and the gold, and Pandu escaped with great difficulty. This calamity was a blow to Pandu's prosperity, and as he had suffered some other severe losses his wealth was greatly reduced.

Pandu was much distressed, but be bore his misfortunes without complaint, thinking to himself: "I have deserved these losses for the sins committed during my past existence. In my younger years I was very hard on other people ; because I now reap the harvest of my evil deeds I have no reason for complaint."

As he had grown in kindness toward all beings, his misfortunes only served to purify his heart; and his chief regret, when thinking of his reduced means, was that he had become unable to do good and to help his friends in the vihara to spread the truths of religion.

Again years passed on and it happened that Panthaka, a young samana and disciple of Nârada, was travelling through the mountains of Kaushambî, and he fell among the robbers in the mountains. As he had nothing in his possession, the robber-chief beat him severely and let him go.

On the next morning Panthaka, while pursuing his way through the woods, heard a noise as of men quarelling and fighting, and going to the place he saw a number of robbers, all of them in a great rage, and in their midst stood Mahâduta, their chief ; and Mahâduta was desperately defending himself against them, like a lion surrounded by hounds, and he slew several of his aggressors with formidable blows, but there were too many for him ; at last he succumbed and fell to the ground as if dead, covered with wounds.

As soon as the robbers had left the place, the young samana approached to see whether he could be of any assistance to the wounded men. He found that all the robbers were dead, and there was but little life left in the chief.

At once Panthaka went down to the little brooklet which was murmuring near by, fetched fresh water in his bowl and brought it to the dying man. Mahâduta opened his eyes and gnashing his teeth, said: "'Where are those ungrateful dogs whom I have led to victory and success? Without me as their chief they will soon perish like jackals hunted down by skilful hunters."

"Do not think of your comrades, the companions of your sinful life," said Panthaka, "but think of your own fate, and accept in the last moment the chance of salvation that is offered you. Here is water to drink, and let me dress your wounds ; perhaps I may save your life."

"Alas! alas!" replied Mahaduta, "Are you not the man whom I beat but yesterday? And now you come to my assistance, to assuage my pain 1 You bring me fresh water to quench my thirst, and try to save my life! It is useless, honorable sir, I am a doomed man. The churls have wounded me unto death,—the ungrateful cowards! They have dealt me the blow which I taught them."

"You reap what you have sown," continued the samana; had you taught your comrades acts of kindness, you would have received from them acts of kindness; but having taught them the lesson of slaughter, it is but your own deed that you are slain by their hands."

"True, very true," said the robber chief, "my fate is well deserved; but how sad is my lot, that I must reap the full harvest of all my evil deeds in future existences! Advise me, O holy sir, what I can do to lighten the sins of my life which oppress me like a great rock placed upon my breast, taking away the breath from my lungs."

Said Panthaka: "Root out your sinful desires; destroy all evil passions, and fill your heart with kindness toward all your fellow-beings."

The Spider Web

While the charitable samana washed the wounds, the robber chief said: "I have done much evil and no good. How can I extricate myself from the net of sorrow which I have woven out of the evil desires of my own heart? My Karma will lead me to Hell and I shall never be able to walk in the path of salvation."

Said the samana: "Indeed your Karma will in its future incarnations reap the seeds of evil that you have sown. There is no escape from the consequences of our actions. But there is no cause for despair. The man who is converted and has rooted out the illusion of self, with all its lusts and sinful desires, will be a source of blessing to himself and others.

"As an illustration, I will tell you the story of the great robber Kandata, who died without repentance and was reborn as a demon in Hell, where he suffered for his evil deeds the most terrible agonies and pains. He had been in Hell several kalpas and was unable to rise out of his wretched condition, when Buddha appeared upon earth and attained to the blessed state of enlightenment. At that memorable moment a ray of light fell down into Hell quickening all the demons with life and hope, and the robber Kandata cried aloud: "O blessed Buddha, have mercy upon me! I suffer greatly, and although I have done evil, I am anxious to walk in the noble path of righteousness. But I cannot extricate myself from the net of sorrow. Help me, O Lord; have mercy on me!"

"Now, it is the law of Karma that evil deeds lead to destruction, for absolute evil is so bad that it cannot exist. Absolute evil involves impossibility of existence. But good deeds lead to life. Thus there is a final end to every deed that is done, but there is no end to the development of good deeds. The least act of goodness bears fruit containing newseeds of goodness, and they continue to grow, they nourish the poor suflFering creatures in their repeated wanderings in the eternal round of Samsâra until they reach the final deliverance from all evil in Nirvana.

"When Buddha, the Lord, heard the prayer of the demon suffering in Hell, he said: "Kandata, did you ever perform an act of kindness? It will now return to you and help you to rise again. But you cannot be rescued unless the intense sufferings which you endure as consequences of your evil deeds have dispelled all conceit of selfhood and have purified your soul of vanity, lust, and envy."

"'Kandata remained silent, for he had been a cruel man, but the Tathagata in his omniscience saw all the deeds done by the poor wretch, and he perceived that once in his life when walking through the woods he had seen a spider crawling on the ground, and he thought to himself, 'I will not step upon the spider, for he is a harmless creature and hurts nobody.'

"Buddha looked with compassion upon the tortures of Kandata, and sent down a spider on a cobweb and the spider said: 'Take hold of the web and climb up.' Having attached the web at the bottom of Hell, the spider withdrew. Kandata eagerly seized the thin thread and made great efforts to climb up. And he succeeded. The web was so strong that it held, and he ascended higher and higher.

"Suddenly he felt the thread trembling and shaking, for behind him some of his fellow-sufferers were beginning to climb up. Kandata became frightened. He saw the thinness of the web, and observed that it was elastic, for under the increased weight it stretched out; yet it still seemed strong enough to carry him. Kandata had heretofore only looked up; he now looked down, and saw following close upon his heels, also climbing up on the cobweb, a numberless mob of the denizens of Hell. 'How can this thin thread bear the weight of all?' he thought to himself, and seized with fear he shouted loudly: 'Let go the cobweb. It is mine!'

"At once the cobweb broke, and Kandata fell back into Hell.

"The illusion of self was still upon Kandata. He did not know the miraculous power of a sincere longing to rise upwards and enter the noble path of righteousness. It is thin like a cobweb, but it will carry millions of people, and the more there are that climb it. the easier will be the efforts of every one of them. But as soon as the idea arises in a man's heart: 'This is mine; let the bliss of righteousness be mine alone, and let no one else partake of it', the thread breaks and he will fall back into his old condition of selfhood. For selfhood is damnation, and truth is bliss. What is Hell? It is nothing but egotism, and Nirvana is a life of righteousness."

"Let me take hold of the spider-web," said the dying robber chief, when the samana had finished his story, "and I will pull myself up out of the depths of Hell."

The Conversion of the Robber Chief

Mahaduta lay quiet for a while to collect his thoughts, and then he addressed the samana not without effort:

"Listen, honorable sir, I will make a confession : I was the servant of Pandu, the jeweller of Kaushambî, but when he unjustly had me tortured I ran away and became a chief of robbers. Some time ago when I heard from my spies that Pandu was passing through the mountains, I succeeded in robbing him of a great part of his wealth. Will you now go to him and tell him that I have forgiven from the bottom of my heart the injury which he unjustly inflicted upon me, and ask him, too, to pardon me for having robbed him. While I stayed with him his heart was as hard as flint, and I learned to imitate the selfishness of his character. I have heard that he has become benevolent and is now pointed out as an example of goodness and justice. He has laid up treasures of which no robber can ever deprive him, while I fear that my Karma will continue to linger in the course of evil deeds; but I do not wish to remain in his debt so long as it is still in my power to pay him. My heart has undergone a complete change. My evil passions are subdued, and the few moments of life left me shall be spent in the endeavor to continue after death in the good Karma of righteous aspirations. Therefore, inform Pandu that I have kept the gold crown which he wrought for the king, and all his treasures, and have hidden them in a cave nearby. There were only two of the robbers under my command who knew of it, and both are now dead. Let Pandu take a number of armed men and come to the place and take back the property of which I have deprived him. One act of justice will atone for some of my sins; it will help to cleanse my soul of its impurities and give me a start in the right direction on my search for salvation."

Then Mahaduta described the location of the cave and fell back exhausted.

For a while he lay with closed eyes as though sleeping. The pain of his wounds had ceased, and he began to breathe quietly; but his life was slowly ebbing away, and now he seemed to awake as from a pleasant dream.

"Venerable sir," said he, "what a blessing for me that the Buddha came upon earth and taught you and caused our paths to meet and . made you comfort me. While I lay dozing I beheld as in a vision the scene of the Tathagata's final entering into Nirvana. In former years I saw a picture of it which made a deep impression on my mind, and the recollection of it is a solace to me in my dying hour."

"Indeed, it is a blessing," replied the samana, that the Buddha appeared upon earth; he dispelled the darkness begotten by ill will and error, and attained supreme enlightenment. He lived among us as one of us, being subject to the ills of life, pain, disease, and death, not unlike any mortal. Yet he extinguished in himself all selfishness, all lust, all greed for wealth and love of pleasure, all ambition for fame or power, all hankering after things of the world and clinging to anything transitory and illusive. He was bent only on the one aim, to reach the immortal and to actualise in his being that which cannot die. Through the good Karma of former existences and his own life he reached at last the blessed state of Nirvana, and when the end came he passed away in that final passing away which leaves nothing behind but extinguishes all that is transitory and mortal. Oh, that all men could give up clinging and thereby rid themselves of passion, envy, and hatred!"

Mahâduta imbibed the words of the samana with the eagerness of a thirsty man who is refreshed by a drink of water that is pure and cool and sweet. He wanted to speak, but he could scarcely rally strength enough to open his mouth and move his lips. He beckoned assent and showed his anxiety to embrace the doctrine of the Tathagata.

Panthaka wetted the dying man's lips and soothed his pain, and when the robber chief, unable to speak, silently folded his hands, he spoke for him and gave utterance to such vows as the latter was ready to make. The samana's words were like music to the ears of Mahâduta. Filled with the joy that originates with good resolutions and entranced by the prospect of an advance in the search for a higher and better life, his eyes began to stare and all pain ceased. So the robber chief died converted in the arms of the samana.

The Converted Robber's Tomb

As soon as Panthaka, the young samana, had reached Kaushambi, he went to the vihâra and inquired for Pandu the jeweller. Being directed to his residence he gave him a full account of his recent adventure in the forest. And Pandu set out with an escort of armed men and secured the treasures which the robber chief had concealed in the cave. Nearby they found the remains of the robber chief and his slain comrades, and they gathered the bodies in a heap and burned them with all honors.

The ashes were collected in an urn and buried in a tumulus on which a stone was placed with an inscription written by Panthaka, which contained a brief report of Mahâduta's conversion. Before Pandu's party returned home, Panthaka held a memorial service at the tumulus in which he explained the significance of Karma, discoursing on the words of Buddha:

By ourselves is evil done.

By ourselves we pain endure.

By ourselves we cease from wrong.

By ourselves become we pure.

No one saves us, but ourselves,

No one can and no one may:

We ourselves must walk the path,

Buddhas merely teach the way.

"Our Karma," the samana said, "is not the work of Ishvara, or Brahma, or Indra, or of any one of the gods. Our Karma is the product of our own actions. My action is the womb that bears me; it is the inheritance which devolves upon me; it is the curse of my misdeeds and the blessing of my righteousness. My action is the resource by which alone I can work out my salvation."

Then the samana paused and added:

"While everyone is the maker of his own Karma, and we reap what we have sown, we are at the same time co-responsible for the evils of evil doers. Such is the interrelation of Karma that the errors of one person are mostly mere echoes of the errors of others. Neither the curse of our failings nor the bliss of our goodness is purely our own. Therefore when we judge the bad, the vicious, the criminal, let us not withhold from them our sympathy, for we are partners of their guilt."

Among the people of the surrounding villages the tumulus became known as "The Converted Robber's Tomb," and in later years a little shrine was built on the spot where wanderers used to rest and invoke the Buddha for the conversion of robbers and thieves.

The Bequest of a Good Karma

Pandu carried all his treasures back to Kaushambî, and using with discretion the wealth thus unexpectedly regained, he became richer and more powerful than he had ever been before, and when he was dying at an advanced age he had all his sons, and daughters, and grandchildren gathered round him and said unto them:

"My dear children, do not blame others for your lack of success. Seek the cause of your ills in yourselves. Unless you are blinded by vanity you will discover your fault, and having discovered it you will see the way out of it. The remedy for your ills, too, lies in yourselves. Never let your mental eyes be covered by the dust of selfishness, and remember the words which have proved a talisman in my life:

Who injureth others,

Himself hurteth sore.

Who others assisteth,

Himself helpeth more.

Let th' illusion of self

From your mind disappear:

And you'll find the way sure;

The path will be clear.

"If you heed my words and obey these injunctions you will, when you come to die, continue to live in the Good Karma that you have stored up and your souls will be immortalised according to your deeds."

Index

Index